DAWSON'S GUIDE

D0978002

TO COLORADO'S FOURTEENERS

Volume 1
The Northern Peaks

The complete mountaineering guide to Colorado's high peaks

Technical Routes

Snow Climbs

Ski Descents

Classic Hikes

Know your limits!

By Louis W. Dawson II

Attention Readers:

The information presented in this book is based upon the experience of the author and his sources and might not necessarily be perceived as accurate by other persons; therefore, extreme care should be taken when following any of the routes described in this book. This book is not intended to be instructional in nature but rather a guide for mountaineers who already have the requisite training, experience and knowledge. An advanced level of expertise and physical conditioning is necessary for even the "easiest" of the routes described. Proper clothing and equipment are essential. Failure to have the necessary knowledge, equipment, and conditioning will subject you to extreme physical danger, injury, or death. Some routes have changed and others will change; avalanche hazards may have expanded or new hazards may have formed since this book's publication.

Blue Clover Press
19650 Blue Clover Lane
Monument, CO 80132
719.488.2941 / Fax 719.636.1184 / Compuserve 71223,1751

Cover photo of the Diamond on Longs Peak by Kennan Harvey.
All other photos by Louis W. Dawson II unless otherwise credited.

Colorado Fourteeners Initiative

The Colorado Fourteeners Initiative is a multi-year, private-public partnership between private organizations and individuals concerned with preservation of the Fourteeners and the federal agencies charged with their management. The goal of the initiative is to mitigate the hiking/climbing impact on the Fourteeners, thereby preserving the peaks' natural integrity and the quality of the Fourteeners' hiking/climbing experience. The initiative provides for the study of hiking/climbing impact, on site mitigation work, and user education. The Colorado Fourteeners Initiative partnership presently includes: the American Mountain Foundation, Colorado Mountain Club, Colorado Outward Bound, Volunteers for Outdoor Colorado, and the U S Forest Service.

Blue Clover Press donates a portion of the proceeds from the sale of this book to support the American Mountain Foundation's role in the Colorado Fourteeners Initiative. For more information on the Colorado Fourteeners Initiative, contact
The American Mountain Foundation
1520 Alamo Avenue, Colorado Springs, CO 80907

Library of Congress Catalog Card Number: 94-71273
ISBN 0-9628867-1-8

Printed in the United States of America

ACKNOWLEDGMENTS

The contributions of many people made *Dawson's Guide to Colorado's Fourteeners* possible. I should mention my first fourteener climb, an ascent of Pyramid Peak in the capable hands of an Ashcrofters Mountain School instructor. That was more than 30 years ago. I've forgotten his name, but I thank him. In the 1960s Dave Farney gave many young mountain men a start through the Ashcrofters. A writer's grant from my late grandfather L.W. Dawson took the sting out of years on the road and at the keyboard. My wife Lisa was a bottomless well of encouragement, as well as a source of nutritional meals and ideas for an office skeleton. John Quinn joined me for many memorable weeks of small town motels, 1:00 AM alarms, and wonderful summits. Indeed, it was his idea to produce this book! Michael Kennedy contributed invaluable editing, advice, and enthusiasm as the idea germinated. Jon Waterman deserves double thanks for advice, editing and encouragement—not to mention friendship through the years. Thanks to Outdoor Research for sundry equipment. Kastle, Dynastar, Miller and Kneissl supplied me with excellent skis. I could not have done all the mixed walking, skiing, and climbing without a pair of Dachstein ski mountaineering boots. Thanks to the Aspen Ski Corporation for the use of their lifts for photography and equipment testing. Glen Randall lent his awesome photography and mountaineering skills during the completion of my "ski the fourteeners project." I've appreciated Paul Ramer's friendship and his help with equipment, especially his fabulous Short Cut ski. Kim Miller of Black Diamond gave me terrific support, both with encouragement and gear. I heartily thank Mountain Smith Packs for their continued help. Lionnel Monaco gave many hours of pixel editing as an unofficial intern. Thanks to Grant Wickes of Micrografx for helping with Picture Publisher image software; using it and Aldus Photostyler, I created the maps and annotated photos.

My special gratitude goes out to Ken Ward, who accompanied me on more than a dozen fourteener climbs and ski descents, plus an equal number of reconnaissance missions and failed attempts; Ken deserves special mention for doing most of the driving while I tickled my laptop computer. A big thanks to physical therapist Karen Church for her help repairing my wheels—and the same thanks to Dr. Michael Berkley. Jim Gilcrest gave me valuable help with several route descriptions.

For the past 12 years, Howie and Mike Fitz and Bob Pfeiffer have focused their love of ski mountaineering on the fourteeners. Among them, they have skied almost 90 different routes. My sincerest gratitude goes out to them for the information and photographs they provided. I wish them luck in their quest for the best in ski mountaineering. Bob's mother Patricia Pfeiffer, an expert historian, gave me invaluable assistance as well.

Ten years ago, the publication of Borneman and Lampert's *Climbing Guide to Colorado's Fourteeners* was an unsung revolution. This book is still the authoritative source for fourteener history and gives a good overview of the peaks. Books such as mine and many others would not be possible without Borneman and Lampert's pioneering efforts.

Moreover, I must acknowledge you, the user of this guide book. After publication you give it the acid test. Without a doubt you'll find mistakes and inconsistencies: that's the nature of an information-intensive project done on a limited budget with the additional constraints of time, weather, and the author's physical abilities—not to mention dated signs and place names. Thus, I'd like to thank in advance those people who take the time to report corrections to me. I can be reached care of Blue Clover Press. Naturally, all such details will be verified and included in future editions. Also, I welcome any reports of fourteener "firsts," especially rock climbs, ski descents, and snow routes.

Finally, thanks also to others too numerous to mention here.

Berg Heil,
Louis W. Dawson II
Carbondale, Colorado

DEDICATED TO MY MOTHER
PATRICIA PILLSBURY DAWSON

"I am fain to confess a deplorable weakness in my character. No sooner have I ascended a peak than it becomes a friend, and delightful as it may be to seek "fresh woods and pastures new," in my heart of hearts I long for the slopes of which I know every wrinkle, and on which each crag awakens memories of mirth and laughter and of the friends of long ago. As a consequence of this terrible weakness, I have been no less than seven times on the top of the Matterhorn."

— A. F. Mummery 1874

TABLE OF CONTENTS

CHAPTER 1: NORTHERN SAWATCH MOUNTAINS

CHAPTER 2: SOUTHERN SAWATCH

CHAPTER 3: MOSQUITO AND FRONT RANGE

CHAPTER 4: THE ELK MOUNTAINS

Table of Contents

FOREWORD

by Jonathan Waterman

When I first met Lou Dawson in May 1978, he was recovering from a spiral leg fracture that gimped him sure as an old man. Although such trauma would have jailed most mountaineers at home, he spent spring and summer guiding in his beloved Colorado Rockies. His natural affinity for suffering, moreover his bull-dog endurance, saw him stiff leggedly racing (and beating) his fittest students over high passes. I left to climb Mount Logan in Canada.

Several years later, in February after I'd climbed Denali, his mother phoned Alaska to tell me an avalanche had broken both of Lou's legs quite badly this time, again in the Colorado mountains. Doctors and friends figured Lou would be hardpressed, physically and psychologically, to perform as a mountaineer. But that Thanksgiving, Lou proved them wrong. He hobbled to the top of Mount Elbert—Colorado's highest alp—bivouacked, then skied to its base at dawn.

He seemed changed after that. He didn't stop mountaineering, but he gave potential avalanche zones wider berths, carried a radio, and volunteered for Mountain Rescue. People who weren't serious mountaineers thought he was still cheeky as ever, but his closest friends knew he had become somewhat of a "Fox of the fourteeners—" determined not only to avoid accidents, but to learn everything he could about the mountains he called home. At the same time, he initiated his most ambitious project: skiing all 54 of Colorado's highest peaks.

It wasn't until the fall of 1989 that I figured out what Lou was really doing. And it was no coincidence I was trying to climb in Nepal. My trip was somewhat of a personal failure because I had hoped to solo a big peak, and I spent a lot of money traveling halfway around the globe only to realize my partner in mountain rime had the answer all along.

Sure, Lou had been climbing in South America, Canada and Alaska. But he had found his Denali's, his Mount Logans and his Himalaya, in the backyard. While I sought mountaineering self-actualization in far ranges, Lou arrived upon Shangri-La in Colorado.

While slouching out of Nepal, I was determined to follow his lead. His brand of backyard mountaineering can be as raw as the arctic extremes of Alaska, and with the exception of extreme high altitude, the fourteeners offer similar technical challenges, scenic backpacking, gentle picnicking, or the ski descents to be expected from any great range in the world. It's also cheaper.

As for the veracity of the guidebook itself, Lou did his field testing—fastidiously checking his odometer, obsessively tapping on his lap-tap computer and incessantly exposing film—as he finished skiing all the fourteeners in the spring of 1991. This was an unprecedented feat. Now, while I am attempt to grovel up the fourteeners in winter, face plant down them in the spring, or sweat up them in the summer, my success is owed to Lou's inspiration, his companionship, and an early draft of his book. Lacking the actual "Fox," this guide is Dawson in a box.

PREFACE

Glen Randall, photo

Lou Dawson at work.

For thirty years I've enjoyed mountaineering all over North America. During those times, upon my return to Colorado, I've always felt the Colorado Rocky Mountains are special. Few mountain ranges in the world have such a blend of easy access, superb terrain, good weather, and wilderness.

Several years ago, my wife Lisa and I made a winter climb and ski descent of Tabeguache Peak. We parked at dawn in the heart of the Sawatch Mountains, clicked into our skis, and climbed up Jennings Creek. As the sun rose, we passed through a grove of stately bristlecone pines. A pale sky held the Methuselah's gnarled branches in a cold embrace. The trees spoke to me: they spoke of countless sunrises and sunsets, the cold light of the moon, and a certain order in the world. I pondered and photographed, then continued up the peak. The trees dropped behind us and, for a few moments during a break, I felt the presence of the bristlecones below. At the summit, I could still hear the voice of those old trees. The world ordered itself, and an emotion of renewal swept through me like a mountain sunrise. All the way down the mountain, and for weeks after, I carried that feeling with me.

A friend once said to me, "if I had one wish—once a week, for eternity, I would climb a mountain." The eternity part of that wish might be a dream, but in Colorado you could easily do a peak a week for a lifetime. The state has countless summits under 13,000 feet, at least 700 peaks between 13,000 and 14,000 feet, and more than 50 "fourteeners" at or over 14,000 feet.

In the past, bean counters have combined USGS criteria with that of the Colorado Mountain Club for a total fifty-four "official" fourteeners. In reality, many other summits in Colorado top 14,000 feet. Nonetheless, the number 54 is a handy measure, and the popular goal of bagging all 54 is an admirable endeavor.

Rather than listing the official fourteeners, or debating what makes a "peak," enhancing your enjoyment of our mountains was my goal in creating this book. To do so, rather than worry about the exact number of "fourteeners," I included the Colorado 14,000 foot summits that I and many others feel have the best climbing, skiing, and hiking. When in need of a criterion I used aesthetics: if it looks and feels like a mountain—it is. If you disagree with the inclusion of any peaks in this guide, simply tear out the offending pages. Your criteria are as good as mine. If your goal is a "grand slam" of the official 54, Appendix 2. gives a list of the best routes for a grand slam.

So, if definitions are vague, why a guidebook for only fourteeners? Rocky Mountain peaks around 14,000 feet in height stand out from other Colorado peaks. They have the greatest vertical drops, summits that leap to the sky, and an imposing majesty that pleases the eye and lifts the spirit. Often, these mountains have the most enjoyable hikes, ski descents, and climbs. For skiers and snow climbers, routes on the fourteeners are the longest, and the extra altitude makes the snow last into late spring or summer. For all these reasons, the fourteeners are heavily used, resulting in trail erosion, crowding, and wildlife impact. While I feel we have the right to climb our peaks as we please, another purpose of this book is to spread the use, thus reducing wear on the crowded routes—hopefully to tolerable levels.

Another issue related to the Colorado peaks, with their abundant road access, is the definition of a "climb." In some circles, a peak climb is said to be 3,000 vertical feet or more. But many people who use that standard have a pesky habit of counting climbs of peaks they traverse to from other peaks. A related issue is mechanized access. How far can you drive up a peak and still say you climbed it? Where does a person in a wheel chair need to start from on the Mount Evans or Pikes Peak road and claim he or she climbed the peak? Standards make sports fun. Mountain climbing, however, is a sport of freedom. As such, we should take a broad definition of "climb." The only rule I'd put into print is a climber must ascend with his or her own muscle power—whatever the choice in vertical feet. Your powered approach to a peak, by car, snowmobile or other, should be your choice (within the law), based on your physical ability, time constraints—and your own feeling of what a "climb" is. Even that standard has its permutations. After all, Himalayan climbers use human powered freight hauling (porters), and most of their approach is done in an airliner. Perhaps another good criterion is challenge—perhaps fun—perhaps both!

While summer hikes and climbs on the fourteeners have been a Colorado tradition dating back before the settlers, the popularity of ski mountaineering on these peaks is on the upswing. People think skiing and they think winter. But winter on the fourteeners is severe, and winter ascents and ski descents are recommended only for a hearty few. Fortunately, the Colorado Rockies have a spring and summer snow season of more than 16 weeks, between March and July. During this time, ski mountaineers and snow climbers have a spectacular playground that can rival the European Alps, without the problems of glacier travel—and without crowds. Beautiful weather and compacted snow, which are terrific for climbing and skiing, are the norms in this spring season. On top of that, avalanche danger is easy to predict and avoid.

When have you "skied" a peak? Again, you should base this on your personal goals, but you can apply a minimum standard. For bragging rights, a good rule is you've skied a Colorado fourteener when you ski the longest vertical drop available on snow. Indeed, several of the longest, most continuous "classic" fourteener ski descents start near, but not exactly, on the summit. For example, most people who ski North Maroon Peak start with a short downclimb. Fortunately for those who like to claim ski descents (myself included), you can ski the majority of fourteeners from the exact summit, while you can ski the few exceptions from a summit ridge or rockpile within 100 feet of the summit. Can you take your skis off and still claim a ski descent? In Europe people often downclimb or rappel sections of routes they claim as ski descents. During his remarkable ski descent of the east face of Pyramid Peak, Chris Landry had to rappel a short section. The conventional wisdom is his was the first ski of Pyramid Peak. I agree.

John Muir said, "go to the mountains and get their good tidings." Indeed, for most people enjoyment—even spiritual succor—is the point of mountaineering. Simply put, mountains make us feel better. On the Colorado fourteeners, Muir's good tidings are within reach for enthusiasts of all abilities. I hope you enjoy these peaks often, and bring the good news back every time you do—and that this book helps you along the way.

Lou Dawson

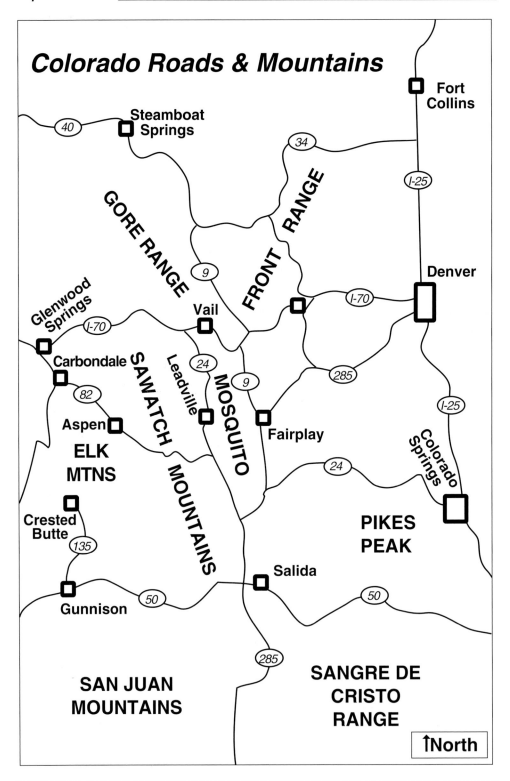

Colorado Roads & Mountains

INTRODUCTION PART 1

HOW TO USE THIS BOOK

The peaks covered in this guide are contained in several mountain ranges which subdivide the north and central Colorado Rockies. The map on the previous page shows these ranges, and the chapters are ordered according to them. These ranges have their gray areas, as do most manmade definitions. But such divisions organize a guide book, and help identify departure points for doing several routes during one trip. Most routes are described in their entirety—with little cross referencing. This results in redundancy, but saves page turning. At the beginning of each route description you will find a data block similar to the following one:

1.2.1	**Mount Massive—Sample Route**	
Ratings:	Summer Climb—Advanced	Ski Descent—Advanced
	Snow Climb—Advanced	
Season:	Summer, or Spring Snow	
RT Data:	8 hours, 6½ miles, 3,891' ↑	
Start:	North Halfmoon Creek Trailhead 10,530'	
1 Day from Rd:	Yes	
Map:	Mount Massive South, pg. 48	
Photo:	pg. 47	

ROUTE NUMBER

The routes are described and numbered consecutively. Referencing is by number. The number is a combination of chapter number, section, and route. For example, in chapter 3, section 4, the second route in the section route is numbered 3.4.2.

PEAK NAME AND ROUTE NAME

Fourteener names are those used on official USGS maps. Route names are those in common usage, including generic designations like "northwest face" where appropriate. Some mountains have been named by locals or mountaineers, but the names are not shown on the USGS maps. These colloquial names are used whenever possible. When peaks have similar names, a range or direction indicator is added, e.g. North and South Wilson.

SUMMER CLIMB RATING

The summer climb rating is for the route after the late spring melt-off. If in doubt about snowcover, use the Snow Climb Rating. From a purely physical standpoint, many fourteener climbs are mere hikes, but even routes rated as Novice are still a mountaineering endeavor. Consider sudden weather extremes, afternoon lightning, and the effects of exertion at altitude, as well as "trails" that pass close to dangerous cliffs and gullies. Indeed, no fourteener route is just a hike, though it might feel that way to a fit climber on a perfect summer day.

Consider the Novice rating as a caveat, not a license for carelessness. In other words, a Novice route usually requires no "hand and foot" climbing, but you should still know your mountain craft. You won't find any "beginner" routes in this book. Beginners should hire a guide or climb with experienced friends.

An Intermediate rated summer climb will have harder route finding and might bring you closer to hazards like cliffs, loose rock, or steep summer snow. For an Intermediate route, you

Hiking in the Sawatch Mountains.

should have climbed other fourteeners, have some knowledge of safe movement on steep, loose rock, and know how to judge the safety of a snow slope. If need be, you should know how to use a rope, crampons, and ice axe.

Advanced rated summer climbs require astute route finding and complete knowledge of mountain craft. If you tackle an Advanced route, you should have climbed many other fourteeners at both the Novice and Advanced level. You should know how to use a rope for 5th class climbing of rock and ice, and you must be expert with crampons and ice axe. In short, a climber on an advanced route should be a seasoned mountaineer or an intermediate level climber accompanied by a guide or experienced friend.

Several climbs in this book involve technical rock climbing. These are rated with the Yosemite decimal system familiar to rock climbers. For example, the North Face Cable route on Longs Peak has a 5.5 rating. Climbs easier than 5.0 which still require a rope are known to many climbers as "4th class." In this book such climbs are rated advanced, and the need for rope work is covered in the text.

SNOW CLIMB RATING

On a Novice rated snow route you will need an ice axe in hand. You should carry crampons, and know how to use them—though they may not be necessary. You must have practiced the ice axe self arrest and know its method and limitations. A rope and related gear are unnecessary, but you should have enough knowledge to recognize and avoid terrain where you might need such equipment.

For an Intermediate rated snow route you must be expert with ice axe and crampons. Use of a rope probably won't be necessary, but you should carry one and know how to use it; it can get you out of some touchy situations. Only experienced snow climbers should climb Intermediate rated routes. An Intermediate route has more fall potential than a Novice route.

If you take on an Advanced rated snow climb, you should be expert with varied crampon techniques and the use of two hand-tools. A rope and climbing hardware may be necessary and should always be carried. Only expert, very experienced mountaineers will be able to handle an Advanced snow route safely and efficiently. Several snow routes are rated Extreme. This rating is reserved for routes with problems such as heavy rockfall danger, mixed climbing (snow, ice, and rock), or formidable route finding.

While most fourteener snow climbs are dry by mid-summer, some gradually become ice climbs. Such climbs require more skill and equipment than their rating indicates.

SKI RATING

A Novice rated fourteener ski route is skiable for mountaineers who can do a solid stem turn and traverse kick turn. Nearby terrain may be steeper and more dangerous. Thus, if you tackle a Novice route, you must be able to distinguish between appropriate terrain and terrain which would get you into trouble. If you tackle a Novice route as a learning experience, consider traveling with a more experienced friend, or hire a guide.

An Intermediate rated fourteener ski route is serious business for any ability level. To do an Intermediate route safely you must have experience with high altitude camping and emergency bivouac. Your skiing skills should be solid intermediate to expert, with experience in poor snow conditions and survival skiing. Some map reading skill is necessary, and you should have a fair degree of mountaineering judgment. Even if you are an experienced ski tourer, a prerequisite for skiing an Intermediate fourteener should be several Novice snow climbs and ski descents.

For safe enjoyment of an Advanced route, you must have a high degree of skill in all aspects of ski mountaineering, including high-angle snow climbing. Some Advanced routes can require belayed rock climbing, especially if you fail to find the best route. Again, if you have never done a fourteener, try a few with easier ratings before you do an Advanced route; that way you'll get a sense of the rating curve.

For an Extreme ski route you must be highly skilled in Extreme skiing and technical climbing. Extreme routes are inherently dangerous because of cliffs and steep snow that may exceed 45 degrees. Nevertheless, the Extreme routes in this guide can be done safely by experienced mountaineers, provided they possess the skill, equipment, and knowledge necessary to tackle the route when the snow and rock are in proper condition. Do not attempt routes rated as Extreme unless you are an elite ski mountaineer.

RECOMMENDED SEASON

This is the season or seasons recommended for climbing the route described. Reasons for recommendations vary. A route with high avalanche exposure might only be recommended for summer after snowmelt. A route with a rough scree gully might only be recommended as a spring snow climb or ski descent.

ROUND TRIP TIME, DISTANCE, AND ELEVATION GAIN

The time and distance are estimates; use them as a general guide. In most cases they assume the descent was made by downclimbing. A ski descent—if it goes smoothly—can shorten the time. Distance varies because of road closures, snow conditions, and individual navigation decisions. A number of routes have long "backpack" approaches. Nonetheless, many of these routes can be done without an overnight by experienced, fit climbers. Such routes often have no defined start other than the trailhead. For these reasons, most routes in this guide, even in the case of those with a backpack approach, are figured from the trailhead. When necessary, additional data is given in the body of the route description.

Elevation gain is figured by subtraction, with additional gain factored in when the route makes more ups and downs. For climbing, elevation gain gives the best estimate of how long a route will take you. After a few peaks, you'll have a rough idea of how long it takes you to climb each thousand feet. With that information, you can use simple math for surprisingly accurate time estimates. To begin, try 1,000 vertical feet an hour while you're actually climbing. For travel on low-angled terrain use two mph in the spring and one mph in the winter. These figures include rest stops.

START, TRAILHEAD

The trailheads are marked on all the maps and are described in the section introductions. For one-day ascents, the trailhead and route start are one in the same: where you park your car. As explained above, routes that require an overnight are usually treated the same way. You can reach most trailheads in an average passenger car, but low-slung cars may encounter problems on even the best dirt roads. If you need a tougher vehicle than a passenger car, the text reminds you that you need either "high clearance 2-wheel-drive" or "4-wheel-drive." In the former case, a pickup truck, van, or passenger car with plenty of clearance will suffice. In the case of 4-wheel-drive, you need at least a stock 4-wheel-drive off road vehicle—not the "all wheel drive" type vehicle; these don't have low enough gearing or high enough clearance. Extreme 4-wheel-drive routes are also noted. These require skilled driving and are not recommended for novice "4-wheelers."

Finding your trailhead is often the crux of fourteener success. Signs are often missing or confusing; roads change; trails are renamed; snow closure varies; roads are gated to prevent erosion. Moreover, guidebook information, by nature, is dated. If you plan a one-day ascent with an early start, it's wise to check the trailhead the day before you start, or camp there.Although you'll have to figure most trailhead changes out for yourself, a stop by the local Forest Service office, map in hand, can save you grief. For snow closure information do the same, and call the county's road maintenance division (see appendix 3.1). In the latter case, you'll need to know the county road number and name (if any). Road numbers are given in the descriptions.

The mileage data in the trailhead descriptions was measured by car odometer. Don't panic if the turnoff doesn't appear at the exact tenth—car odometers differ and are inexact. When mileage is described from a town, assume your starting point is the center of the town unless otherwise noted.

If you're short on time, or short on strength for an overnight pack, consider vehicle access. Indeed, climbers with medical problems or disabilities will find Colorado's copious road access allows them to enjoy many peaks that would otherwise be impossible. After melt-off, many high trailheads are accessible with a 4-wheel-drive vehicle or bicycle. During snow season these same roads are often popular snowmobile trails. Local snowmobile clubs and guide services can help with snowmobile transport on these routes. Motorcycles and bicycles work well for roads that are dry but still gated later in the spring. For example, the paved Maroon Creek Road is gated long after most of the road is free of snow. More than one climber has peddled a bicycle or put-putted up those 7 miles.

Parking your vehicle at a remote roadhead can tempt criminals. At the very least, do not leave valuables in your car. More than one luckless mountaineer has returned from a nice climb only to find his/her car window broken and a subsequent monthly bill which traces a trail of check and credit card purchases across the continent!

ONE DAY FROM ROAD

Winter and late spring ascents often involve more than one night out, especially when snow closure forces a long approach. If this is the case, that fact is noted in this portion of the data block.

MAPS

In most cases the maps in this guide are all you'll need for field navigation. But some complex routes might require a full-size USGS topographic map. In this case, use the book map for reference. Routes are marked with a dark line and reference number corresponding to route number in the text.

For road navigation use text maps or 7.5 minute topos in conjunction with the Forest

Service Forest Visitor maps and Colorado state road maps. The National Forest maps are updated more often and cover larger areas. Thus, they are outstanding for the big picture, but poor for backcountry navigation. All these maps are available at mountaineering stores and Forest Service regional offices. You can buy USGS maps via mail order from the United States Geological Survey, or at the USGS map outlet at gate 5 of the Denver Federal Center (see appendix7).

PHOTOGRAPHS

The Colorado Rockies have a split personality. For about four months a year they rise as gray monoliths through the summer haze. In winter, spring, and early summer, the same peaks sparkle with snow. With variation like this, no photograph can reflect the true nature of a route—it only shows how it was for a moment. With the type of photo reproduction used here, it's much easier to see terrain variations with snow to define them. Thus most of the photos show the mountains with their white mantle. This should pose no problem for summer climbers, since it's easy to imagine the mountain with no snow.

ROUTE DESCRIPTIONS

Used with this book's maps, the route descriptions give you plenty of information, but they are not an inch-by-inch account. You will find enough detail for you to enjoy the routes in the traditional mountaineering sense—that is, a feeling of adventure combined with enough safety to ensure your being able to enjoy the mountains another day. One important warning: our mountains are a dynamic and ever changing land. Though great pains were taken to verify the accuracy of facts in this guide, trails close, landslides occur, signs deteriorate. Take time to verify the written description with your map, talk to locals about your route, and stay aware of your surroundings—safe mountaineering is impossible with a connect-the-dots attitude.

SAFETY NOTES

This section mentions any safety problems specific to the route, as well as general reminders. The latter may be repetitive, but bear repeating. Included in the Safety Notes is information about "sunhit." This is the approximate time the sun hits the top of the route, an essential factor for safe spring season snow work or early summer starts to avoid lightning. For more on timing your start, see the appendices.

PLACE NAMES AND NAME CONVENTIONS

Place names add interest to a map, give us a sense of history, and allow precise communication about routes. Where possible traditional common usage names are used in lieu of commemorative names that often appear only on the map. Unnamed points are referred to by their marked elevation, e.g. Point 12,380'. Variations from "official" names are clarified on the text map (see the Peak Name section above for more information). On occasion, a name is used that was either suggested to the author by other climbers or used in other publications. Readers are encouraged to correct these names or suggest alternatives.

Note the abbreviations used in this book. United States Forest Service is shortened to USFS. Compass directions are abbreviated when they describe direction of travel. For example you would head "E" up the "north" side of the creek.

APPENDICES

The appendices are an essential aid for your planning. They include listings of routes by difficulty, recommended routes, routes you can climb or ski in a day, a sunrise table with tips on starting times, map lists, and other useful information. To some climbers, the recommended routes are the most valuable part of this guide. For those who'd like ski all the peaks, do their "grand slam,"or just pick the best route for their ability, these charts are the ticket.

Michael Kennedy, photo

Near the summit during a winter ascent of Capitol Peak Northwest Buttress.

INTRODUCTION Part 2

FOURTEENER CRAFT Safe Mountaineering

Mountain climbing is a craft. If you're a novice, the learning process can be overwhelming. Some information is obvious, but you can bog down in detail. Still other parts of the craft are best learned from a teacher. It's frustrating. Thus, many people give up learning after they master the basics, then substitute a dilatory attitude that can cause the "didn't have to happen" accident. With a dangerous craft like climbing, knowledge will give you a balance between risk and reward that tips the scale in your favor.

If you're new to mountain climbing, a good way to learn quickly and safely is from guides, climbing schools, and friends. A caveat about friends: Often, you'll end up simply following them, with little real learning. Your friend should be a willing mentor. With such training you can gain adequate skill in three or four seasons—so long as you keep enough modesty to "know what you don't know."

Are you an expert? If so, can you boast equal skill in route finding, weather prediction, avalanche hazard evaluation, first aid, skiing, snow and rock climbing, and general knowledge of the alpine world? The sad fact is many expert mountaineers learn the basics, then plateau where their skill level is "good enough." Often, they mistake their conquests as a sign of great skill, while luck may play a more vital role than they realize. Pluck and luck only go so far—a craftsman must be skilled. Following is a brief sketch of Colorado mountain craft. Novices can use this as a basic outline; experts can check for any voids in their know-how.

ROCKFALL DANGER

The fourteeners were formed by a variety of processes. The most important was a huge uplift of the land that began 70 million years ago. As the land rose, it was attacked by water erosion and, in more recent geologic time, the glaciers of the Ice Ages. The uplifted rock of sedimentary origin, as well as much of the igneous rock in the Rockies, is fractured and loose. Climbing such rock can be like tailgating a gravel truck—only more lethal. The only fourteeners solid enough to keep rock climbers happy are Longs Peak and parts of The Crestones. Yet even these peaks have their share of incontinence.

To travel safely in loose rock terrain, NEVER CLIMB ABOVE ANOTHER CLIMBER. Always move side by side or one at a time. Take care not to stray onto steeper loose rock. Even with utmost care you may still find yourself on rock that gets steeper and looser by the step. In this case don't force your route. Backtrack immediately and look for a safer line; a short traverse will often lead around a steeper area. Wear a helmet for all but the easiest hiking routes, and if you do dislodge a rock, yell *rock!* to warn those below you.

Beware of spontaneous rockfall in gullies. Loose rock stabilized by a freezing night will fall at first sunhit—another reason to start early. Snow climbers may encounter less rockfall danger, but it's amazing how fast rocks roll down a couloir full of frozen spring snow.

MOUNTAIN WEATHER

Lightning, hypothermia, poor visibility, snow avalanches—nothing causes more accidents than weather.

Summer weather—as we usually think of it—never occurs above 13,000 feet in Colorado. It does stop snowing, however, and you can sometimes climb in a t-shirt. But your t-shirt will often stay in your pack. Indeed, you can have full winter conditions on the fourteeners during any month. One common story is of a party climbing on a sunny "summer" day; a storm moves in, and in minutes the mountain is covered with a thin layer of treacherous ice. What's more, every summer you hear reports of exposure accidents and near misses during cold and windy rain storms. Dressing properly, timing your trip, and using good judgment are all ways to avoid problems from inclement weather.

Unseasonable cold is a grim prospect. But heat can also be a problem—summer or winter. To prevent overheating, start hydrated and stay hydrated (carry at least a 2 liters of water and drink several cups each hour), wear clothing easy to ventilate and shed, and do so as soon as (or before) you break a sweat. Heat exhaustion or heat stroke can ruin a trip just as effectively as a lightning bolt.

High altitude sunlight, with less atmospheric filtration, will injure your skin. You can sunburn in less than an hour, and cumulative damage can cause skin cancer. Moreover, thinning of the earth's ozone layer has increased this danger. Fortunately, skin protection is easy: at least every two hours, slather full block sunscreen (SPF 16 or more) on your exposed skin. Don't forget the backs of your hands, your neck, and your ears. For added protection wear a long brimmed hat (add a piece of cloth to the back of your hat for ear and neck protection). Remember sunglasses and carry backup eyewear.

Lightning is a common weather hazard on the fourteeners, and even strikes in the winter, though this is rare. In summer, avoid lightning by starting your trip early in the morning—you must be off the summit before the afternoon thunder clouds build. A good rule of thumb is to leave exposed ridges or summits by noon.

If you're on a high point when thunder booms or electricity crackles, quickly move down so you aren't the highest object around. You should be at least several hundred feet below ridge crests and summits, preferably lower. While you wait out a storm, squat with your feet together as protection against ground bolts. Deep caves offer good protection, but stay out of shallow overhangs where a ground-bolt could use you as a connection between the overhang and ground below. Remember, lightning is a hazard like the avalanche: an encounter will most likely leave you on the losing end.

Winter temperatures in Colorado can drop below -40° Fahrenheit. Combined with ubiquitous wind, this makes frostbite and hypothermia real dangers. On a winter ascent of Pikes Peak, climbers reported a temperature of -30° F, with 50 mph winds—a wind chill of more than 100° below zero! Some winters little snow falls. Depth hoar crystals form within these thin snowpacks, causing extreme avalanche danger (see Early Winter Subseason below). Conversely, such drought winters have the best weather for climbing: cold but clear.

During heavy winters, strong storms move through the mountains one after the other, sometimes up to three a week. Climbing during these winters can mean many aborted trips. Slide danger can be dreadful, and trail-breaking is almost impossible in the loose deep snow. Yet every winter has a bit of everything: sparse snow periods and periods of constant storm. So take heart; some climbing is possible during even the heaviest winters.

A fourteener winter ascent can be a splendid experience. The keys to safety and success (and enjoyment) are timing and perseverance. Ideally, start your trip on short notice. This allows you to catch the snowpack in the 24 hour window after the last storm (for avalanche stability) but before the next. Short notice starts are hard if you have an inflexible job, or you're from out-of-state. In this case begin your trip, but have an alternate plan in case your chosen time falls during a storm. For options, take a valley tour or ski at a resort. Above all, don't let time constraints force you into weather you'd otherwise avoid. If you can, wait for good weather; remember—most Colorado storms last only several days. It's likely you'll get a few days of good weather between storms.

In Colorado, snowshoes or skis are necessary for almost all winter climbing. While most climbers use skis, snowshoes are used by non-skiers or climbers on technical routes where carrying skis would be awkward.

Forecasting Tips

1. Use your altimeter to check the barometric pressure: steadily falling pressure usually indicates an approaching storm; steadily rising barometric pressure usually indicates clearing weather.
2. Precipitation has little chance of continuing when the barometric pressure is more than 30.10 (again, use your altimeter).
3. When the temperature during a storm drops to less than 5° F, snowfall will rapidly diminish.

4. Cirrus clouds can precede a storm by 24 hours or more. (A ring around the moon is caused by thin cirrus.)
5. Thickening and lowering clouds (usually approaching from the west) indicate an approaching storm.
6. Thickening mountain wave clouds indicate increasing moisture, increasing winds aloft, and a possible approaching storm.
7. Mountain wave clouds and snow plumes on ridges indicate high winds at mountain top levels.
8. Thinning and lifting clouds indicate clearing weather. The end of a storm is often indicated by the lowest point of the barometric pressure curve (see tip 1), a wind shift, and the sudden appearance of ice coated snow crystals or graupel (snow that looks like small styrofoam pellets).
9. Current weather reports on radio, especially NOAA Weather Radio (VHF band), are your best sources for accurate forecasts while mountaineering.

STREAM CROSSING

If you climb mountains in Colorado, you must cross open streams—during any season. Stream crossing is tricky. You can slip on icy or wet logs; you can break through snow bridges. During spring you'll confront streams in spate with snow melt.

If you're on a summer trail, look for a log crossing or foot bridge. During snow season, you might find a snow or ice bridge. In spring most snow bridges melt, but you might find a bridge formed by avalanche debris. Be certain such bridges are sturdy, especially later in the day when the snow softens. If all else fails, you'll have to wade or rock-hop across. During spring plan for the daily flood cycle. At higher elevations, streams will be at their lowest in the early morning, then become a raging torrent by late afternoon.

Rock hopping is tough. Stream rocks are often slick and may have a coating of morning ice (or ice all day in winter). Thus, you might end up wading anyway. Wading is unpleasant but safe if you do it right. Wear your boots with no socks or inner boot. Leather boots will absorb a little water. Even so, they won't end up much wetter than they would from a normal day's sweat. If you wear plastic boots, the water will be even less of a problem—just pour it out when you're done. If you're wading in the winter, take care that your feet are warm and your circulation is good before continuing on the trail.

Wading deep fast streams is perilous. Belaying the wader can lessen the danger. But belaying must be done properly—people have drowned while tied to the end of a rope. The proper method is to use two lines. Set one as far as possible upstream above the wader, the other on the bank where he starts across. The upper line keeps him from being washed down the stream; the lower line is used to pull him in if he gets in trouble. It is easy to set up this system with two belayers but tricky with one. For the one belayer method, station yourself on the bank where the wader starts. The upstream rope goes from you, upstream through an anchored carabiner, then back down stream to the wader. The lateral rope goes from you directly to the wader. Use a belay brake on the upstream rope; the force of moving water can outdo the strongest belay hand. Roped stream crossing works well on smaller streams—in "big water" a person in trouble will drown before you can haul them in.

STEEP SNOW

Climbers die every year from sliding falls on snow. Thus, no discussion of safe snow climbing and steep skiing would be complete without a review of the self arrest—the time honored method for stopping such falls.

For snow climbers and mountain skiers the self arrest has four forms. These depend on gear. Climbers should learn to use their ice axe. Skiers can use specialized self arrest grips on their ski poles. These are less effective than an ice axe. Yet skiing while holding an ice axe is dangerous and awkward, so arrest grips can be useful. If you have ski poles, but no arrest grips or ice axe, you can perform a self arrest with your pole tips. This is awkward and ineffective. Lastly, if you have nothing, you can try to arrest with your hands and boot toes. This is

A ski pole self arrest may work, but an ice axe is better.

bogus—but good to practice so you know why you need a tool for an effective arrest.

A successful self arrest is a skilled acrobatic maneuver. You must practice until it becomes instinct. If you're new to the game, a snow climbing course is your best bet for learning. If you're an expert, you should still practice periodically.

Self arrest has one other important aspect: whether you're climbing or skiing, wear nonskid clothing. Slick nylon can turn a small slip into a deadly slide/fall. Wool blend knickers and ski pants are nonskid, as is pile fabric. Cordura nylon is better than slicker nylons. Experienced snow climbers and backcountry skiers have a name for slick nylon shell pants: "death pants."

SKI SAFETY

Most backcountry skiing accidents are the result of skiing out of control and without regard for hidden obstacles. In general, to ski safely in the wilderness you should "survival ski." To survival ski means to ski in control. You must anticipate hazards, fall as little as possible, and if a fall is inevitable, do it in a way that makes the consequences less serious. Practice survival skiing at the ski resort; then use it in the backcountry.

Backcountry skiing on the fourteeners adds a few wrinkles to ski safety: mainly steep snow. The danger in skiing steep snow is a that fall might result in the dangerous sliding fall I mentioned above under "self arrest". You can't evaluate this danger by slope angle alone. A 38° powder slope might present no danger of a fall, but the same slope covered with frozen spring snow could be deadly. Even low-angled slopes can be dangerous given certain conditions, such as rain glaze.

Learning to judge life threatening "fall potential" is hard. Plainly, you can not gain experience on the actual slopes in question. Again, what you must do is practice your self arrest on slopes with safe runouts. Lots of self arrest practice on slopes with different angles and snow conditions will give you the background you need for judgment—and for correcting your mistakes!

SNOW CLIMBING

Most of the safety aspects of steep snow are covered above under Ski Safety, yet steep snow climbing has its own set of problems. Foremost is the question of rope use. Many snow climbers are convinced that connecting their group with a rope increases their safety. The theory is if one person slips, the others can drop into a self arrest and stop the fall. In reality this technique may not work. If the fall happens when the party is inattentive, they'll be jerked off their feet and fall in a tangle of bouncing packs, people, and ropes. Climbing literature abounds with accounts of such falls.

All things considered, snow climbers should only tie together while using anchored belays, moving through a crevasse area on a glacier, or negotiating a corniced ridge. In other rare situations climbers might travel "in coils" to save the time of tying in and untying (time saved can greatly increase safety). If you must safeguard novice climbers on steep snow, you can make roped travel safer with fixed ropes. Used quite often by Outward Bound, and in the past by mountain clubs in the Northwest, fixed ropes provide almost fail-safe protection. For example, a group of 4 climbers could carry several 165 foot ropes. All party members are equipped with a climbing harness and ascending device. When they reach steeper terrain, they tie all the ropes together (if need be), and the best climber in the group climbs the snow while on belay from the bottom. He can protect himself

Climbing for a spring ski descent.

with rock or snow anchors if needed (in that case the ropes would be used for individual pitches rather than being tied together). When he reaches his destination (or runs out of rope), he anchors the rope, and the party climbs together while protecting themselves with their ascenders. The beauty of this system is it averts the danger of unanchored roped travel without sacrificing the huge amounts of time to belay climbers one at a time.

The routes in this book seldom require rope work. Nevertheless, unusual snow or ice conditions or a sick partner can change the easiest climb into a technical problem. So on all but the easiest routes, carry a lightweight rope. If you do carry a rope, be sure you know the fundamentals of belaying and rappelling. Indeed, a rope can get you out of hairy situations, but like any tool a rope is only as good as its user.

Also, don't hesitate to set anchors and belay your skiing in steep terrain. A belayed ski descent is a legitimate application of mountain craft. Purists might scoff— you cannot argue the beauty of an individual challenging a mountain solo, with nothing but skis, axe, and crampons—but most of us would forgo the "edge" in favor of many years of mountain enjoyment—protected by the safety of a rope.

It's immeasurably safer and more efficient to climb snow with crampons and ice axe. Make these items a standard in your kit if snow climbing is remotely possible. The same goes for the excellent ski crampons available for alpine touring ski bindings. Crampon technique for snow is simple. For low-angle work, walk with a normal gait. Steeper angles require more technique: balancing on your front points or using a series of traverses to keep your feet flat or a combination of the above. "Snow school" with a guide service is a good way to learn snow climbing.

Crampons give you security, but conversely they also cause falls. One noxious occurrence, "snow balling," happens when snow sticks to your boot soles. It gets so thick your crampon points won't bite. Some models of crampons have a plastic sheet that helps prevent snow balling. Silicon spray helps, too. Sometimes nothing works and you must whack the snow off your crampons before every step. A sharp rap with your axe works well. The other common trip-up occurs when your crampon catches your other leg's clothing or crampon strap. Prevent this with a careful gait and heavy fabric gaiters which a crampon point is less likely to penetrate. Many snow climbers dull their crampons slightly to make them less likely to catch on clothing, but this makes them less sure on ice.

AVALANCHE SAFETY

In fourteener country, snow is on the ground from fall to late spring—a span that can cover more than 6 months! During that time, avalanche danger is always possible. Snow slides are a terribly fickle phenomenon. Great strides have been made in avalanche prediction, but experts are still "dead wrong" much too often. Yet you can reduce avalanche risk to an acceptable level, chiefly by choosing times and routes for your climbing that will expose you to less hazard. This is done by the practices of "hazard evaluation" and "hazard avoidance."

Avalanche!

To practice "hazard avoidance," choose your route to avoid areas exposed to slides. Such navigation seems basic: for avalanche terrain you need a slope of 25° or more—and snow. But route finding in slide terrain is as subtle as celestial navigation, and just as hard to master. You must put in hours of book study (see bibliography)—and many days in the mountains. The subtleties arise because of slight terrain variations that make the difference between safe and dangerous routes.

To make sense of the terrain, subtle or not, you must identify slide danger: this is "hazard evaluation." Again, the key is education. If you are a novice, begin your study with books, advice from others, and perhaps a session with an avalanche school. Combine your study with practice. Indeed, "experience is the best teacher"—but you must temper your experience with caution. With practice you'll be able to pinpoint times when your intended routes are an acceptable risk.

The best way to be safe from snow slides is to stay off avalanche slopes and out of run-out zones. Below timberline, heavily timbered terrain can give you these danger-free routes. Just remember: light timber is no insurance against slides. As the saying goes, "if the trees are close enough together to make you cuss, they're safe." Above timberline, rock ribs and ridges provide safe lines to the fourteener summits.

In many situations skirting a run-out or not crossing a slope are impractical choices. If your hazard evaluation skills are good, you may make a decision to expose your party to minimal hazard. Above all, don't let summit fever cloud your judgment. You can come back another day—the mountain will still be there.

RULES OF THUMB FOR ROUTE FINDING IN AVALANCHE TERRAIN

1. **At Home:**
   - Call the Forest Service avalanche information number.
   - Check group and yourself for essential items and knowledge:
     Survival gear, avalanche transceiver, shovel, self-rescue capability, route finding
   - Know previous weather, current weather, and forecast.
   - Check map and guide book for your route's avalanche exposure.
2. **Identify Avalache Paths, Runouts, and Staring Zones.**
   - Prepare at home with map study
   - Use constant vigilance in the field
3. **Make an Extra Effort to Find and Use Routes with No Hazards.**
   - Areas blown clear of snow
   - Early morning frozen snow (in the spring)
   - Heavy timber
   - Slope angle below 26 degrees or over 50 degrees
   - Ridges
   - Valley floor (with an eye out for danger above)

IF YOU MUST TRAVEL OVER AVALANCHE SLOPES

4. **Be Willing to Turn Back; Evaluate Slide Probability Via:**
   - Snow pit study
   - Recent snow accumulation (wind or precipitation)
   - Sunrise and nighttime low temperature (spring season)
   - Slide activity on other slopes
   - Knowledge of past avalanche cycles
   - Forest Service avalanche phone
5. **Travel one at a time over lowest-angled portion of path.**
6. **Identify and use islands of safety.**
7. **Avoid starting zones.**
8. **Use an anchored belay while crossing smaller slopes.**
9. **If, as a last resort, you must descend a small avalanche slope, first belay a tester in the staring zone. If he can trigger a slide it will make the path safe for the rest of the group.**
10. **Expedient avalanche rescue is only possible with the use of an electronic avalanche transceiver and a good shovel—every person in your party should carry these items.**

Deep hard sastrugi such as this may indicate stable, wind-compacted snow.

MINIMIZE AVALANCHE RISKS

1. Wind

Year around in the Rockies the wind hammers the lands above timberline. Areas where the wind scours or packs the snow may be avenues of safety. The Northeast Ridge of Mount Elbert (1.2.6) is often in this condition, as is the North Ridge of Holy Cross (1.1.1). Areas with no snow are obvious, while windpacked snow is less distinct. Look for patches of vegetation and ground to get an idea of how deep the pack is, and keep an eye out for sastrugi (means "frozen ocean"; see photo) patterns more than several inches deep. These indicate major wind erosion and compaction.

Windscoured areas present several problems. First, they are uncommon below timberline, so you can't count on wind scour for a safe approach. Second, if wind has been strong, snow may have been transported from scoured areas and deposited as a dangerous hair-trigger slab on other slide paths above timberline. Most experts are extremely careful when they deal with paths of this sort. Yet down in the trees, many of the same people blithely cross horrendous slide runouts without thought of the snow above. To prevent this mistake, include all the snow above you in your "sphere of awareness." Third, because wind deposited snow varies so greatly by exposure, climbers can easily traverse from a safe scoured area to an unsafe slab that is literally inches away. For the reasons above, careful route finding should go hand-in-hand with crystal-ball guesses about snow stability at high altitudes.

2. Timing

Snow is most likely to slide within 24 hours after being deposited (by wind or storm) at a rate of 1 inch an hour or more for 9 hours or more. Thus, by using this simple rule of thumb you can better your odds: wait at least 24 hours before exposing yourself to avalanche slopes that have been newly loaded. Avalanches may still fall after this period—but they are less likely. Even with less loading than described above, this 24 hour rule is still a good standard.

The cyclic nature of slide danger can help you in another way: simply pick a route that has already avalanched. If no other slides are possible, either from more snow in tributary paths or from a collection area above the path, climb it. Bed surface snow (that which remains after an avalanche) has been known to slide on rare occasions, but only when it is a thick slab over another sliding surface—an easy thing to check with a quick snow pit.

3. Seasons of the Snowpack

Colorado avalanche danger varies by four subseasons: Early Winter, Mid-to-late Winter, Spring, and Summer. You can use qualities unique to these seasons for help with your safety decisions.

Snowpack/Early Winter: During this subseason from about October to January, the Colorado peaks have a thin snowpack, weak sunlight, and very cold temperatures. Almost every year an unstable layer of temperature gradient snow crystals (depth hoar) forms in the snowpack. This depth hoar layer is so loose it's hard to climb or ski, and it forms a perfect trigger and sliding surface for avalanches. During most years many avalanches run in the early winter Season.

Nonetheless, the early winter season can be safer in two scenarios. First, every few years the early winter season is cut out by heavy snow falls. In that situation the snowpack mimics mid-to-late winter season snow—without the dangerous depth hoar layers. In the second scenario, at the start of a normal early winter season you can find fairly safe snow before the depth hoar forms. This snow, however, is usually thin and infirm, making for laborious climbing and dangerous skiing because of hidden obstacles. Perhaps the safest early winter seasons are those with little or no snowfall. In this event skiers will weep, but the fourteeners can be climbed on foot and snowshoe via their summer routes with no avalanche danger.

For the expert mountaineer early winter can be a bittersweet time on the fourteeners. It's always cold and slide danger is often extreme. Yet the short days with their longer dusks and dawns have a subtle beauty worth enjoying. With proper hazard evaluation and avoidance, you can climb and ski the fourteeners in the early winter. But only experts should venture; less experienced winter mountaineers should stick to safer valley excursions.

Snowpack/Mid-to-Late Winter: In this subseason, usually between January and early March, warmer temperatures and deep snow retard the depth-hoar formation that makes the early winter snow so dangerous. The thick snowpack collapses under its own weight. It either stabilizes by virtue of the snow crystals adhering to each other (sintering), or avalanches with the new snow's weight as a trigger.

If the snow slides to the ground (a "climax avalanche"), stability may result if the slide cleans out the depth-hoar and new snow builds up fast enough and thick enough to sinter and not develop more depth-hoar. Climax avalanches in the mid-winter season often lead to "repeater" slides. In this event, a layer of depth hoar crystals remains on the slide path after the slide, or new snow isn't deposited quickly enough to halt the formation of new depth-hoar. Danger develops again when new snow is deposited over the depth hoar.

You can climb and ski safely during many days in the mid-to-late winter season. Some days, however, are extremely dangerous. During these periods skiers are even killed during "safe" valley tours. To travel safely in this season, you must practice your hazard evaluation and avoidance, and take avalanche hazard reports seriously. If hazard in your area is rated as extreme, or an avalanche warning is in effect, stay away from all avalanche terrain. If you lack the skill to identify such terrain, travel with someone who can.

Snowpack/Spring: During the spring subseason, a period of 12 to 16 weeks between late March and July, the snowpack begins to thaw and compact. This process is contingent on elevation, aspect, and weather. Thus, one slope can still have a mid-winter snowpack while another has a spring snowpack.

The outstanding attribute of spring snowpack is avalanche danger is almost totally predictable—and thus avoidable. This is a marked contrast to Colorado's deserved reputation as a winter slide trap. Spring snow is predictable because spring avalanches are almost always one of two types: the wet snow slide or the direct action slide.

Direct action slides are those that happen during or just after storms when new snow slides off of the older snow underneath.They are common in the spring because frozen spring snow makes a good sliding surface. Direct action slides are easy to avoid: just stay out of avalanche terrain during and shortly after spring storms.

Wet snow slides are possible only when most of the snowpack is thawed and saturated with water. Fortunately the thawing process follows a daily cycle, freezing by night and melting by day. While the snow has a solid frozen shell, it will not avalanche (for total safety, climb or ski under these conditions). In the morning, as soon as the sun hits, this shell begins to thaw. In the afternoon thawing takes place in earnest and avalanches are common. Keep in mind you are dealing with slopes of varied aspect, so the morning sun hits them at different times. A north or west slope will warm much later than a south or east slope. This book provides the approximate time when the sun first hits the routes and appendix 5 is a detailed treatise on timing a snow climb or ski descent.

Beware of one "gotcha": after a warm or cloudy night only a thin shell of snow will freeze—or not freeze at all. Either occurrence makes the snow unsafe. You can test for the freeze by digging and probing. While the whole snowpack will not freeze, it should have a solid frozen shell too thick to kick a boot through. Also, check the air temperature when you get up in the morning. If you're at a high camp, the temperature must be in the low thirties for a proper freeze. Yet the air temperature need not drop to freezing for the snow surface to freeze; radiant cooling also helps the freezing process—hence the need for a clear night. At lower elevations it is hard to use temperature to evaluate the snow above. Try adding 2 degrees to 31 degrees for every thousand feet below 11,000 feet. If the morning temperature is warmer than that, take time to carefully evaluate the snow as you climb. (Take similar precautions after nights with cloudy skies.) Don't hesitate to leave earlier if you doubt your timing—you can always lounge on the summit if it's too dark to descend. As one climber said, "you can never start too early for a real adventure."

One caveat about the spring season: sometime, usually in May, a major slide cycle occurs when the snow from 10,000 feet on up finally gets saturated with water. You don't want to be traveling during this time, since whole valley sides may run. You can avoid this cycle by paying attention to Forest Service avalanche reports, as well as by making your own observations while driving into the higher valleys. Look for consecutive warm days and nights combined with a deep snowpack from heavy March storms or a heavy winter.

For a fabulous alpine holiday, time your skiing or snow climbing to coincide with the spring season. You'll find the perfect crampon surface on the frozen morning snow. Often you'll find a layer of "corn snow" covering the snowpack. Corn is so fun to ski some mountain skiers seek out the stuff like pilgrims.

Snowpack/Summer: Eventually the freezing, thawing, and compaction described above leads to a dense snowpack almost free of avalanches. You'll find this mature snow in late spring and summer, at high altitude. Fourteeners have a lot of it. Mature snow only slides when it undergoes rapid melting, such as several inches of warm rain or unusually hot weather. It is decent for skiing, but usually has lots of embedded rocks and sun cups. If you climb or ski in mid-summer this is the snow you will find. Cramponing mature snow is delightful. It's also the only way you can safely climb such snow. Indeed, many climbers are hurt or killed climbing on mature snow without proper gear and technique.

BE FOREWARNED: THESE SEASONS MAY OVERSIMPLIFY THE PROBLEM

After a winter with a "bad" snowpack, (that with many dangerous weak layers), the potential for slab avalanches can persist through spring and on into summer. Moreover, snow can fall during any month. Since most late spring or summer slide danger is caused by thawing snow, you can avoid hazard by starting your climb early. For example, in June of 1992 two people were killed in a slab avalanche in an east facing couloir on South Maroon Peak. They were climbing during late morning. Several other people had climbed the same snow earlier in the morning—those people are still alive.

Many nonseasonal factors alter snowpack stability. Suncrust layers, surface hoarfrost, and wind loading are a few examples. What's more, pinpointing these snow subseasons is complicated by many things. Their durations vary from year to year and by exposure. For example, a mountain could have spring-season snow on a south face, while the north face snow still behaves like a mid-to-late winter pack. To identify snow subseasons, study the descriptions below. Keep a record, perhaps a journal or just a good memory, of the winter's crucial avalanche factors. These include snowfall, wind activity, thaws, and slide cycles. Supplement your own field experiences with this information. To get a sense of conditions, speak with mountaineers who have recently traveled in the area. Ski patrol snow-safety people, who deal with slide danger every day, are another good source. Finally, make regular calls to the local Forest Service avalanche information number (see directory in this book). This number provides information on seasonal trends and also gives a general hazard rating.

It is impossible to be one hundred percent sure about any avalanche slope. The best defense is total defense: avoid avalanche slopes whenever possible and turn back at the slightest provocation (see "Winter Routes" below). Use the following rules to triple check your safety habits.

During snow season, backcountry deaths in the Rockies usually result from avalanches. Nevertheless, many snow-season backcountry accidents and medical emergencies result from causes other than snow slides. Mountaineers should take care not to be blinded from these hazards by avalanche paranoia.

ROUTE FINDING AND ORIENTEERING ON THE FOURTEENERS
Orienteering

Orienteering means finding exact locations—and navigating between them. When climbing and skiing on the fourteeners, you use orienteering mostly on your approach to the peak. Intricate routes, such as those on Pyramid Peak, may require orienteering during the actual climb.

The essentials for effective orienteering in the Colorado Rockies are topographic maps (those reproduced here will suffice for all but the most complex routes; such routes are noted in the text), a good quality altimeter, a compass, and skill. The former items can be purchased at any mountaineering store. Skill requires practice. Treat each of your backcountry trips, no matter how simple, as route finding exercises. Start with simple routes, like Mount Bierstadt from Guanella Pass. Then graduate slowly to complex routes such as Pyramid Peak. Above all, know your limits. If you doubt your abilities to follow a route, hire a guide or climb with a friend who knows the route. Have patience—learning orienteering requires a long apprenticeship.

The importance of your altimeter for orienteering is paramount. It, a compass, and a topographic map are the only tools that allow you to safely navigate in low visibility conditions. The trick to using your altimeter is to keep it calibrated. An altimeter reads air pressure, which is constantly changing. To counteract this you must recalibrate at every chance. Calibration is simple but takes discipline: each time you reach a location with a known elevation, check your altimeter and set it to the known elevation if it deviates. Mountain tops, passes, huts, stream confluences, and trailheads are good places for recalibration.

Once your altimeter is calibrated, you can identify your exact progress up a valley, along a mountainside, or along a ridge. Do so by map-plotting the intersection of your route with your elevation. For flawless route finding, use your compass as well and estimate how far you have traveled (based on a known travel speed from other trips).

Though compass work is often secondary to map and altimeter, it can be invaluable. This is especially true in poor visibility when you have no clearly defined drainages or ridges to follow. This situation is quite common in the alpine bowls of the Rockies. Another use of your compass is for low altitude travel in darkness. Snow climbers and skiers are often in this situation.

Use a compass with a flat see-through base and rotating needle housing. Usually, you use your compass to "orient" your map. This means positioning the map to match the surrounding terrain so you can visualize your route. You then navigate from an oriented map just as you would with a floor-plan or road map.

What you must remember about compass orientation is two "norths" confuse the issue: magnetic north and geographic north. The vertical borders of the map line up close to geographic north—but your compass shows magnetic north. This difference is known as declination. The simple way around this problem is to use the direction rays on your map. Rotate your compass needle housing until the north-south lines are parallel to the long edges of the triangular base. Simply line up the edge of the compass base with the MN line on the direction rays, then rotate the map and compass until the compass needle is pointing to the N on the needle housing. Your map is now oriented. Take heed, orienting by compass is easy, but an oriented map is no help unless you know your location and can identify surrounding terrain. In other words, use your map before you get lost!

On rare occasions when you encounter dense timber, fog, or white-out snow, you will utterly depend on your compass. This demanding form of compass use is called "following a bearing." Simply put, by combining map and compass (and compensating for declination) you figure out your direction of travel. You then use your compass needle and dial to spot a landmark that marks your travel direction, and you travel toward your landmark. In situations with limited visibility, use nearby landmarks and repeat the process each time you reach the landmark. With complete lack of visibility, such as in fog, you may have to use a companion as a marker. Using your compass, you direct her movements as she walks, then have her stop while she is still in sight. You then move to your "human landmark" and repeat the process. This is an effective, albeit tedious, method. One problem is you must follow a straight line—a hard task if you need to avoid avalanche slopes and other obstacles. What do you do with complete lack of sight, such as night travel? Hold you're compass in front of you and check it every couple of minutes—it's surprising how quickly you'll walk a circle when you have no points of reference.

SNOW SEASON CLIMBING

Trail Breaking

At most times in the winter, as well as spring afternoons, skiers and snow climbers sink into the snow with every step. If you're on foot, this is fondly termed postholing and can be one of the most strenuous things you'll ever do. Share the labor by changing leads often. Use a rhythmic pace at your endurance level. You can tell you are at your endurance level by being able to converse; if you are gasping too hard to talk, you won't last long. Remember to eat and drink regularly—about once an hour is a good schedule.

Finding Good Snow

The fourteeners never have a total snow cover. Wind and sun strip various exposures, and from year to year different ranges have more or less snow depending on how storms track. Nevertheless, from late October through July, climbable and skiable snow exists in the Rockies. If you suspect problems with snowcover, try to check your intended route from a road.

In the winter, more skiers are stymied by trap crust than any other snow condition. This variety of breakable crust sucks your skis down under the surface and prevents them from turning. But you can ski trap crust—and even have fun in the process. Most skiers handle trap crust with rebound turns. These are jump turns that use the springboard effect of your skis to pop you up out of the snow. Regular jump turns use wild leaps to do the same, but take more energy and provide less control. To do a rebound turn, first commit yourself to the fall line using proper anticipation; then, when completing your first turn, aggressively press your skis into the snow with a little extra leg extension. Let the skis snap back and, as they do, pull them out of the snow with leg retraction. While your skis are still above the snow, change their direction just enough to make them keep turning when they are back in the snow. A smooth but aggressive rhythm helps with rebound turns. So does practice.

In the spring and summer, finding good snow is a question of daily timing and slope aspect. In general, you'll find the least reliable spring snow on eastern slopes. These slopes get warmth from the morning sun, then continue to gain warmth later in the day from the warm afternoon air; this process heats eastern exposures more than other exposures. In the early spring look for good skiing on south facing slopes, and in the late spring and summer look for turns on the northern exposures (see appendix 5). Another factor is that Colorado's winter storms follow three different tracks: north, middle, and south. Each year one or two of these regions will have more snow than the other(s). A few phone calls to Forest Service supervisors' offices (see appendix 3.4) will give you an idea of where the snow is the deepest and at what elevation the snowcover begins.

A CLIMBER'S RESPONSIBILITIES

We climb, hike, and ski the backcountry for many reasons—the feelings of freedom and well-being are at the top of the list. You can't beat a crampon climb up a swooping snow gully to a summit, then launching off for a long ski run. Or watching the sunrise from a four-teener. Or hiking a long ridge high above the timber.

Yet the grim fact is all mountaineering has risks, and occasionally a mountaineer must be rescued. This costs money—sometimes a lot of money. Most county sheriff departments are required by law to rescue those in need, no matter what the cost. Rescues cause financial problems. For example, during the winter of 1986-1987, Summit County, Colorado, used up its whole emergency budget digging out avalanche victims.

Thus, the politics of rescue have boiled down to economics and led to proposals that limit or ban our use of the backcountry. Fortunately, a fair solution to this problem exists. In 1987 a law was enacted in Colorado that takes a surcharge from every hunting and fishing license fee and places the funds into a state rescue fund. In 1992, the law was expanded to include snowmobile, all-terrain-vehicle, and boat registrations. In 1994, the law was again expanded to include a rescue certificate that anyone who uses the backcountry can buy, including mountaineers. If you don't already buy a license or registration that includes this rescue surcharge, you can buy the $1.00 rescue certificate wherever fishing licenses are sold. While purchase of this certificate is optional, it is highly recommended.

Safe mountaineering on the fourteeners is a complex craft; at times it is tedious, most often spectacular, and always rewarding. Surely, one of the lures of climbing is the feeling of well-executed craft. A responsible commitment to safe mountain travel will let you to take that feeling home, time after time. Enjoy our glorious mountains—but enjoy them with care.

Hope you never need one of these.

INTRODUCTION Part 3

EQUIPMENT

Today's mountaineering equipment is lightweight, durable, and well-designed. Nevertheless, the demands of summer mountain climbing, ski mountaineering, and snow climbing cause equipment to fall short. Choosing the right gear for your style of mountaineering is a key to enjoying the fourteeners. The following is intended only as a brief equipment primer. For up-to-date information refer to magazine equipment reviews and shop employees.

Clothing

Though mankind was brought naked into the world, Eden was not at 14,000'. In any season, you should dress with care for a climb on the Colorado fourteeners. A warm day in July might see you in shorts and t-shirt, but let the clouds roll, and you'll be reaching for more clothing. It's in your pack, yes?

The key to dressing for mountain climbing is "layering." This simply means wearing several thin garments rather than fewer thicker ones. Layering allows precise temperature control and gives you efficient insulation by virtue of trapped air pockets.

For spring and summer climbs, carry (or wear) synthetic fabric shorts or hiking pants, longsleeved shirt, and sun hat. Avoid cotton; it's propensity for holding moisture, and subsequent evaporation cooling, can quickly chill you to the point of danger. People have died in the mountains because they wore cotton. When the temperature drops, remove damp clothing and dress in a light turtle neck and tights, both made from any of the excellent synthetic fibers. Colder still, dig out your jacket made of acrylic "pile" fiber and another pair of thicker tights. Lastly, for wind or wet put on your "shell garment." Your shell should be pants and jacket made from a waterproof/breathable fabric. Carry gloves and a warm hat for "full" conditions.

Earlier, I covered the importance of non-skid clothing for snow climbing and steep skiing. Several companies make excellent climbing pants and jackets made from rough twill-like fabrics with good friction. Many mountaineers have found traditional stretch wool ski pants, combined with gaiters, make good outer wear for snow or ice climbing.

Skiers will want attire suitable for their specialized movements. Wool/lycra blend ski pants with padded knees make good leg covering and have the added benefit of higher friction if you take a sliding fall. Special ski gloves help your grip, and shell jackets and pants cut for ski motion help you move.

In winter stick with the layering concept, just carry more layers. During the coldest days even waterproof/breathable shell fabrics may trap too much moisture. In this case use non-waterproof breathable nylon shells, known as "wind shirts" or "wind suits." Shell garments that combine jacket and pants, known as "one-piece suits" are terrific for winter climbing. Some of those designed for alpine skiing use breathable uncoated fabric and are perfect for extreme cold. Others are made from waterproof/breathable fabrics and work well for all but the coldest times. Women, and perhaps both sexes, should consider having a full crotch zipper installed in their shells (some are sold with this included). Indeed, obeying nature's call in a blizzard can be dangerous if you must partially undress.

Footwear

Your footwear should suit your style. If you're bagging peaks during a dry summer day, lightweight fabric hiking shoes might be your choice. For rougher climbs and backpack approaches, mid-weight boots, usually made from leather, are better. For snow or mixed snow and rock your best choice is a pair of modern plastic mountain boots. Use gaiters, whatever your choice in footwear. See below for information on ski boots.

Sun Protection

As mentioned in Mountain Weather (Introduction I), ultraviolet (UV) radiation will ruin unprotected eyes and skin. Use sunglasses with certified UV filtration, preferably 100%. On spring snow use side shields on your sunglasses or add a small flap of tape for the same effect. Skiers, winter climbers, and even spring snow climbers should carry goggles. Modern ski goggles with double layer lenses are good. Again, be sure these are certified to filter the dangerous UV rays. Another advantage of carrying sunglasses—and goggles—is you're covered if you lose either.

Light

Carry an artificial light source whenever you climb. If you're serious about safety, you'll start many of your climbs in the dark. And you never know when yours or someone else's problems will require you to be out at night. The best light source is a lightweight battery-operated headlamp. Carry a spare bulb and batteries. Winter climbers should note: Nicad and Lithium cells give the best performance in the cold. Rechargeable Nicads also save money and cause less pollution. Handheld flashlights are useless for climbing.

Water Container

Hydration is crucial for mountaineers. Summer or winter, your lowly canteen takes on new meaning. Wide-mouth plastic bottles make the best water jars. Most hold about a quart, so carry two on longer climbs. In summer larger parties can save weight by filtering or treating water from streams to replenish their supplies.

Winter mountaineering in the Elks.

During the colder winter months, frozen water can be an acute problem—sucking on a block of ice is no way to stay hydrated. To keep your water from freezing, fill your bottle in the morning with hot water or tea, wrap the bottle in extra clothing, and stow it in your pack as close to your back as possible. Some people carry an unbreakable thermos or one of the insulated jars available in mountaineering stores. The latter will cool sooner than a real thermos, but they never freeze. Another good method is to carry one of the new collapsible bladders in your pack near your back with a tube to your mouth. These resist freezing, and since you can consume the water at a constant rate, you metabolize it more efficiently.

Climbing equipment

When you pick technical climbing gear for most fourteener climbing, make weight as much a gear criterion as anything else. If your gear is too bulky and heavy, it will probably be left behind. Only a few routes in this guide require more than lightweight twelve point crampons, a short lightweight ice axe, and a small diameter 150-foot rope. Wear a helmet in snow gullies, on the steeper climbs like those in the Elk Mountains, and while you extreme ski. Carry minimal anchoring gear ("protection") on the more technical routes. Details for technical gear are covered in the route descriptions. Usually, a few slings, carabiners, and nuts will suffice. Of course, routes exist that require more equipment, such as the climbs on the east face of Longs Peak. High-angle wall climbs such as those are not covered in this book (see bibliography).

Ski Equipment

Ski mountaineering gear has evolved rapidly in the past decade; mountaineers now use everything from nordic racing skis to alpine gear with non-lift bindings. Two pivotal changes stand out: the first is the development of ski equipment that enables mountain skiers to make turns without latching down their heels. This gear is sometimes called "telemark" equipment and is termed "free heel" ski equipment in this guide. Free heel skiing is harder than using a latched heel. But it has its place. For tours that involve a lot of distance, or much hiking, the free heel rigs offer a bit less weight and boots with good walking comfort. But free heel ski boots are poor for snow, rock, and ice climbing. Moreover, the inherent limits of free heel downhill skiing make steep descents in difficult snow the province of an elite group of skiers willing to spend hundreds of days a year perfecting their technique.

If you don't qualify for that select group of free heel skiers, the other exciting change in equipment is the evolution of incredibly light, warm, versatile, and durable alpine touring (AT) ski equipment. These set-ups consist of alpine width skis, specially designed plastic boots, and release bindings that latch down your heel for downhill skiing but unlatch for vertical heel movement while walking.

Modern AT equipment works well for any ski touring other than track skiing, and it has many advantages over free heel gear. Intermediate level alpine skiers can click into AT skis and enjoy ski descents impossible for them with a free heel set up. Additionally, AT boots are designed to double as climbing boots. They work well for snow and ice climbing, are adequate for moves on easy rock, and are warm and dry. For those who tackle hairy ski descents, AT equipment gives a level of safety through control not possible with a free heel. Many folks choose free heel gear because they think it is lighter than AT equipment. In reality you can get AT boots that weigh less than free heel boots, and AT skis weigh about the same as free heel skis. AT bindings add weight, but very little. In the balance, the added efficiency of skiing downhill on AT gear more than makes up for the slight increase in weight. The fourteeners are a good place for AT ski equipment.

Whatever type of skis you use, climbing skins are a must. The mohair type are the lightest, but mountaineers have found the durability and extra grip of the synthetic nylon skins more than makes up for the slight weight increase. If you use AT gear, buy bindings with detachable ski crampons—these are a godsend. Adjustable length ski poles are useful for skiing steep terrain—lengthen them for solid pole plants. Or adjust them to different lengths for a long traverse. Most brands also clamp together to make a long avalanche probe, which can double as a snow depth tester for shelter building. One caveat about adjustable poles: they add another layer of mechanical complexity to your system. In extreme conditions, such as winter fourteener ascents, adjustable poles have been known to collapse or break.

Some ski poles have optional self arrest grips. These are an obvious choice for extreme skiers. Yet snow climbers should consider them as well, since it is efficient to use ski poles for low-angle snow climbing. In doing so, it's nice to have something more in your hands than ski pole grips. Another caveat: for performing a self arrest, ski pole arrest grips are half as effective as an ice axe, so use them thoughtfully.

Even today's superb gear can break. Analyze the frailty in your equipment and carry a well-thought-out emergency repair kit that includes essential spare parts and tools, fire starting items, and clothing repair items. Two things every repair kit should have are malleable wire and duct tape, otherwise known as *god on a roll.*

Gear does not the climber make. Be realistic about your skills and the limits of your equipment. Pick appropriate routes using the ratings in this book. Gradually escalate the difficulty of your climbs—in a learning curve you can stay alive with.

1

NORTHERN SAWATCH MOUNTAINS

On the Mount Elbert Trail, looking west towards the summit, fall.

USFS Forest Visitor Maps: San Isabel National Forest, White River National Forest

Colorado's Sawatch mountain range extends from Interstate Highway 70 on the north, south to Salida and US Highway 50. Its spine forms the Continental Divide. In this book, the Northern and Southern Sawatch are separated (somewhat arbitrarily) by the North Cottonwood Creek drainage and road. Vail, Minturn, Aspen, Leadville and Buena Vista are the gateway cities for the Northern Sawatch. Good accommodations can be had in any of these towns (Aspen and Vail are expensive). Of particular note is the Mount Princeton Hot Springs Lodge on the Cottonwood Pass Road. The Lodge pool is perfect after a long day of mountaineering.

If any one range in Colorado has the easiest climbs, as well as the most accessible snow climbing and skiing, the Northern Sawatch is it. (The Southern Sawatch has similar terrain, but a lack of snow). The Sawatch peaks have big vertical drops, and a good balance between rounded snow humps like Mount Elbert (Colorado's highest) and aretes like Mount of the Holy Cross. Summer hikers and climbers will find the Sawatch to be friendly mountains. All the standard summit routes are easy, and the many wilderness trails in the range could keep a backpacker busy for several lifetimes. All the peaks have worthy winter routes via ridges safe from avalanches, and most are within a day's travel from parking, winter or summer. The spring skiing is exceptional.

SECTION 1.1
Mount of the Holy Cross (14,005')

Mount of the Holy Cross is well known for its cross-shaped, east-facing snow fields; the vertical portion of the snow field forms the famous Cross Couloir. Many people believe the Cross to have religious significance, and Christians frequently make the pilgrimage to view the Cross from Notch Mountain. For pilgrims of a more secular bent, the Cross provides a good snow climb or extreme ski descent, and the peak's North Ridge (1.1.1) is an enjoyable hike, climb, ski descent, or winter adventure.

Mount of the Holy Cross was probably first climbed by miners or Indians. The Cross Couloir was first skied in 1977 by Vail residents Tom and Mike Carr. This was certainly one of Colorado's pioneer extreme descents. Presently, the Cross gets several ski descents each season. With a cliff band near the bottom that most skiers must downclimb or avoid by leaving the couloir, it doesn't rate as a classic ski descent—but it's close. As a snow climb it's sublime but still escapes classic status because the cliffs keep most parties from climbing the entire couloir. The peak's first winter ascent was made in winter of 1943 by Russel Keene and Howard Freedman, 10th Mountain Division soldiers stationed at Camp Hale. They described wading through bottomless Colorado powder during their climb—things never change!

ROADS AND TRAILHEADS

USGS Maps: Minturn, Mount of the Holy Cross
USFS Forest Visitors Map: White River National Forest

While the following descriptions are written as if you're driving from Interstate Highway 70 and south on U.S. Highway 24, you can also reach these trailheads by driving north from Leadville on U.S. Highway 24. To do so, use a "backwards" look at the descriptions to find the well-signed turnoffs from the highway onto the Homestake and Tigiwon Roads.

Tigiwon Road and Half Moon Campground
For a wilderness approach to Mount of the Holy Cross, you can use Cross Creek from a trailhead a short distance up the Tigiwon Road just outside of Minturn. A more popular approach is to drive the Tigiwon Road to Half Moon Campground (open in summer to normal autos). From the campground you can deviate to your route of choice. Call the White River National Forest (Appendix 3.4) for road closure information.

Half Moon Trailhead and Fall Creek Trailhead
To reach the Tigiwon Road, take Interstate 70 east from Glenwood Springs or west from Vail and turn off at the Minturn exit (171). Drive 2 miles S on Highway 24 to Minturn. Continue south through Minturn, and at 4.8 miles from I-70 turn right onto the dirt Tigiwon Road (usually has a good sign). Drive the Tigiwon Road (high clearance 2-wheel-drive) 8 miles to an obvious parking area (10,280'; road's end) near Half Moon Campground. Though you won't see Mount of the Holy Cross from the Tigiwon Road, watch for a view of Notch Mountain at 11.9 miles from I-70. The Half Moon Trailhead is at the upper end of the parking area, and the Fall Creek Trailhead is at the lower end of the parking area, on the south side of the road. Both trailheads have good signs.

The Tigiwon Road is closed in winter near the highway. In this case, though the trail is usually packed by snowmobiles, you are looking at a long 8 mile slog up to the campground, then onto the route of your choice. You can avoid the slog by using a snowmobile.One option is to contact the snowmobile guide service in Minturn and pay them to drop you and your gear off at Half Moon Campground (see directory Appendix3.2). The road usually opens in mid-June.

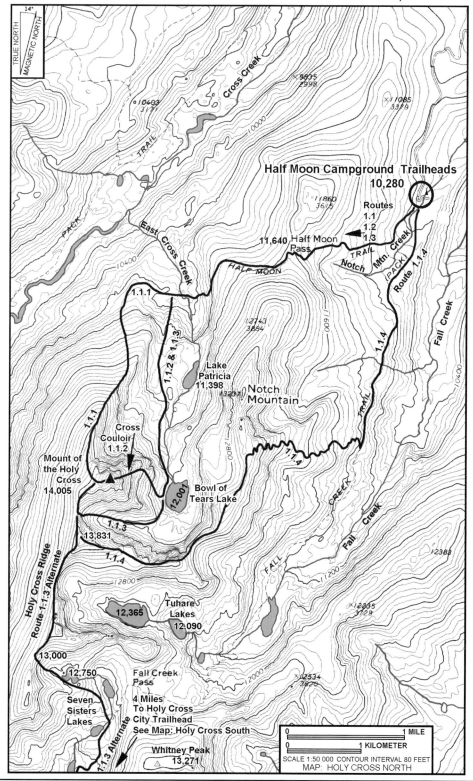

14°

TRUE NORTH
MAGNETIC NORTH

Cross Creek

×9835
2998

×11403
3471

×11085
3379

TRAIL

10000

PACK

Half Moon Campground Trailheads
10,280

×11860
3615

Routes
1.1
1.2
1.3

East Cross Creek

11,640 Half Moon
Pass

Notch

Mtn. Creek

TRAIL (PACK)

Route 1.1.4

10400

HALF MOON

Fall Creek

1.1.1

12745
3854

11600

1.1.4

10400

1.1.2 & 1.1.3

Lake
Patricia
11,398

13237

Notch
Mountain

1.1.1

Cross
Couloir
1.1.2

TRAIL

Mount of
the Holy
Cross
14,005

12800

1.1.4

12,001

Bowl of
Tears Lake

FALL

CREEK

Fall Creek

1.1.3

13,831

1.1.4

Holy Cross Ridge

Route 1-1.3 Alternate

12800

12388

12800

12,365

Tuhare
Lakes
12,090

×12385
3729

12000

11200

13,000

12,750

Fall Creek
Pass

×12534
3820

Seven
Sisters
Lakes

4 Miles
To Holy Cross
City Trailhead
See Map: Holy Cross South

0   1 MILE
0   1 KILOMETER
SCALE 1:50 000 CONTOUR INTERVAL 80 FEET
MAP: HOLY CROSS NORTH

1-1.3 Alternate

Whitney Peak
△ 13,271

Northern Sawatch Mountains 🚶 37

Homestake Road—Holy Cross City Trailhead

Take Interstate 70 east from Glenwood Springs or west from Vail and turn off at the Minturn exit (171). Drive 2 miles S on Highway 24 to Minturn and continue through Minturn. Eleven miles from Minturn (measured from the Turntable Restaurant) you'll come to the well - signed Homestake Road (dirt, 2-wheel-drive). Drive the Homestake Road 8 miles and take a right on Forest Service Road 704; drive 2.2 miles, take another right, and continue 2 miles to intersect the Holy Cross Jeep Trail at 10,320'. Park here at the Holy Cross City Trailhead or drive a tough 4-wheel-drive road several miles to the wilderness boundary just below Hunky Dory Lake. In winter, the Homestake Road is a popular snowmobile and ski trail. Snow closure is at a parking area near the highway. The road opens in early June.

1.1.1	Mount of the Holy Cross—North Ridge	
Ratings:	Summer Climb—Intermediate Ski Descent—Intermediate	
	Snow Climb—Intermediate	
Season:	Summer/Spring	Winter
RT Data:	12 hours, 13 miles, 4,723' ↑	multi-day, 37 miles, 6,843' ↑
Start:	Halfmoon Campground 10,280'	Tigiwon Road snow closure 8,160'
1 Day from Rd:	Yes, with road open or snowmobile	No
Map:	Holy Cross North, pg. 37	
Photos:	pgs. 39, 41	

This route is a fine summer hike, a classic winter ascent, and a less demanding ski descent than many of the peaks in this guide. In the spring the summit and parts of the ridge can be quite dry. In late winter you'll often find skiable snow from the summit or slightly lower.

Summer after snow melt-off: drive to Half Moon Campground (see section introduction). If you're doing the climb in one day, start well before sunrise. From the campground, hike 1,360 vertical feet and 1½ miles W to scenic Half Moon Pass. From the pass, follow a well-traveled trail (as marked on the USGS Mount of the Holy Cross map) that leads down into East Cross Creek.

Once you're in East Cross Creek, immediately climb SW onto the North Ridge of Holy Cross. At the 11,000' level contour around to the west side of the ridge and climb up through trees to timberline. At timberline regain the ridge and follow it to 13,400'. Traverse out onto the west face from here and continue on to the summit. Descend your ascent route.

Spring snow season: Assuming the Tigiwon Road is closed by snow (section introduction), get yourself to Half Moon Campground early enough in the day to continue the 1,360 vertical feet and 1½ miles to a scenic bivouac on Half Moon Pass. Your strategy here is to camp at the first high point of the trip, before you drop to East Cross Creek.

From your bivouac at the pass, drop W to the fringe of the timber, then take a gradual dropping contour W for slightly less than 1 mile to a sparsely timbered shoulder at 11,200'. Descend this shoulder down to about 11,000', then follow a series of aspen groves and brush-filled gullies down into East Cross Creek at around 10,600'. With compacted spring snow you can find a bit of skiing here but be careful of cliff bands.

Once you're in East Cross Creek, follow the summer directions above. Descend your ascent route. On your return climb out of Cross Creek, stay off numerous small avalanche slopes by sticking to the heinous but safe brush and aspen trees.

Winter: Follow the spring snow season directions above. Travel may be rough down into Cross Creek. Persevere. You can avoid numerous small avalanche slopes by bushwhacking aspen trees and brush.

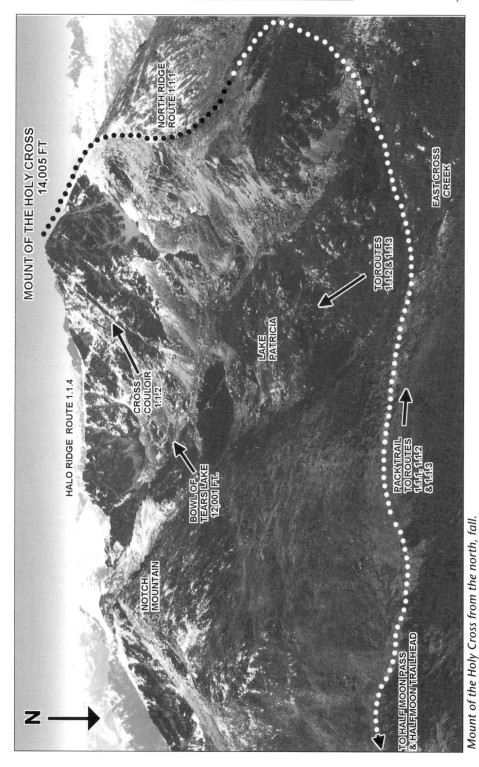

N

MOUNT OF THE HOLY CROSS
14,005 FT

NORTH RIDGE ROUTE 1.1.1

EAST CROSS CREEK

HALO RIDGE ROUTE 1.1.4

CROSS COULOIR 1.1.2

TO ROUTES 1.1.2 & 1.1.3

LAKE PATRICIA

BOWL OF TEARS LAKE 12,001 FT.

PACK TRAIL TO ROUTES 1.1.1, 1.1.2 & 1.1.3

NOTCH MOUNTAIN

TO HALF MOON PASS & HALFMOON TRAILHEAD

Mount of the Holy Cross from the north, fall.

Safety notes: Because this route takes a ridge traverse, you'll have little rockfall danger. Remember that such traversing keeps you up above timberline for much of the climb, so watch for thunder clouds and start early. With snow this route is fairly safe from avalanches. Give some room to the slope to the south as you do the traverse on the west side of Half Moon Pass. Take care with steep slopes between Halfmoon Pass and East Cross Creek and in the timber on the west side of the North Ridge. Rule of thumb: the only timber truly safe from slides is that which you must work to get through. Remember, the slope to the west of the summit could avalanche given unstable snow conditions. This slope can be avoided if you stick to the north ridge. Add several hours to standard sunrise for sunhit.

1.1.2	Mount of the Holy Cross—Cross Couloir	
Ratings:	Ski Descent—Extreme	Snow Climb—Advanced
Season:	Spring or Summer Snow	
RT Data:	12 hours, 13 miles, 4,723' ↑	
Start:	Halfmoon Campground 10,280'	
1 Day from Rd:	High camp recommended	
Map:	Holy Cross North, pg. 37	
Photos:	pgs. 39, 41	

The Cross Couloir is certainly the best known snow gully in Colorado. Every spring it tempts climbers and skiers from all over the state. Climbers will find good crampon conditions into early summer, but rockfall and technical difficulties increase as the snow gets sparse. Early spring is best for skiing since the cliff areas melt out early. Many people belay in the steeper sections, and few skiers or climbers do the whole couloir—they usually enter and exit above the cliff band.

Spring or summer snow: Follow the directions above for the North Ridge (1.1.1). Cross East Cross Creek, continue W a short distance, then climb up the west side of the East Cross Creek drainage 1½ miles to 11,600' (½ mile below Bowl of Tears Lake). The couloir is obvious. It begins with a steep rocky section often devoid of snow, then eases back to the basic Rocky Mountain snow gully (steepest section 43 degrees). If the lower section of the couloir looks forbidding, an easier climb can be had by continuing up the valley to the south end of Bowl of Tears Lake. Indeed, for most climbers this is the best route. From Bowl of Tears Lake take a steep northerly climbing traverse up the east face of Mount of the Holy Cross and intersect the Cross Couloir at 12,740', above the cliff bands. This intersection is critical, since access to the couloir is blocked by its cliffy sides above and below this point. Descend the south ridge or descend the couloir back to your entry point.

Safety notes: Be wary of the steep rocky section lower in the couloir. Do not glissade. Several climbers have died after taking slide/falls over these cliffs. Indeed, during low snow years, many couloirs in Colorado offer safer climbing and skiing. To avoid avalanche danger, ascend and descend the Cross Couloir on frozen or just thawing consolidated spring snow. Most parties should consider starting from a high camp at the Bowl of Tears. This side of Holy Cross is shaded by the close proximity of Notch Mountain, but the upper part of the Cross Couloir still gets sunhit just after standard sunrise. Remember your crampons and ice axe. Due to rockfall, once this route is dry it is not recommended.

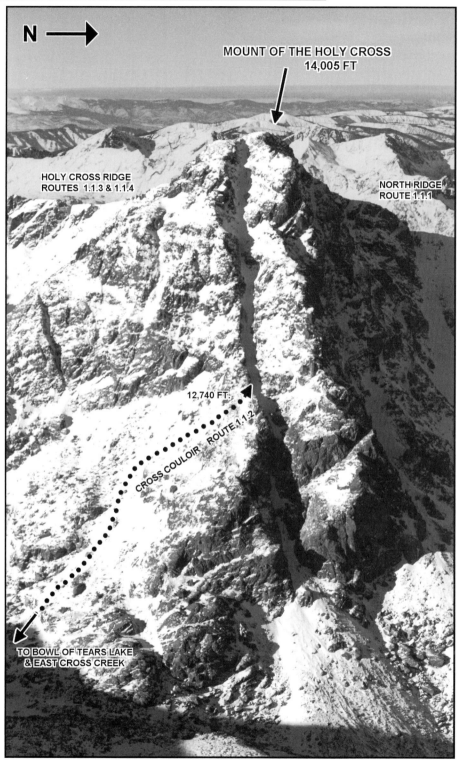

N →

MOUNT OF THE HOLY CROSS
14,005 FT

HOLY CROSS RIDGE
ROUTES 1.1.3 & 1.1.4

NORTH RIDGE
ROUTE 1.1.1

12,740 FT.

CROSS COULOIR ROUTE 1.1.2

TO BOWL OF TEARS LAKE
& EAST CROSS CREEK

Mount of the Holy Cross from the east, early winter.

1.1.3	**Mount of the Holy Cross—Holy Cross Ridge**	
Ratings:	Ski Descent—Advanced	Snow Climb—Advanced
Season:	Spring or Summer Snow	
RT Data:	12 hours, 13½ miles, 4,723' ↑	
Start:	Halfmoon Campground 10,280'	
1 Day from Rd:	Best with a high camp; one day for strong groups	
Maps:	Holy Cross South, pg. 43; Holy Cross North, pg. 37	
Photo:	pg. 41	

Holy Cross Ridge, the south ridge of Mount of the Holy Cross, is a classic crest dividing the Homestake drainage from the Cross Creek drainage. The following route, which gains the ridge close to the summit, is harder than the North Ridge route, but has a wilder feel than the trade routes such as the North Ridge (1.1.1). This route mounts Holy Cross Ridge via a steep hidden cirque. Due to loose rock it's best done as a snow climb in spring or early summer. After the snow melts, use the alternate approach described later in this route description.

Spring or summer snow season: Follow the Half Moon Pass Trail into Cross Creek and follow Cross Creek up to Bowl of Tears Lake (see route 1.1.2). From the south end of the lake, continue south for several hundred vertical feet, then swing W and climb to the south summit ridge (Holy Cross Ridge) via a cirque with a small tarn. The cirque steepens as you near the ridge, and early season climbers may encounter a cornice. Skiers will probably want to leave their skis below the ridge crest. Take the ridge to the summit. Return via the same route or do a traverse by descending the North Ridge (route 1.1.1).

Alternative Southern Approach after snow melt-off (Rated Advanced in spring or summer; not recommended for winter)

If you're up for a long day or overnight, and you want solitude, you can run the complete Holy Cross Ridge from the Holy Cross City Jeep Road. Unlike the route above, which is only safe with a good snowcover, this option goes with or without snow. And with 3,685 vertical feet and 14½ miles round trip, it's a marathon effort.

Drive to the Holy Cross City Jeep Road (see section introduction). Hike up the jeep road and, instead of taking the road to Holy Cross City, continue on the old jeep trail up the drainage to Hunky Dory Lake (11,300'). Continue past Hunky Dorry Lake and stay on the trail as it swings north, becomes the Fall Creek Trail, and leads you into the basin holding Seven Sisters Lakes. Leave the trail at about 12,200', climb the drainage to the highest and northern-most lake in the basin (12,750'), then continue from the lake to the crest of Holy Cross Ridge (13,000'). Beat the ridge (easy ground but high elevation) 1½ miles N to the summit of Mount of the Holy Cross. Return via your ascent route.

1.1.4	**Mount of the Holy Cross—Halo Route**	
Ratings:	Summer Climb—Advanced	Snow Climb—Advanced
Season:	Summer/Spring	Winter
RT Data:	14 hours, 16 miles, 4,825' ↑	multi-day, 32 miles, 5,845' ↑
Start:	Halfmoon Campground 10,280'	Tigiwon Road snow closure 8,160'
1 Day from Rd:	Summer — Yes	Winter — No
Maps:	Holy Cross South, pg. 43; Holy Cross North, pg. 37	
Photos:	pgs. 39, 41	

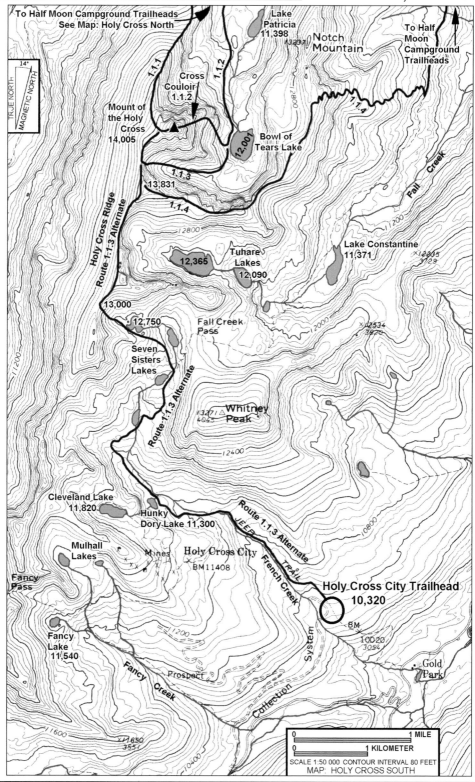

While quite a trudge for most pilgrims, aerobic animals enjoy this route. It also works well as a winter climb to avoid avalanche danger that's more prevalent on other routes.

Summer, or spring snow season: Drive to the Fall Creek Trailhead (see section introduction). Hike S on the well-defined Fall Creek Trail. After a gradual climb through 2¼ miles of conifer forest, turn right (11,170') onto the obvious Notch Mountain Trail. Climb the Notch Mountain Trail to the Notch Mountain Shelter on the ridge of Notch Mountain at 13,080'. This shelter was built in 1924 to accommodate hundreds of pilgrims who came to view the Cross.

Now your lengthy trek on the Halo Ridge begins. Enjoy the vista and strike S along the south ridge of Notch Mountain. After a mile of easy ground, stick with the ridge as it swings west, gets rougher, and leads another 1¼ miles to point 13,831' on Holy Cross's south ridge, also known as the Holy Cross Ridge (see route 1.1.3). Follow the ridge N for ½ mile to the summit. Descend your ascent route.

Winter: Plan on at least one night out or use a snowmobile for the Tigiwon Road. Follow the summer route described above. To avoid avalanche paths, deviate from the exact route of the Notch Mountain Trail onto ribs and ridges. The crux of the winter route, as it was for the first ascent soldiers, is wading through Colorado's deep snow. Halo Ridge is covered with boulders and scree. After the umpteenth time punching a boot through the snow between two blades of scree, many a would-be summiteer has seen the last of the day glimmer into twilight and turned back to camp with the summit unattained.

Safety Notes: The limiting factor with this route is its length. Summer climbers should be fit and pick a day with less likelihood of lightning. In winter, the Notch Mountain Shelter provides a decent bivouac. Take a shovel to dig out the snow and a bivy sack to keep spindrift off your sleeping bag. At the narrow parts of the ridge, beware of slide starting zones on either side.

SECTION 1.2
Mount Elbert (14,433'), Mount Massive (14,421'),
North Mount Massive (14,370')

Mount Massive and Mount Elbert form one of Colorado's great massifs. Stately Mount Elbert is a classic peak with one prominent sub-peak. Massive is a gigantic three mile long ridge with three summits over 14,000'. It would not be farfetched to call all three summits separate fourteeners! Indeed, in this book North Mount Massive is treated as a separate peak. Massive and Elbert provide good hikes and skiing on almost every flank and ridge. Just lay out a map, cover your eyes, and point—you'll come up with a hike or ski route. For snow climbers the two peaks are rather plain, but they both make good winter climbs.

As the highest peak in Colorado, Mt. Elbert is a popular climb. The traditional routes, Mt. Elbert Trail (1.2.7) and the Northeast Ridge (1.2.6), get crowded on weekends and holidays. You'll see fewer souls on the Echo Canyon route (1.2.9). Skiers and winter climbers will have the mountain to themselves.

Several befuddling aspects, mostly arising from trail marking, add spice to hikes and climbs on Massive and Elbert. First, portions of the Main Range Trail shown on the USGS maps are not accurate. This is due to rerouting of the trail over the years. Second, the Main Range Trail is used for part of the Colorado Trail, which extends from Durango to Denver. As a result, the names Main Range Trail and Colorado Trail are often synonymous. To reduce confusion, these sections are called Colorado/Main Range Trail herein. The Colorado Trail is marked with small white triangles that say COLORADO TRAIL. Because the Colorado Trail was recently established, these markers can be more obvious than Main Range Trail markers. In legal wilderness, the trail is usually marked with tree blazes (marks made with a hatchet in the bark of trees).

If you're headed for Mount Elbert or Mount Massive, you have plenty of choices for lodging. In summer and late spring, you can camp at several Forest Service campgrounds on the Halfmoon Road near the Colorado/Main Range trailheads described below. Several Forest Service campgrounds are located on Colorado State Highway 82 near the Black Cloud Gulch and Echo Canyon trailheads. These open in late spring. A good bet for deluxe lodging in the same locale is the Mount Elbert Lodge near the Black Cloud Gulch Trailhead.

Leadville (10,152') is the highest city of its size in the United States. This charming old mining town was created in the 1800's by the gold and silver boom that civilized much of Colorado. Lodging and dining in Leadville are both fun and affordable. Harrison Avenue is the main street through the old part of town ("oldtown"). Here you'll find the fabulous restored Hotel Delaware, as well as other affordable motels. For dining try the Golden Burro or Golden Rose cafes on Harrison Avenue, or authentic Mexican food at The Grill at the west end of Elm Street.

ROADS AND TRAILHEADS

> **USGS Maps:** Mount Elbert, Mount Massive, Leadville South
> **USFS Forest Visitors Maps:** White River National Forest, San Isabel National Forest

Halfmoon Road

After snow melt-off the Halfmoon Road (dirt, medium clearance 2-wheel-drive) leads deep into the heart of the Northern Sawatch. To reach the Halfmoon Road, start on Harrison Avenue in oldtown Leadville. Drive S out of Leadville 3.7 miles on Highway 24 to the Fish Hatchery Road (State Road 300). Take a right (W) on to the Hatchery Road, drive .8 mile, and take a left turn onto County Road 11. Drive 1.0 mile S on Road 11 to the actual Halfmoon Road (good sign). Take a right on the Halfmoon Road (enjoy a good view of Mount Massive straight ahead) and drive 4.7 miles to Halfmoon Campground. (Don't confuse this with Halfmoon Campground near Mount of the Holy Cross).

Colorado/Main Range Trailheads

From Halfmoon Campground, continue 1.8 miles to parking for the Colorado/Main Range Trailheads (10,060') at 6.4 miles from the Hatchery Road. The parking area is obvious on the right (N) side of the road. The trail for Mount Massive leaves from the north end of the parking area. For the Mount Elbert route, walk 100 feet back down the road (E) to obvious trailhead signs on the south side of the road.

South Halfmoon Creek Trailhead

For the South Halfmoon Creek Trailhead, continue 1.9 miles with high clearance 2-wheel-drive to an obvious fork (possibly marked with a Forest Service road stake with the number 110.3A). The South Halfmoon Creek Trailhead (10,330') is next to the river several feet down the left fork. This trailhead has no signs, and you'll find plenty of parking.

North Halfmoon Creek Trailhead

To reach the North Halfmoon Creek Trailhead, park 2-wheel-drive at the South Halfmoon Creek Trailhead mentioned above. Continue on foot (or with 4-wheel-drive) up the the right fork .6 miles to the trailhead (10,530') which is to the right (N) up off the road. If you cross a bridge over the creek you've gone too far. The trailhead is marked with several signs.

Snow closure varies on the Halfmoon Road. Early winter snow closure can be as high as Halfmoon Campground, with the road open to Halfmoon Campground by mid-May. Melt-out is complete by mid or late June. Mining activity can change this. The Halfmoon Road is a designated multiple use trail shared in winter by skiers and snowmobilers. Check road conditions with the Forest Service in Leadville (see Appendix3.4).

Colorado State Highway 82

Highway 82 is a classic Colorado mountain road that connects Glenwood Springs (Interstate 70) with the Arkansas River Valley (Leadville and Buena Vista). You use Highway 82 to access Mt.

Elbert from near the town of Twin Lakes on Colorado State Highway 82 via Black Cloud Gulch, Echo Canyon, and the Mt. Elbert Trail. To reach Twin Lakes, drive Highway 82 for 40 miles E from Aspen (over scenic Independence Pass), or 6 miles W from U.S. Highway 24. Twin Lakes has all-season gas, food, and lodging. If you come from the west, remember that Independence Pass is closed in the winter. In that case you'd reach U.S. 24 via Interstate 70 or U.S. 50.

Twin Lake's history will interest backcountry skiers. In January of 1962 a gigantic avalanche fell from Gordon Gulch, wiped out several homes, and killed nine people. Old timers in the area recalled that the Gordon Gulch slide had run that far about 70 years before, but to the untrained eye the area where the homes were built looked like a secure forest. If you look sharply as you drive you can see the foundations of the homes that were wiped out. The trees are growing back.

Black Cloud Gulch Trailhead

For the Black Cloud Gulch Trailhead, drive 4.1 miles W from Twin Lakes on Highway 82. The trailhead (9,690') is marked by a small sign on the north side of the road.

Echo Canyon Trailhead

To reach the Echo Canyon Trailhead, drive 6.1 miles W on 82 from Twin Lakes to a sign and driveway on the north side of the road near several buildings. Drive up the driveway a short distance to parking (9,967'). Avoid private property.

Mount Elbert Trail Trailhead

For the Mount Elbert Trail, drive E from Twin Lakes on Highway 82. At 2.4 miles turn left (N) onto Lake County Road 24 (paved). If you're driving a low clearance vehicle, or want room to park on a weekend, drive Road 24 for 1.2 miles to Lakeview Campground. Follow signs in the campground for the Mount Elbert Trailhead (9,600') at the northwest end of the camp-ground. To avoid confusion, remember that you use the Colorado Trail to get from this trail-head to the actual Mount Elbert Trail.

With a high clearance or 4-wheel-drive vehicle, the following variation for the Mount Elbert Trail Trailhead knocks about 2 miles and some vertical off the climb: Despite the signs, don't turn into Lake View Campground. Instead, continue on Road 24 past the campground .1 mile to an overlook turn-out on the left. Several yards past the turn-out take a left (W) on a dirt road marked with a motor vehicle route sign. This road is suitable for high-clearance 2-wheel-drive, but it can be slippery when wet. Drive the dirt road 1.8 miles to parking at its terminus near a creek (10,440'). Parking is obvious. A well-used trail leads from parking to the Mount Elbert Trail.

Road 505 (A.K.A. Upper Fryingpan Road)

Road 505 is used to reach North Mount Massive from the west. This approach requires a great deal of driving for people from the Eastern Slope, but Western Slope climbers enjoy this convenient trailhead. Road 505 is a dirt spur off the paved Fryingpan Road. It was built for maintenance on the Fryingpan Arkansas water diversion project. In winter Road 505 remains snowcovered, and it's shared by skiers and snowmobilers. Early in spring (early May) the road is plowed 6 miles to its end in the Upper Fryingpan drainage (skiers take note). After it's plowed it's gated on occasion, but usually open.

To reach Road 505, drive to Basalt on Highway 82 between Aspen and Glenwood Springs. Drive E through Basalt on Midland Avenue (the main street), which soon becomes the Fryingpan Road (County Road 104). Drive the Fryingpan Road from Basalt 26.5 miles to the Biglow fork. Take the right (S) fork and continue 5.9 miles up pavement. Here the Upper Fryingpan Road is obvious as it turns to the right off the pavement. A small sign has the numerals 505, and there may be a larger Forest Service sign here as well, which indicates FRYINGPAN LAKES. Drive Road 505 six miles to parking at road's end near a valve station

---

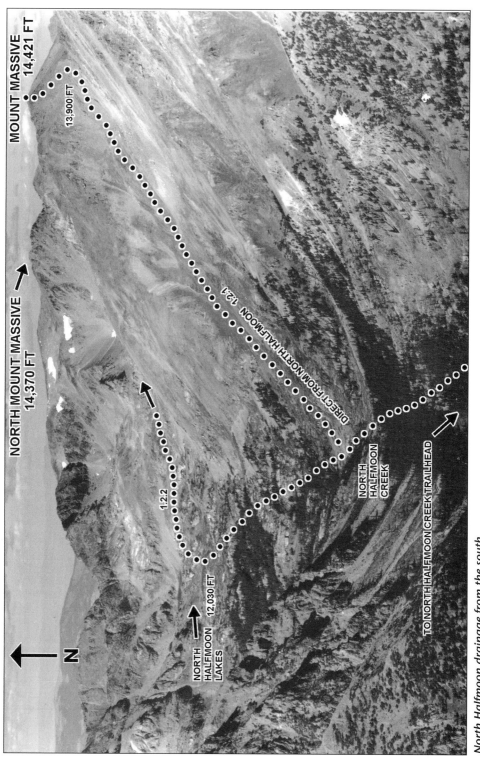

MOUNT MASSIVE 14,421 FT

13,900 FT

NORTH MOUNT MASSIVE 14,370 FT

DIRECT FROM NORTH HALFMOON 1:2.1

1:2.2

NORTH HALFMOON LAKES 12,030 FT

NORTH HALFMOON CREEK

TO NORTH HALFMOON CREEK TRAILHEAD

N

North Halfmoon drainage from the south.

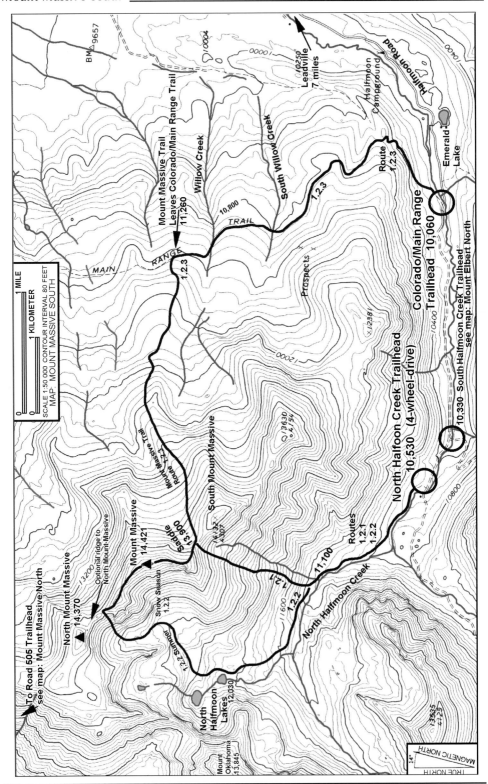

(10,000'). In winter, park on a widened part of the Fryingpan Road near the start of Road 505 or slightly farther up the main road at the plow turnaround. (Mileages above are measured from Alpine Bank in Basalt).

1.2.1 Mount Massive Direct from North Halfmoon Creek

Ratings:	Summer Climb—Advanced		Ski Descent—Advanced
		Snow Climb—Advanced	
Season:	Summer, or Spring Snow		
RT Data:	8 hours, 6½ miles, 3,901' ↑		
Start:	North Halfmoon Creek Trailhead 10,530'		
1 Day from Rd:	Yes		
Map:	Mount Massive South, pg. 48		
Photo	pg. 47		

Summer after snow melt-off: Drive the Halfmoon Creek Road (section introduction) to the North Halfmoon Creek Trailhead. Hike the North Halfmoon Creek Trail to 11,100' (about 2 miles, depending on parking). Leave the trail here, swing right, continue a short way up the North Halfmoon Creek drainage, then climb to your right (NE) up an obvious gully to a saddle on the summit ridge at 13,900'. Use your altimeter and map to be certain of this gully, since other gullies lead to rugged terrain on South Mount Massive (14,132'). From the saddle climb the ridge ¼ mile W, then stay on the ridge as it swings N to the summit of Mount Massive. Descend the same route.

Spring snow season: Snow climbers will find steep snow on the summer route above. Skiers who want the steep, and are willing to forgo an exact summit descent, can stick to this route.

Safety Notes: Summer climbers with shaky knees may want to descend via the Mount Massive Trail. Snow season climbers should allow plenty of time to avoid thawing snow. Figure sunhit for standard sunrise, since snow near the top of the route faces east.

1.2.2 Mount Massive from North Halfmoon Lakes

Ratings:	Summer Climb—Intermediate		Ski Descent—Advanced
		Snow Climb—Intermediate	
Season:	Summer	Winter	Spring
RT Time:	8 hours, 10 miles	multi-day, 20+ miles	8 hours, 9 miles
	4,001' ↑	4,821' ↑	3,901' ↑
Start:	North Halfmoon Creek	Halfmoon Road	North Halfmoon Creek
	Trailhead, 10,530'	snow closure 9,600'	Trailhead, 10,530'
1 Day from Rd:	No		
Map:	Mount Massive South, pg. 48		
Photo:	pg. 47		

Fit fourteener aspirants will enjoy this climb. The route takes Mount Massive from the same drainage as the direct route (1.2.1); it's easier—but much longer. It's a beautiful winter route, but seldom done because of the long distance. Spring skiing on this side of Mount Massive is a joy. Steep bowls abound, and sunhit is late. You'll probably need a high camp, however, and the snowcovered access road can be a tiresome slog.

Summer after snow melt-off: Drive to the North Halfmoon Creek Trailhead (section introduction). Hike a well-used trail 2½ miles to a point on the east side of lower North Halfmoon Lake (12,030'). Continue climbing north from the lower lake ¼ mile to 12,400'. Pause here to study your map. The summit of Mount Massive is up to your right—up a dreadful talus slope. While this route is a good snow route, you can avoid the talus by climbing another ¼ mile towards the summit to 12,720'. At this point start climbing directly north, up a drainage to the left of a tower-studded precipice. At 13,400' in the upper part of the drainage, swing right (NW) and climb another 680 vertical feet to the crest of Mount Massive's north ridge. You are now about a mile from the summit, but you've avoided frustrating scree.

Nip south over a false summit above the aforementioned precipice, then walk an elegant ridge to Mount Massive's summit. Descend your ascent route.

Spring snow season: Park as high as you can drive on the North Halfmoon Creek Road. If you park below the trailhead, remember to add more distance and vertical to your trip plan. Stay on the North Halfmoon Creek Trail as it passes through timbered areas to 11,200'. You'll find sheltered camping in the trees just below here. From 11,200' take a climbing traverse to 11,800'. Then stay between the two streams and follow a series of steep sections and shelves

Moonrise over Mount Massive seen from near North Halfmoon Lakes, winter.

up to lower North Halfmoon Lake.

Pass to the right (E) of Lower Halfmoon Lake, then climb to another shelf at the 12,440 foot level. From here ski or walk (depending on snow conditions) up the west side of Mount Massive to a saddle (14,200') ¼ mile north of the summit. Follow the ridge south to the summit. For a ski descent drop W off the summit, traverse to a point near your ascent route, then ski your ascent route.

Winter: Though long on miles (unless the road is open due to mining or you use a snowmobile) a winter climb of Massive via Halfmoon Creek makes a terrific expedition. Park at the Halfmoon Road snow closure. Ski the snowcovered road up the long valley to the North Halfmoon Creek Trail (section introduction).

Safety notes: Winter: The Halfmoon Road crosses several slide runouts, and above 11,000' the route crosses numerous avalanche paths. Because this is the west side of the mountain the snow is often windscoured, compacted, and stable. Such conditions, or a spring snow pack, would insure a safe trip. With unstable snow you can follow several ribs and ridges to the summit, most notably the one directly east of lower North Halfmoon Lake. Unfortunately this ridge is discontinuous, especially at the beginning, thus forcing you to cross avalanche slopes. Use your hazard evaluation skills.

Summer climbers should take normal precautions and be careful of rockfall on talus slopes. Watch for climbers above you. Add 2½ hours to standard sunrise for sunhit.

1.2.3	**Mount Massive via the Mount Massive Trail**	
Ratings:	Summer Climb—Novice	Ski Descent—Advanced
	Snow Climb—Intermediate	
Season:	Summer or Spring	Winter
RT Data:	12 hours, 14½ miles, 4,341' ↑	Multi-day, 20 miles, 4,821' ↑
Start:	Colorado/Main Range Trailhead	Halfmoon Road snow closure
	10,060'	9,600'
1 Day from Rd:	Summer or Late Spring	Winter
	Yes	No
Map:	Mount Massive South, pg. 48	
Photo:	pg. 52	

Summer after snow melt-off: This is the easiest route up Mount Massive, but it's long on distance.

Drive the Halfmoon Road to the Colorado/Main Range Trailhead (10,060') on the right (N) side of the road. From parking at the trailhead, hike NE then N on the well-defined Colorado/Main Range Trail 3½ miles to 11,260'. Here take care to locate the Mt. Massive Trail, which heads W from the Colorado/Main Range Trail at a (sometimes) signed intersection.

Leave the Colorado/Main Range Trail and power up the Mount Massive Trail 2½ miles to a saddle on the summit ridge at 13,900'. From the saddle climb the ridge ¼ mile W, then stay on the ridge as it swings N to the summit. Descend your ascent route.

Spring snow season: This side of Mount Massive provides the best summit ski descents. You'll need a very early start or high camp to avoid the consequences of an early sunhit. You may be able to drive to the Colorado/Main Range Trailhead. If that is the case, by all means use that trailhead. If the Halfmoon Creek Road is closed at Halfmoon Campground (or before), a good gambit for this route is to take a direct line from snow closure up through dark timber to the Mt. Massive Trail. Then follow the Mt. Massive Trail to the summit as described in the summer route above. You must have impeccable map, compass, and altimeter skills to navigate through the dark timber. If in doubt slog the Halfmoon Road and take the

Colorado/Main Range Trail. But the extra mileage this entails defeats the purpose of this east side route, which is to give direct access.

Many groups of skiers and snow climbers have failed on the direct line mentioned above, usually for two reasons: they either encounter hard trail breaking or impossible route finding in the huge forest on the lower east facing slopes of the peak. Yet as a ski route this is one of the classics and thus worth the effort. Use it as a test of your orienteering skills.

Winter: Again, the direct dark timber variation described above will save you miles of trekking on the snowcovered road. But you must be an expert orienteer. Also, if deep trail breaking is probable in the forest, the extra miles on the Halfmoon Road and Colorado/Main Range Trail might actually be easier. Halfmoon Road is usually packed by snowmobile, and the Colorado/Main Range Trail is likely to be packed by skiers. Be very careful to find the Mt. Massive Trail, since trail signs at the intersection can be covered with snow. "Mount Massive Trail," of course, is only a generalization of the route you would take in the winter, depending on snow conditions. But down in the trees following the trailcut can save you from more bushwhacking. For your descent enjoy the general route of the ascent. If you do this one in good style you're ready to teach an orienteering class—good luck.

Safety notes: Summer climbers need only be concerned with weather hazards—so long as they pay attention to their map. During snow season, slide hazard is nil until you reach timberline. If need be, you can find a safe ridge route, but these ridges are hard to gain without some exposure. Snow season climbers who challenge the dark timber must use an altimeter to find the Colorado/Main Range Trail. Use standard sunrise for sunhit.

Mount Massive from the east, summer.

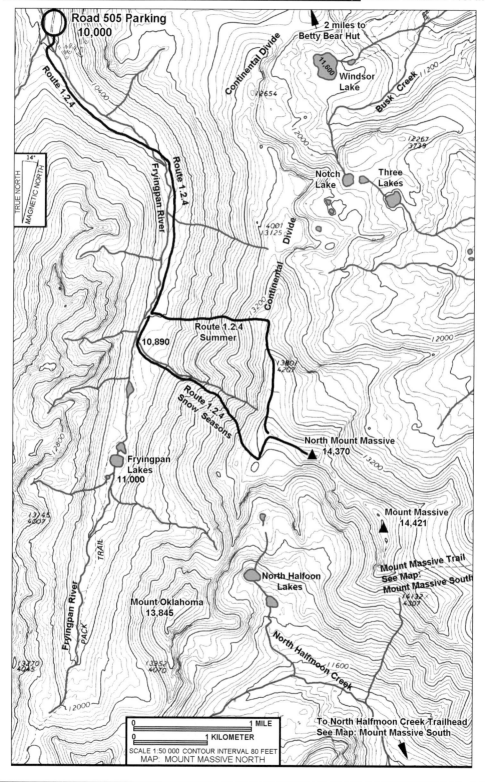

Road 505 Parking
10,000

2 miles to
Betty Bear Hut

Windsor
Lake

Route 1.2.4

Continental Divide

Busk Creek

Route 1.2.4

Fryingpan River

Notch
Lake

Three
Lakes

TRUE NORTH
MAGNETIC NORTH
14°

Continental Divide

Route 1.2.4
Summer

10,890

Route 1.2.4
Snow Seasons

North Mount Massive
14,370

Fryingpan
Lakes
11,000

Mount Massive
14,421

TRAIL

Mount Massive Trail
See Map:
Mount Massive South

North Halfoon
Lakes

Fryingpan River

PACK

Mount Oklahoma
13,845

North Halfmoon Creek

To North Halfmoon Creek Trailhead
See Map: Mount Massive South

0   1 MILE
0   1 KILOMETER
SCALE 1:50 000 CONTOUR INTERVAL 80 FEET
MAP: MOUNT MASSIVE NORTH

1.2.4	**North Mount Massive from the Fryingpan Drainage**	
Ratings:	Summer Climb—Intermediate	Ski Descent—Advanced
	Snow Climb—Intermediate	
Season:	Summer or Spring	Winter
RT Data:	11 hours, 12 miles, 4,370' ↑	2 or 3 days, 5,250' ↑
Start:	Road 505 terminus 10,000'	Fryingpan Road 9,120'
1 Day from Rd:	Yes, in summer and after Road 505 is plowed	
Map:	Mount Massive North, pg. 53	
Photo:	pg. 55	

Mount Massive is a long ridge studded with 14,000' bumps. The true summit is flanked by two bumps that aesthetically qualify as paks, and many climbers feel that any one of the three summits counts for a fourteener hit. North Mount Massive is one of these bumps, and it happens to be a convenient climb for people from western Colorado.

Also, you can climb this side of Mt. Massive from the 10th Mountain Hut Association Betty Bear Hut. This hut is open both winter and summer. It's quite a distance from the hut to the optimum winter routes, but summer hikers will find the hut is a good base for climbs of North Mount Massive. See the *Colorado 10th Mountain Trails* guidebook (bibliography) for Mt. Massive routes from the Betty Bear Hut.

Summer after snow melt-off: Drive to the end of the Upper Fryingpan Road (section introduction) and park near the valve station (10,000'). Cross an obvious foot bridge over the river, then hike a well-defined pack trail about 3 miles to the 10,800' in the Fryingpan River drainage. Look up to the east and pick a likely looking flank for a hard hike/climb to 13,500' on the Continental Divide ridge. The farther up the valley you start, the rockier the climbing. Hike the ridge to the summit of North Mount Massive (14,370'). Descend your ascent route.

Spring snow season: Though this side of Mount Massive is often windscoured, couloirs trap enough snow for excellent snow climbs and ski descents. One advantage of these routes over Massive's eastern routes is a late sunhit.

Instead of using the foot bridge and summer trail, start to the left (N) of the creek in a small clearing adjacent to the valve station. You'll probably start in the dark, and it's easy to get disoriented in the timber here. To stay on track, climb close enough to the creek to use it for navigation. Once in sparser timber, follow a series of clearings and denser patches of timber several miles up the Fryingpan drainage to 10,890'. Keep looking to your left and you'll see a very obvious cut through the trees leading up to a wide deep couloir. Climb this couloir to 11,700'. Here, swing right and climb an obvious couloir which leads to a low-angled area on the ridge southwest of the summit. Continue along the ridge to the summit. Descend your ascent route.

For a lower-angled, slightly longer route, continue up the valley to another obvious snow couloir/bowl that drops from the summit ridge. Hundreds of other snow climbs and ski routes exist on the peaks in this valley, and it's common for mountaineers to set a base camp at timberline and ski a half dozen peaks in as many days.

Winter: Use the summer route. Follow windblown ribs to avoid avalanche danger. An alternative is to head E from the Betty Bear Hut and gain the long north ridge (Continental Divide) that connects to Mount Massive. You can then follow this ridge to the summit. It's mostly a hike, but a very long one at extremely high altitude.

Safety notes: If you've got knee problems, skip hiking this route—the descent involves an arduous 3,000' vertical drop. Snow climbers and skiers will find the best conditions during the spring season. In the winter, stick to windblown ribs to avoid avalanche danger and take care with the many slide paths dropping into the Fryingpan River Drainage. Add 3 hours to standard sunrise for sunhit.

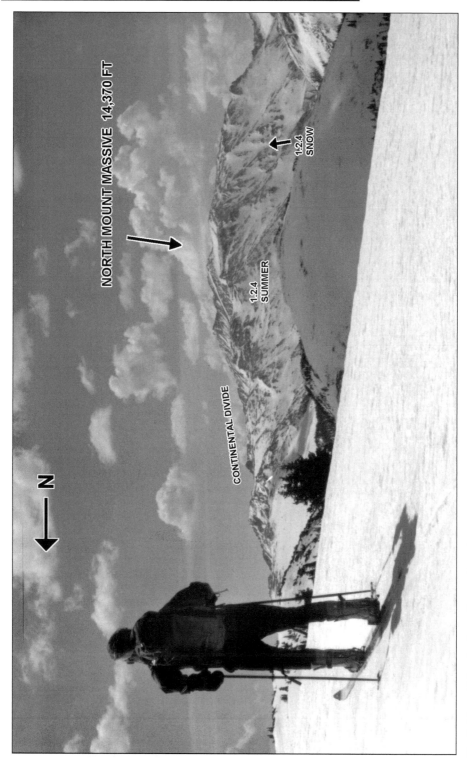

North Mount Massive from the west, spring.

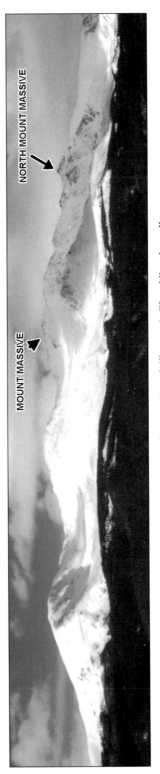

Winter panoramas of Mount Elbert and Mount Massive from the east (Leadville area). The skiing is endless.

1.2.5	**Mount Elbert—South Halfmoon Creek**	
Ratings:	Snow Climb—Intermediate	Ski Descent—Advanced
Season:	Spring Snow	
RT Data:	8 hours, 7 miles, 4,103' ↑	
Start:	South Halfmoon Creek Road 10,330'	
1 Day from Rd:	Yes, with open road	
Map:	Mount Elbert North, pg. 58	
Photo:	pg. 60	

Spring snow season: As a Sawatch classic for snow climbing and skiing, it's best to climb this couloir from a camp at 11,200' in South Halfmoon Creek. Fit mountaineers, however, can take advantage of a late western sunhit and perhaps do this route in one day from the trailhead. Later in the spring the Halfmoon Road may be open to its intersection with the South Halfmoon Road. In that case this route can be done as a day trip by most parties. This side of Mt. Elbert, when devoid of snow, is a huge scree field. Thus, other routes are better for summer climbs.

Depending on snow closure, from Halfmoon Campground follow the Halfmoon Road to parking at the South Halfmoon Creek Trailhead (section introduction). Cross a broken down bridge S over Halfmoon Creek and climb an old jeep trail 2 miles to 11,200'. Look up to your left and spot a prominent break in the timber at the base of the the spectacular gully leading to Elbert's summit. Climb through the break then up the gully. Descend your ascent route.

Safety notes: This avalanche gully is only safe with frozen spring-season snow.

Winter climbing: This can be a reasonable winter route provided you use wind-scoured ribs for avalanche-safe travel. The gully may be filled with wind-hardened, avalanche-safe snow, but don't count on it. The Northeast Ridge Route (1.2.6) is a more accessible winter line, and includes an avalanche-safe ridge. Add 2½ hours to standard sunrise for sunhit.

1.2.6	**Mount Elbert—Northeast Ridge**	
Ratings:	Summer Climb—Novice	Ski Descent—Advanced
	Snow Climb—Intermediate	
Season:	Summer/Spring	Winter
RT Data:	9 hours, 8½ miles, 4,373' ↑	2 days, about 11 miles, 4,833' ↑
Start:	Colorado/Main Range Trailhead 10,060'	Halfmoon Road snow closure 9,600'
1 Day from Rd:	Yes	No
Map:	Mount Elbert North, pg. 58	
Photos:	pgs. 60, 62	

This is an excellent route for a summer hike or climb or winter ascent of Mount Elbert. Skiers should not count on a summit ski descent, as the upper parts of this route are often windscoured.

Summer after snow melt-off: Start from the South Colorado/Main Range Trailhead on the Halfmoon Road (see section introduction). Park and hike S on the Colorado/Main Range Trail ¾ mile to a high point (10,600') in the timber (you are actually on the true East Ridge of Elbert). Continue S on the trail as it gradually drops. Look for an unsigned trail turning off to the right about

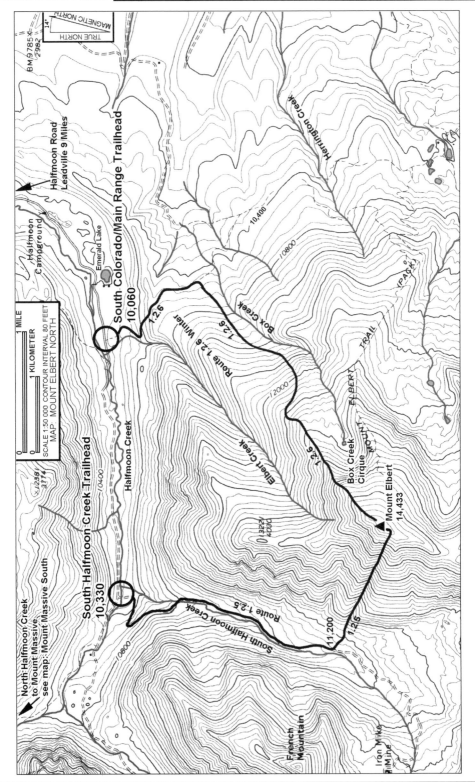

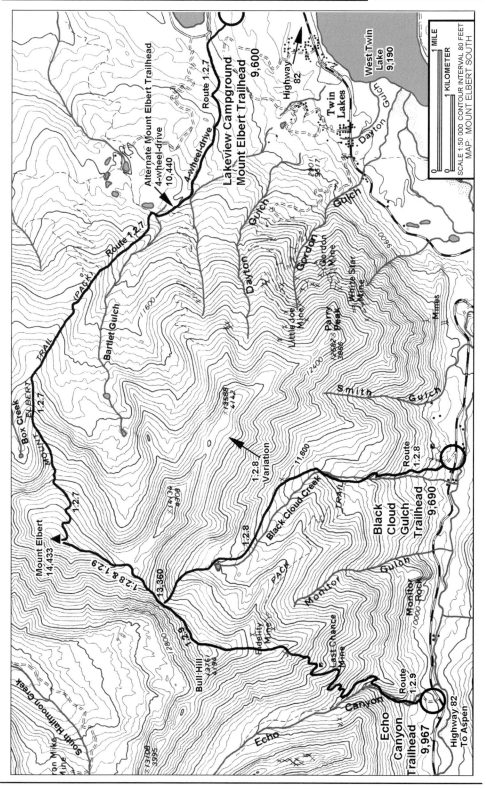

Mount Elbert from the west, spring.

½ mile after you begin the gradual descent. Take this trail and follow it up the right (N) side of the Box Creek drainage to timberline. When you break through the trees, identify the Box Creek cirque above you. Your route continues up the right side of the Box Creek drainage, gradually gaining the crest of the east ridge at 12,600' near the base of the Box Creek cirque. Follow the ridge to the summit and descend your ascent route.

Spring snow season: To begin, use the summer route above. If the Halfmoon Road is closed, consider the Mount Elbert Trail route (1.2.7). Take the Colorado/Main Range Trail to the first high-point at 10,600' on Elbert's east ridge. Instead of dropping south as the summer route describes, simply turn right off the trail, climb the northeast ridge through timber to treeline, and stick with the ridge to the summit. Without skis, descend the ridge. Skiers can make turns down the ridge, perhaps dropping more to the south for better snow between the ridge crest and Box Creek.

Experts can ski the Box Creek cirque. To do so drop east from the summit towards the right (S) side of the cirque. At 13,800' drop into the cirque and ski an obvious couloir on your right. This route avoids a steeper cliff area in the middle of the cirque headwall and is rated expert. As with all steep ski descents, it would be a good idea to use it as your ascent route so you'll know what to expect.

Winter: Drive to the Halfmoon Road snow closure, then ski the Halfmoon Creek Road to the South Colorado/Main Range Trailhead (section introduction). This trailhead can lack signs, or the sign can be covered with snow. It's important to get on the trail because it leads through dense dark timber. To find it, combine the following directions with those in the section introduction. While skiing up the snowcovered Halfmoon Road, positively identify Emerald Lake on your left as you pass it at 10,000'. You'll ski up a short hill, still on the Halfmoon Road, then after skiing about ½ mile farther you'll come to the intersection of the Halfmoon Road with the South Colorado/Main Range Trail, on the left (South) side of the road (10,060'). If you ski past the intersection, you'll cross a culvert over Elbert Creek 100 feet farther up the valley. During heavy snow years, this culvert may be your only method of identifying the trail, since the signs will be covered.

Take a left onto the South Colorado/Main Range Trail. Ski up the trail as it traverses the north flank of Mount Elbert. At the two mile point (10,400') leave the trail and climb SW through a forest up to the crest of the wide and lower-angled portion of the east ridge (12,400'). From here follow the east ridge to the summit.

Descend the ridge. Or if you feel avalanche conditions allow you can descend the huge east bowl or the north flanks of the peak. Stay out of the Box Creek cirque. In both cases you'd take the Colorado/Main Range Trail back to the Halfmoon Road.

Safety notes: During any season, be prepared for wind and cold on this exposed ridge route. For snow season climbers, avalanche problems are minimal because the route sticks to a ridge. But you may encounter dangerous cornices. The steep pitch just below the summit can avalanche given extremely unstable snow. You can avoid this pitch by sticking to the ridge rocks. Subtract one hour from standard sunrise for sunhit.

1.2.7	**Mount Elbert—Mount Elbert Trail**	
Ratings:	Summer Climb—Novice Ski Descent—Intermediate	
	Snow Climb—Novice	
Season:	Summer/Spring	Winter
RT Data:	9 hours, 11¼ miles, 4,833' ↑	12 hours or overnight, 11¼ miles, 4,833' ↑
Start:	Mount Elbert Trailhead at Lakeview Campground 9,600'	
1 Day	Summer/Spring	Winter
from Rd:	Yes	No
Map:	Mount Elbert South, pg. 59	
Photo:	pg. 62	

Mt. Elbert has seen ascents by almost every conveyance known to man—automobile, bicycle—you name it, they have all been to the highest point in Colorado. Most of these novelty ascents have used the Mount Elbert Trail. You won't see much other than the occasional horse or bicycle these days, so this trail is usually a nice hike. You can follow an obvious tread all the way to the summit. Thus, it makes a good first fourteener for people with physical limitations. Try an ascent of this route during an October Indian-summer day; you won't be disappointed.

Summer after snow melt-off: Drive to the Mount Elbert Trail Trailhead via Lake County Road 24 (see section introduction: Highway 82). From parking, hike the Colorado/Main Range Trail (marked with small white triangles nailed to trees) as it follows a jeep trail (you can 4x4 this; see section introduction). At 2 miles the jeep trail becomes a foot trail, which then crosses a log bridge over a creek, then follows an easy grade though elegant aspen forest for ⅛ mile to a fork with good signs indicating the Mount Elbert Trail. Pause to view the beautiful ponds on your right, then take a left (W) onto the famous Mount Elbert Trail.

Immediately, you know this trail's purpose as it climbs straight up a steep hill W through forest to cross a creek at 10,960'. The trail swings N after the creek and climbs out of Bartlett Gulch ½ mile to 10,400' on Mt. Elbert's grand east ridge. After ½ mile up through sparse trees on the ridge you break timberline at 11,600'. Looming ahead is the summit. Take heart, the obvious trail you're standing on continues up the ridge one mile to a shelf at 12,400', then climbs steeply to the base of the summit scree-dome (13,600'). For map practice, stop here and decide whether you can see the true summit. Continue up the trail as it traverses a short distance, then climbs a series of switchbacks to the top. Descend via the same route.

Enjoy the terrific view from the summit. Mount Massive looms to the north over the deep chasm of the Half Moon drainage. La Plata Peak is the huge rocky fist to the southwest. You can easily spot a dozen fourteeners from the top of Mount Elbert (hint: many are west in the Elk Mountains).

Spring Snow Season: Use the route above. In the early spring you won't be able to drive the dirt road portion of the auto route. In that case use the winter round-trip data.

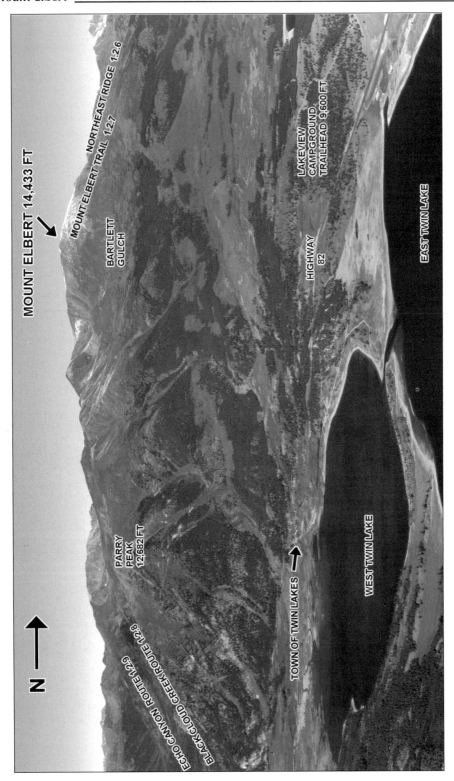

MOUNT ELBERT 14,433 FT

MOUNT ELBERT TRAIL 1.2.7

NORTHEAST RIDGE 1.2.6

BARTLETT GULCH

LAKEVIEW CAMPGROUND TRAILHEAD 9,600 FT

HIGHWAY 82

EAST TWIN LAKE

PARRY PEAK 12,682 FT

ECHO CANYON ROUTE 1.2.9

BLACK CLOUD CREEK ROUTE 1.2.8

TOWN OF TWIN LAKES

WEST TWIN LAKE

N

Mount Elbert from the south.

Skiers will enjoy the ascent route provided the East Ridge is not too windscoured. For more consistent (but steeper) skiing, try the upper basin in Bartlett Gulch. This option is rated Advanced. Advanced level skiers can try Horseshoe Cirque (route 1.2.6) at the head of the Box Creek drainage.

Winter: Use the summer route described above. Park at the overlook turnout on Lake County Road 24.

Safety notes: Don't let the nature of this route lull you into false security. You're still above timber where the weather can change by the moment. Winter climbers, provided they use windscoured areas for safe passage, will find this route is reasonably safe from avalanches. For sunhit, use standard sunrise minus about one hour.

1.2.8	**Mount Elbert via Black Cloud Gulch**	
Ratings:	Summer Climb—Advanced Ski Descent—Advanced	
	Snow Climb—Intermediate	
Season:	Summer, or Spring Snow	
RT Data:	10 hours, 8 miles, 4,743' ↑	
Start:	Black Cloud Gulch Trailhead 9,690'	
1 Day from Rd:	Yes	
Map:	Mount Elbert South, pg. 59	
Photo:	pg. 62	

This route is slightly more direct than the Echo Canyon (1.2.9) route. Summer climbers use it for variety, but first-time Elbert climbers are better off on the Echo Canyon route or Mount Elbert Trail (1.2.7) routes. Skiers will find plenty of vertical on the Black Cloud Gulch route, but it doesn't usually allow a summit ski descent.

Summer after snow melt-off: Drive Highway 82 to the Black Cloud Gulch Trailhead (section introduction). Park, then take care to find a steep trail leading up the right side of the creek. Follow this trail 1½ miles to 11,600'—a grunt. Continue to follow the creek up the valley through beautiful alpine terrain, pass a small tarn (12,400'), and climb NW to an obvious saddle (13,360') northeast of Bull Hill. From the saddle head NE along the ridge 1¼ miles to the summit. Don't let the first false summit fool you; it's a long ridge! Descend via the same route or nip over Bull Hill and descend the Echo Canyon (1.2.9) route. For a steeper climb, you can climb N from the mining area at 11,600', then follow the southeast ridge to the summit.

Spring snow season: Use the route above. For a good ski or snow climb variation break right (N) at 11,700' and ascend a gully system to Mount Elbert's south summit (14,134'). Continue on to the main summit if you have time. Ski or downclimb the gully you ascended. You must have advanced ski and snow climbing skills for this option.

Safety notes: Winter climbing on this route is not recommended. As with many other Sawatch fourteeners, you'll be cresting a ridge for some time, so beware of lightning. Add two hours to standard sunrise for sunhit.

1.2.9	**Mount Elbert from Echo Canyon**
Ratings:	Summer Climb—Intermediate
Season:	Summer
RT Data:	10 hours, 9¾ miles, 4,466' ↑
Start:	Echo Canyon Trailhead 9,967'
1 Day from Rd:	Yes
Map:	Mount Elbert South, pg. 59
Photo:	pg. 62

Climbers who like technically easy routes will enjoy this fine tour with plenty of high-ridge vistas. The route is not recommended for snow climbing.

Summer after snow melt-off: Drive Highway 82 to the Echo Canyon Trailhead (section introduction). Hike up a driveway (avoid private property), then continue up Echo Creek to 10,600'. Leave the drainage here and climb NE up through the Last Chance mining area 1½ miles and 2,000 vertical feet to 100 vertical feet below the summit of Bull Hill. Skirt around the right (E) side of Bull Hill ½ mile to the NE ridge connecting to Mount Elbert. You'll need to descend this ridge a bit to Black Cloud Saddle (13,360') at the head of Black Cloud Creek.

From Black Cloud Saddle, continue NE up the obvious ridge a mile to the summit. Beware of false summits—a mile of ridge at this altitude can last forever. Descend the same route or do a traverse of the peak with a descent of any other route in this section.

Safety notes: This is a long, arduous journey. Start early and watch the weather. Add 2½ hours to standard sunrise for sunhit.

SECTION 3.1
LA PLATA PEAK (14,336')

Hulking La Plata Peak dominates the view to the southeast from the summit of Independence Pass. The peak is easy to identify by its long and jagged northeast ridge. This is the Ellingwood Ridge, one of the Colorado fourteeners' better known "scramble" mountaineering routes. Don't let the foreboding Ellingwood Ridge give you an extreme first impression; La Plata has plenty of hike, snow climb, and ski routes. Take your pick.

ROADS AND TRAILHEADS

USGS Maps: Mount Elbert, Independence Pass, Mount Harvard
Forest Service Visitors Map: San Isabel National Forest

La Plata Gulch Trailhead

Drive Colorado State Highway 82 (see section 2 trailheads) 8.8 miles E from the Independence Pass Summit or 8 miles W from the town of Twin Lakes. Turn south off the highway onto the well-signed South Fork Road. Drive past fenced private land on the left for .4 miles. Park at the obscure and unsigned La Plata Gulch Trailhead on the left (E) side of the road (10,160'). A small turnout has room for two cars; if it is full, park on the highway. If you come from Independence Pass, take time at the pass to study a grand view of the peak.

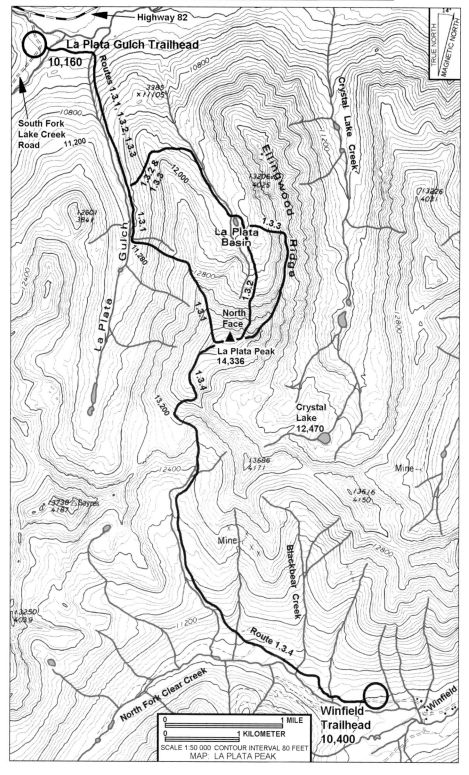

LA PLATA PEAK 14,336

N

ELLINGWOOD RIDGE ROUTE 1.3.3

NORTH FACE 1.3.2

NORTHWEST RIDGE 1.3.1

12,760 FT

La Plata Gulch

La Plata Basin

La Plata Peak from Independence Pass, looking southeast, spring.

South Fork of Lake Creek Road

Since the same approach is used for all routes from this trailhead, the lower section of trail is described here: from the trailhead take a well beaten path SE a few hundred feet to a log bridge over a shallow but scary gorge containing the South Fork of Lake Creek. From here the trail is obvious as it swings N for a short distance, then swings E and becomes fainter as it leads along the south side of the Lake Creek Valley. Many people have problems navigating this trail. The trees are dense. The trick is to take a slightly climbing contour E to intersect La Plata Creek—and not let the bushwhacking deflect you from your course. You'll find cairns on occasion, but some parties have reported that the wrong trail was marked! A recent Colorado Mountain Club work group improved and marked the trail, and reported good log bridges over South Fork Lake Creek and La Plata Creek. Use your altimeter and compass, and study your map before you leave.

Winfield Trailhead

Drive US Highway 24 for 16 miles S from downtown Leadville or 14.5 miles N from Buena Vista (as in section 4 introduction) and turn W onto the well-signed Clear Creek Reservoir Road (Chaffee County 390). Drive the Clear Creek Reservoir Road 11 miles (from Highway 24) to the Winfield Townsite. In Winfield you'll hit a T intersection. Take a right (N), and the road will lead you ½ mile to 2-wheel-drive parking in the North Fork of Clear Creek drainage. If you're headed for the south La Plata Peak routes, using 4-wheel-drive to get farther is hardly worth it, since several desperate mud bogs block the way, and you'll save less than a mile of walking. Don't confuse this trailhead with the South Fork of Clear Creek Trailhead, which you also get to from Winfield (see section1.5 of this chapter).

1.3.1 La Plata Peak—Northwest Ridge

Ratings:	Summer Climb—Intermediate		Ski Descent—Advanced
	Snow Climb—Intermediate		
Season:	Summer/Spring		Winter
RT Data:	7 hours, 8 miles, 4,176' ↑		12 hours, 8 miles, 4,176' ↑
Start:	La Plata Gulch Trailhead 10,160'		
1 Day from Rd:	Yes		
Map:	La Plata Peak, pg. 65		
Photos:	pgs. 66, 69		

Summer after snow melt-off: Park at the La Plata Gulch Trailhead on the South Fork of Lake Creek Road (section introduction). Use the trail described in the section introduction to travel along the south side of the Lake Creek Valley to La Plata Gulch Creek. Cross the creek and follow the east side of La Plata Gulch about 2 miles to the 11,280'. Climb E out of the gulch up the west flank of La Plata Peak to the crest of the northwest ridge at about 12,700'. You'll see many possible routes up through the west flank's patchwork of scree, boulders, and snow. Several trails are well beaten; one has been marked by Colorado Mountain Club. Stick to it to prevent erosion trail braiding.

Once you gain the ridge it yields a simple route to the summit. As you relax on the summit, study the exciting Ellingwood Ridge. Your next climb perhaps? Descend your ascent route.

Spring snow season: Because of its low 10,000' start this route is best skied in the early spring. But if you're willing to hike through the lower woods, it can be rewarding later. Snow climbers will probably find the best snow in early June, but conditions vary from year to year. You can evaluate this route from the summit of Independence Pass.

Winter: This is the best winter route for La Plata. Yet Highway 82 may not be open to the trailhead. In that case, plan on a multi-day expedition or use a snowmobile for the closed highway, which is a popular snowmobile route.

Safety notes: Beware the stream crossings for this route if you miss the log bridge. Portions of the stream follow a deep chasm that could be dangerous in the dark. The route is reasonably safe in the winter if it's wind-scoured. If not, start lower down on the ridge to avoid avalanche slopes. In spring use the early start tactic.

Add 3 hours to standard sunrise for sunhit.

1.3.2	La Plata Peak—North Face	
Ratings:	Ski Descent—Extreme	Snow Climb—Advanced
Season:	Spring or summer snow	
RT Data:	7 hours, 8 miles, 4,176' ↑	
Start:	La Plata Gulch Trailhead 10,160'	
1 Day from Rd:	Yes	
Map:	La Plata Peak, pg. 65	
Photos:	pgs. 66, 69	

Spring snow season: This aesthetic route will give you excellent climbing and superb skiing. At a minimum of 48 degrees it's a good choice if you're just starting with extreme skiing. To begin, follow the trail to La Plata Gulch Creek described above under "Roads and Trailheads." From your intersection with the creek climb an unimproved but well-marked trail about 1 mile up La Plata Gulch to 11,100'. From here take a climbing traverse to the NE up to a large step at 11,800' on the northwest ridge of La Plata Peak.

From the aforementioned step, take a dropping traverse SW into La Plata Basin, then make your way up to the base of the north face. Use Ellingwood Ridge to landmark the left (E) side of the face.

As you approach the north face you'll see many snow routes to the summit. The best route is an obvious continuous gully system that starts to east (left) of center, then leads up to the beginnings of the Ellingwood Ridge a few feet to the east of the summit. The ski descent takes the same route.

Safety notes: When these gullies have snow or ice they are good technical mountain routes. After they dry out the rockfall danger is severe. Skiers should climb their descent route. In the spring, sun hits the upper parts of these couloirs several hours after standard sunrise. If you're skiing, climb it first.

1.3.3	La Plata Peak—Ellingwood Ridge	
Ratings:	Summer Climb—Advanced (possible ropework)	
Season:	Summer	
RT Data:	12 hours, 9 miles, 4,176' ↑	
Start:	La Plata Gulch Trailhead 10,160'	
1 Day from Rd:	Yes	
Map:	La Plata Peak, pg.65	
Photos:	pgs. 66, 69	

Named after its first ascender, famed climbing pioneer Albert Ellingwood, Ellingwood Ridge is one of the classic fourteener ridge routes of Colorado. To climb it safely you must have good technical route finding and climbing skills. Carry a rope and small amount of rock climbing hardware.

Summer after snow melt-off: To begin, take the first part of the La Plata Peak North Face route (1.3.2) to 12,000' in La Plata Basin. Head E up any likely looking couloir to the crest of Ellingwood Ridge, then climb the ridge to the summit. With careful route finding all the aretes on the ridge can be skirted to the side. For more excitement try climbing several aretes. Be ready to rappel if you do so. Descent is via the Northwest Ridge (1.3.1).

Since the route above only takes the upper part of the ridge, some climbers get a lower start. To do so stay lower in La Plata Basin and traverse to the scree apron at timberline on the north end of the ridge. Hike up the apron to the first part of the ridge. Climbing the ridge from the beginning is much more time consuming and involves several sections of hand-and-foot climbing. You might ask why you'd access this start from La Plata Basin, when Highway 82 is just north of the scree apron. Problem is, hiking directly up from the highway means you must cross Lake Creek. You'll see several bridges in the area, but they're on private property and the river is too deep to wade.

Safety notes: Plan your climb to avoid afternoon lightning. You can escape from the ridge crest down many scree gullies, especially on the east side of the ridge. Carry a rope and know how to use it. This route is not recommended for winter because of avalanche danger on the approach. One of the few deaths by avalanche on a fourteener occurred in 1960 when a climber was caught in a slide during his approach for a winter attempt on the ridge. Avalanche danger is also a problem during spring snow season because the route takes the better part of a day, thus forcing a descent of dangerous thawing snow. For sunhit on the ridge use standard sunrise time.

With a dusting of fall snow, La Plata Peak juts from the horizon south of Mount Elbert.

1.3.4 — La Plata Peak–South Face from Vicksburg

Ratings:	Summer Climb—Intermediate Ski Descent—Advanced Snow Climb—Intermediate
Season:	Summer, or spring snow season
RT Data:	10 hours, 6½ miles, 3,936' ↑
Start:	Winfield Trailhead 10,400'
1 Day from Rd:	Yes
Map:	La Plata Peak, pg. 65

As a less crowded and slightly less challenging way up La Plata, this route is a fine choice. Hikers will enjoy the pristine tundra, and the spring skiing is terrific!

Summer after snow melt-off: Drive to the Winfield Trailhead (see introduction). From parking, walk the jeep trail 1¼ mile W to 10,730', where a gated road heads to the right. Walk the gated road for several hundred feet. Leave the road, head W to cross the stream, then take a climbing traverse upvalley ¼ mile W into the next gulch (a little map work here will help).

Grunt 2,000 vertical feet up the gulch to a beautiful hanging basin at 12,000'. Continue climbing near the stream course to 12,400'. As the terrain steepens, head up near the left stream course to the left (W) shoulder of the basin. Gain the shoulder at 13,200'. Take the shoulder up to 14,000' on La Plata's southwest ridge. Catch your breath, then follow the airy ridge ½ mile NE to the summit.

Spring snow season: The upper part of this route has good snow climbing and skiing. But in early spring Clear Creek road may only be open up to the Rockdale vicinity, thus mandating a valley slog up the snow covered road. Consider a high camp or snowmobile ride so you can hit the good skiing early in the morning. The road opens to Winfield sometime in May.

For the most part, use the same route as the summer description above. At 12,400', you may be able to take a more direct snow line up to the main ridge.

Safety notes: This is a long arduous route. The trailhead and approach are easy, but during the climb pay attention to your map and altimeter. Use standard sunrise time for sunhit.

Skiing near Independence Pass, La Plata Peak on right horizon.

SECTION 1.4
Mount Oxford (14,153'), Mount Belford (14,197'), Missouri Mountain (14,067')

This cluster of peaks has one of the best concentrations of summer climbs, ski routes, and snow climbs in the Sawatch Mountains. For full enjoyment of this area, whatever the season, work from a base camp in Elkhead Basin at the head of Missouri Gulch. This fabulous expanse of alpine tundra is worth enjoying in the afternoon and evening after a morning of mountaineering. If your goal is to check three more fourteeners off your list, it's possible to do a summer climb of all three from Vicksburg. Be fit for this marathon.

Mount Belford and Mount Oxford are almost the same mountain. Indeed, they are commonly bagged in the same day (with excellent alpine hiking or skiing). Missouri Mountain is a majestic peak with fine views and several good hikes and climbs. During spring snow season, Missouri's north ridge has abundant ski runs that could keep you busy for a week.

A good alternative for access to these peaks is to basecamp in Missouri Basin at the head of Pine Creek. Though hard to reach, this is one of the most spectacular high mountain basins in Colorado. It easily lives up to its nickname—"Where God Lives." Missouri Basin is a fun day trip from a camp in Elkhead Basin.

Summer climbers will find plenty of camping on the trailhead access roads. Your best bet for lodging is any of the motels in Buena Vista.

ROADS AND TRAILHEADS

USGS Maps: Winfield, Mount Harvard
USFS Forest Visitors Map: San Isabel National Forest

Vicksburg/Clear Creek Reservoir Road (Chaffee County 390), Vicksburg Trailhead
To reach the Vicksburg Trailhead, follow US Highway 24 to the Clear Creek Reservoir Road. Turn off 15 miles north of Buena Vista or 20 miles south from oldtown (downtown) Leadville (sign for Vicksburg and Chaffee County Road 390). Turn off here and drive the Clear Creek Reservoir Road 7.6 miles to the Vicksburg ghost town. If you're headed for Elkhead Basin via Missouri Gulch, park across the road from Vicksburg in the obvious trailhead parking area (9,640').

Pine Creek Trailhead—Missouri Basin
Drive north from Buena Vista 13 miles or south 23 miles from oldtown Leadville on US Highway 24. Turn southwest off the highway (near a trailer park) onto Chaffee County Road 388. Drive Road 388 (dirt, 2-wheel-drive); at .7 mile turn right to an obvious parking area atop a rough hill (8,700'). The actual trailhead is several hundred feet west from parking, at a gate that enters the private land of the Pine Creek Ranch. Signs here make it clear that you must respect private property and pay a small fee for crossing ½ mile of ranch (an honor system container is available for this).

Rockdale Trailhead, Cloyses Lake Trailhead
Drive US Highway 24 for 16 miles S from downtown Leadville or 14.5 miles N from Buena Vista (as in section 1.4 introduction) and turn W onto the well-signed Clear Creek Reservoir Road (Chaffee County 390).

For the Rockdale Trailhead, drive 9.5 miles to the Rockdale townsite (9,986'). Identify Rockdale by the row of cabins just south of the road. Summer parking is abundant while snow season parking is poor. Your best bet during snow season is in a wide spot about 100 feet down the road from Rockdale. In summer with 4-wheel-drive, you can cross the creek S from Rockdale, then drive a jeep trail 2.5 miles to Cloyses Lake 4-wheel-drive parking (10,860'). Obey private property signs in this area.

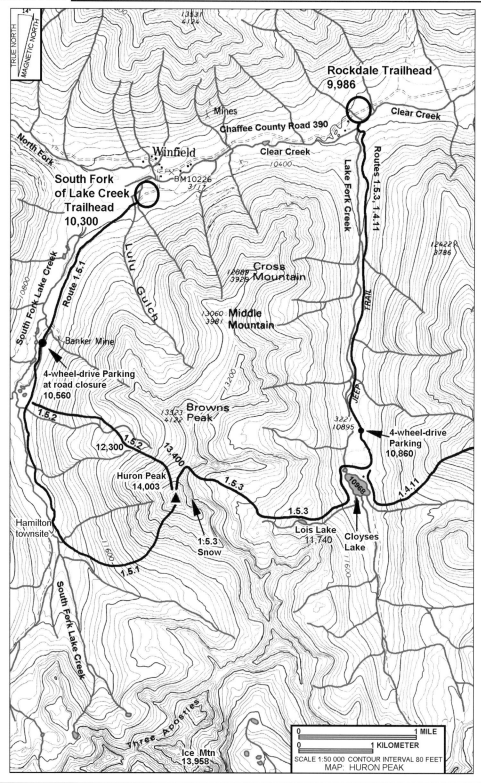

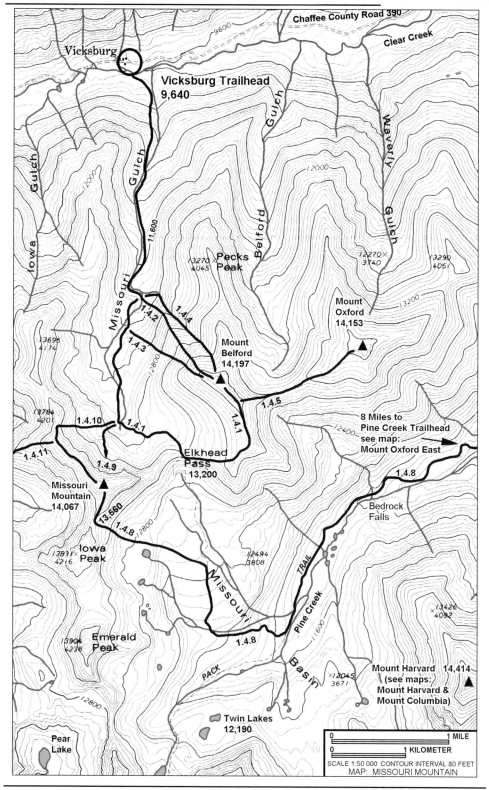

1.4.1	**Mount Belford from Elkhead Basin via Elkhead Pass**	
Ratings:	Summer Climb—Novice Ski Descent—Intermediate	
	Snow Climb—Novice	
Season:	Summer or Spring	Winter
RT Data:	12 hours, 9 miles, 4,557' ↑	multi-day, 9 miles, 4,557' ↑
Start:	Vicksburg 9,640'	
1 Day from Rd:	Yes, in summer; high camp recommended for snow or skiing	
Map:	Missouri Mountain, pg. 73	
Photo:	pg. 77	

This easy ridge route gets you a nice summit. It's a terrific hike. For good skiing and snow climbing, do this route in late winter or early spring. It loses its snowcover fast. List checkers will prefer the more direct line of the Northwest Flank route (1.4.2).

Summer after melt-off: You can start the trip two ways. If you're fit and have limited time, do the whole route in one day from Vicksburg on the Clear Creek Reservoir Road (section introduction). Climbers with mortal thighs should backpack to a high camp at about 11,500' in Elkhead Basin, relax, then climb in the morning. This allows a round-trip of only 4 miles and about 2,700' gain.

Whatever your choice in schedule, from the trailhead parking hike across a foot bridge over Clear Creek, then climb the well traveled switchback trail into Missouri Gulch. Climb easy tundra up Elkhead Basin SE to Elkhead Pass at 13,200'. From here follow the south ridge of Mount Belford to the summit (easy ground with some scree). The ridge route is obvious. Descend the same route. Fit summer climbers can shorten this route by climbing E up the huge scree face from 12,700' in Elkhead Basin.

For the "double bagger" day, continue to Mount Oxford via the obvious connecting ridge (1.4.5). You can also throw a triple if you grab Oxford and Belford, descend to Elkhead Basin, then climb Missouri Mountain (see routes in this chapter). You'll sleep well after that.

Spring Snow Season: Use the summer route above. Novice skiers and snow climbers should stick to the same route for descent. Remember, with snow climbing and skiing it's best to descend your ascent route when possible.

Winter: Take the summer route and plan on at least one night out.

The trail from Vicksburg up to Elkhead Basin can be extremely hard in winter. You may encounter dense trees, trail breaking in steep powder snow, and a trailcut that's hard to find.

Safety notes: This is an obvious ridge route. During snow season, the ascent from Elkhead Basin to Elkhead Pass takes you through avalanche terrain. This route follows all different exposures. Use sunrise time for first sunhit.

In upper Missouri Gulch, spring.

MOUNT BELFORD 14,197 FT

N

1.4.2	**Mount Belford—Northwest Flank**	
Ratings:	Summer Climb—Intermediate	Snow Climb—Intermediate
Season:	Summer or Spring	Winter
RT Data:	11 hours, 6½ miles, 4,557' ↑	multi-day, 6½ miles, 4,557' ↑
Start:	Vicksburg 9,640'	
1 Day from Rd:	Yes, in summer	
Map:	Missouri Mountain, pg. 73	
Photo:	pg. 74	

Other than a snow climb up the West Face Couloir (1.4.3), the Northwest Flank is the most direct route up the west side of Mount Belford. It's a good summer climb and is probably the most popular way to "bag" Mount Belford. Because of windscour this can be a fairly safe winter route—but don't expect much skiing or snow climbing.

Summer after snow melt-off: Follow route (1.4.1) to Elkhead Basin. Set a high camp in Elkhead Basin or, if you're strong, do the trip in one day from Vicksburg. In either case, hike to 11,800' in Elkhead Basin. From here, as you look up east at the huge bulk of Mount Belford, identify the deeply cut northwest gulch. Your route is the obvious shoulder that forms the right side of the gulch. An intermittent trail (with occasional good tread) leads up the shoulder to the summit. Don't mistake the Central Couloir (on Belford's west face) for the northwest gulch. The northwest gulch is a much deeper cleft and contains a stream. Descend via your ascent route—it's a knee banger.

Spring snow season: Use the summer route above. This route is usually windscoured, but still makes a good climb if you aren't seeking snow. For better snow climbing, consider the Northwest Gulch (1.4.4) or Central Couloir (1.4.3).

Winter: Since it is direct and windscoured, this is usually the best choice for a winter climb of Mount Belford.

Safety notes: Watch for rockfall from parties above you. Winter climbers should be sure that all snow is either windscoured or compacted. For sunhit, add about 3 hours to standard sunrise.

1.4.3	**Mount Belford—West Face Central Couloir**	
Ratings:	Ski Descent—Advanced	Snow Climb—Advanced
Season:	Spring snow	
RT Data:	overnight, 9 miles, 4,557' ↑	
Start:	Vicksburg 9,640'	
1 Day from Rd:	High camp recommended for snow or skiing	
Map:	Missouri Mountain, pg. 73	
Photo:	pg. 74	

Spring snow season: This is a beautiful snow climb and borderline extreme ski. It is not recommended without snow. From a high camp in Elkhead Basin (section introduction and route 1.4.1), snow climb the obvious gully system that splits the west face of Belford. Start from about 12,000' in Elkhead Basin. The lower part of the couloir, where it necks down, has a short 44 degree steep section. As you climb higher the couloir becomes less pronounced. As it fades, trend slightly to the right, then climb directly to the summit. The upper slopes are angled between 32 and 40 degrees. Descend your ascent route, or head down the ridge to Elkhead Pass (1.4.1).

Safety notes: Climb and ski this avalanche path only when snow conditions are most stable. For sunhit, add about 3 hours to standard sunrise.

1.4.4	Mount Belford—Northwest Gulch	
Ratings:	Ski Descent—Advanced	Snow Climb—Advanced
Season:	Spring snow	
RT Data	overnight, 8½ miles, 4,557' ↑	
Start:	Vicksburg 9,640'	
1 Day from Rd:	High camp recommended, one day possible	
Map:	Missouri Mountain, pg. 73	
Photo:	pg. 74	

Spring snow season: This is an excellent introductory snow climb or ski route for good skiers with little mountain experience and for climbers in the learning stage.

Hike to 11,800' in Elkhead Basin. Looking up west at the bulk of Mount Belford, identify the deep cleft of the Northwest Gulch. It's marked on the map by a stream that branches off the Missouri Gulch stream at 11,800'. Follow this gulch to the summit of Mount Belford. Descent is via the same route or descend the ridge to Elkhead Pass (1.4.1). You can also continue to Mount Oxford. (see route 1.4.5)

Safety notes: This route follows an avalanche path. Ski and climb it only when the snow is the most stable. For sunhit, add several hours to standard sunrise.

1.4.5	Mount Oxford via Mount Belford	
Ratings:	Summer Climb—Intermediate	Ski Descent—Advanced
	Snow Climb—Intermediate	
Season:	Summer or Spring	Winter
RT Data:	12 hours, 9½ miles, 5,927' ↑	multi-day, 9½ miles, 5,927' ↑
Start:	Vicksburg 9,640'	
1 Day from Rd:	Summer or spring high camp recommended, one day possible	
Map:	Missouri Mountain, pg. 73	
Photo:	pg. 77	

Climbers are fenced from Mount Oxford by dangerous stream crossings and large roadless areas to the east and south. As a result, the most efficient route uses the connecting ridge from Mount Belford. Yet with a low intervening saddle (13,490'), connecting these two peaks involves a painful amount of vertical—especially as a same-day ascent from Vicksburg. To ease the pain, a high camp in Elkhead Basin is a good idea. Or, if you enjoy backpacking, consider climbing Mount Oxford from Pine Creek via its Southeast Flank or East Ridge (1.4.6; 1.4.7).

Summer after melt-off: To bag both peaks in the same day, climb Mount Belford via any of the routes in this chapter. Hike the obvious connecting ridge ¼ mile SE then 1 mile NE

MOUNT BELFORD 14,197 FT

1.4.5
SKI

BELFORD
GULCH

1.4.1 & 1.4.5

1.4.5

13,490 ft

1.4.1

N

During the last leg to Mount Oxford, you get a good view of Belford's east side.

to the summit of Mount Oxford. You have to wind around a few rock outcrops, but most of the ridge is easy tundra and scree. Descend the same route, including climbing from the saddle back over the summit of Belford, or walking down the ridge S then W to Elkhead Pass. The latter option has slightly less vertical—but more distance.

Spring snow season: Climbers can follow the summer route described above and use the same route for descent. For good skiing, from the summit of Belford ski E about 700 vertical feet into Belford Gulch. Staying high in Belford Gulch, traverse to the 13,490' Oxford/Belford saddle. Climb the easy ridge from the saddle to the summit of Oxford.

Ski from the summit of Oxford back into Belford Gulch (drop as far down as your fitness allows you to re-climb), then climb back to the Oxford/Belford saddle. Slog the ridge back to the summit of Belford, then enjoy a descent of Mount Belford via the Central Couloir (1.4.3) or Northwest Gulch (1.4.4). You may be tempted to ski Belford Gulch, but this is not recommended because of steep bushwhacking and lack of a bridge over Clear Creek. Likewise, Waverly Gulch, by all reports, has good skiing—but steep brush and lack of a bridge make it less appealing. Nonetheless, you could still ski either route down to timberline, then climb back up.

Winter: This peak's ridges provide good avalanche-safe winter routes. Use route 1.4.2 for Mount Belford, then follow the summer route described above.

Safety notes: High altitude ridge traverses take time. Get an early start—especially for snow climbing or skiing. Add 3 hours to standard sunrise for sunhit on the west side of Mount Belford.

1.4.6	**Mount Oxford from Pine Creek**	
Ratings:	Summer Climb—Intermediate Ski Descent—Intermediate	
	Snow Climb—Intermediate	
Season:	Summer or Spring	Winter
RT Data:	14 hours, 16½ miles, 5,603' ↑	overnight, 16½ miles, 5,603' ↑
Start:	Pine Creek Trailhead 8,850'	
1 Day from Rd:	Yes, in summer or spring; no, in winter	
Map:	Mount Oxford East, pg. 79	
Photo:	pg. 81	

Are you fit and fleet? If so, use this route to get away from the crowds.

Summer after snow melt-off: Park at the Pine Creek Trailhead (section introduction). Walk the beaten Pine Creek Trail 4 miles to its intersection with the Colorado/Main Range Trail (10,400'). Turn right (N) and hike the Colorado Trail to a ridgetop at 11,655'. Leave the trail here and follow the broad ridge W to the summit of Waverly Mountain. Drop a few vertical feet SW from Waverly Mountain to a major saddle, then follow Oxford's east ridge 1 mile to the summit. Descend your ascent route.

Spring snow season: Use the summer route above. Leave skis near the summit of Waverly Mountain.

Winter: Use the summer route above. You'll probably need a high camp.

Safety notes: Allow plenty of time. Use your map, compass, and altimeter. Winter climbers can avoid avalanche danger by using timber and ridges. Use standard sunrise for sunhit.

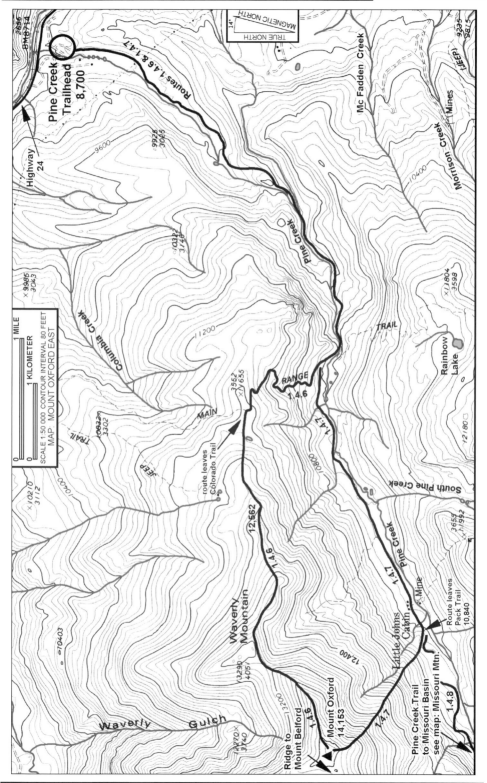

1.4.7	**Mount Oxford—South Flank from Pine Creek**
Ratings:	Summer Climb—Advanced Ski Descent—Advanced
	Snow Climb—Advanced
Season:	Spring or Summer snow
RT Data:	14 hours, 16½ miles, 5,303' ↑
Start:	Pine Creek Trailhead 8,850'
1 Day from Rd:	Consider a high camp for this route.
Map:	Mount Oxford East, pg. 37
Photo:	pg. 81

Summer after snow melt-off: Park at the Pine Creek Trailhead (section introduction). Walk the beaten Pine Creek Trail 6¼ miles to 10,840', just after you cross a small stream. Leave the trail here and hike/climb NW up a steep rib to the summit of Mount Oxford. Descend your ascent route or the East Ridge (1.4.6).

Spring snow season: You may find skiing or snow climb alternatives in the steep drainage to the east of the summer route. Skiing in this area is rated Advanced to Extreme.

Safety notes: You'll need strong legs, strong will—and plenty of time if you don't camp. Use standard sunrise for sunhit.

1.4.8	**Missouri Mountain—South Ridge from Missouri Basin**	
Ratings:	Summer Climb—Intermediate Ski Descent—Intermediate	
	Snow Climb—Intermediate	
Season:	Summer or Spring	Winter
RT Data:	overnight, 27 miles, 5,217' ↑	expedition, 27 miles, 5,217' ↑
Start:	Pine Creek Trailhead 8,850'	
1 Day from Rd:	No	
Maps:	Mount Oxford East (start of route), pg, 79; Missouri Mountain (end route), pg. 73	
Photo:	pg. 81	

All but the ultra-marathoner should do this route as a backpack trip.

Summer after snow melt-off: Park at the Pine Creek Trailhead (section introduction). Hike the Pine Creek Trail 10 miles to 12,480' in Missouri Basin. Leave the trail and climb NW then W to the prominent saddle (13,560') between Iowa Peak and Missouri Mountain. Follow Missouri's rocky but easy south ridge to the summit. Descend your ascent route.

Spring snow season: Use the summer route above. Enjoy skiing in Missouri Basin.

Winter: Are you set for a multi-day winter expedition? Anyone who does this winter climb is ready for the great ranges.

Safety notes: Take the usual precautions and remember how far from help you are. Use standard sunrise for sunhit.

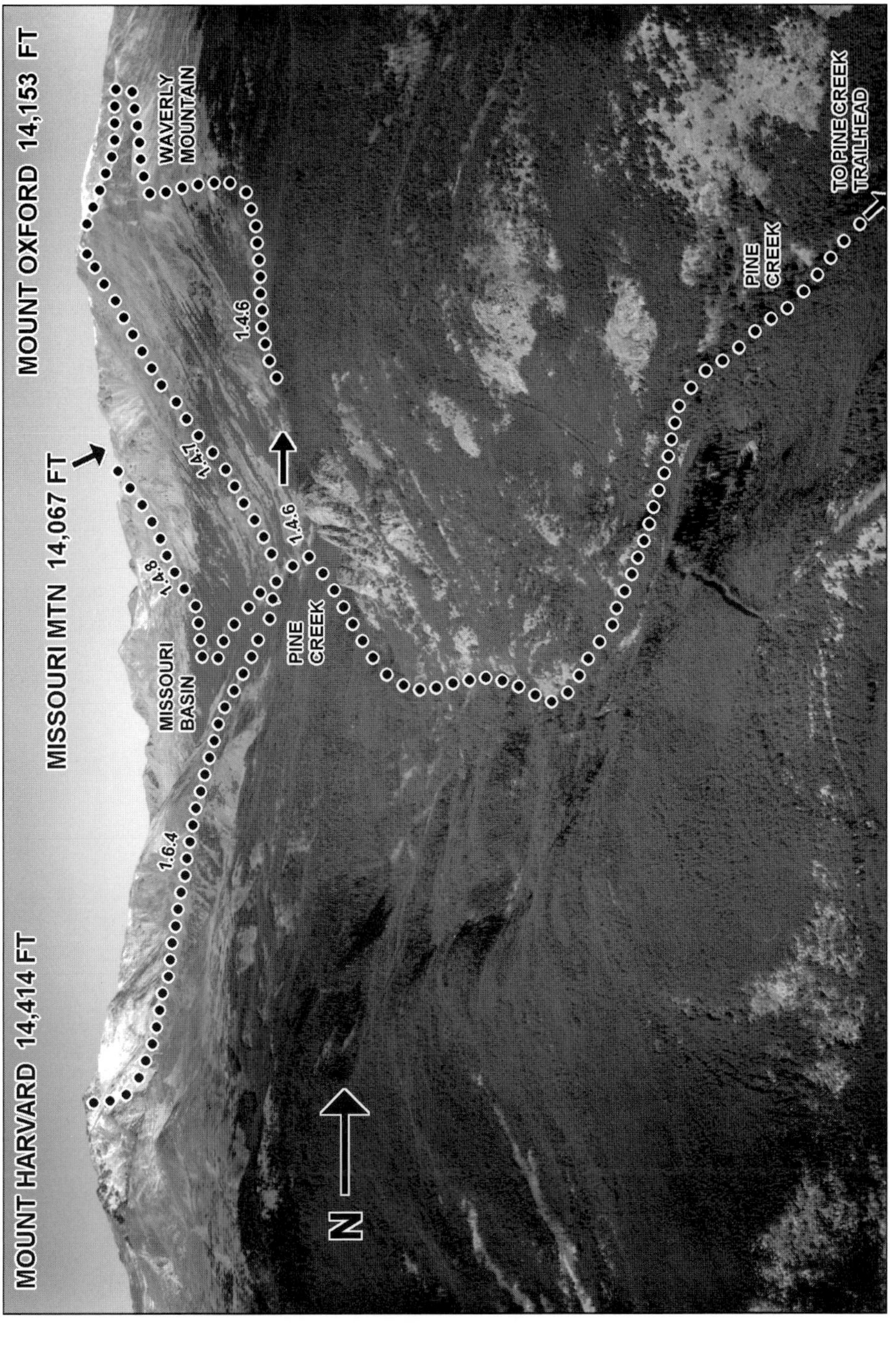

MOUNT HARVARD 14,414 FT

MISSOURI MTN 14,067 FT

MOUNT OXFORD 14,153 FT

WAVERLY MOUNTAIN

MOUNT HARVARD 14,414 FT

1.6.4

1.4.8

MISSOURI BASIN

1.4.7

1.4.6

PINE CREEK

1.4.6

PINE CREEK

TO PINE CREEK TRAILHEAD

N

Pine Creek and Missouri Basin from the east.

1.4.9	**Missouri Mountain—North Face from Elkhead Basin**	
Ratings:	Ski Descent—Extreme	Snow Climb—Advanced
Season:	Spring or Summer snow	
RT Data:	12 hours, 9 miles, 4,427' ↑	
Start:	Vicksburg Trailhead 9,640'	
1 Day	Yes,	
from Rd:	but high camp is better	
Map:	Missouri Mountain, pg. 73	
Photo:	pg. 82	

If you're accustomed to the easy scree faces of Mount Oxford and Mount Belford, this route on Missouri Mountain may be a shock. No easy trail leads to the summit. You must climb a steep gully with snow, perhaps ice, and possible rockfall. Nonetheless, it's a pleasant climb if you're careful. With snow cover the gully is a fine snow climb and superb ski descent.

Spring or summer snow season: Follow route 1.4.1 from Vicksburg up to Elkhead Basin. Take time in Elkhead Basin to study Missouri Mountain. Examine the east summit ridge carefully. If you think of the ridge as starting at Elkhead Pass, the summit is the farthest W (right) bump on the ridge—farther to the west than most people would think. For a

Camp in Elkhead Basin.

double check, examine the photograph in this book, and pay attention to your map. Notice that several gullies drop from the ridge a bit to the left (E) of the summit. With complete snow cover, the couloir nearest the summit is a good climb and ski descent. Its steepest section is about 43 degrees. An easier route, which is less obvious from below, takes a slightly lower angled gully that starts to the right (W) of the summit, then heads up and left. Several more gullies drop from the east ridge farther from the summit. Don't confuse these with the summit gullies.

Take the west side of Missouri Gulch Creek to the 12,600' level in Elkhead Basin. Climb W up a small headwall that leads to a lower angled area at 13,000', just below the obvious gullies that split the north face of Missouri Mountain. Continue to your gully of choice.

Safety notes: This is adult mountaineering. All climbers should have an ice axe and know how to use it. Snow climb and ski these couloirs only at the most stable times, preferably early in the morning on compacted spring snow. Due to rockfall, these gullies should only be done as snow climbs. Add several hours to standard sunrise for sunhit. Many people are confused by these gullies and climb the steeper more dangerous chutes farther to the east of the summit. Take time to read your map.

1.4.10	**Missouri Mountain—Northwest Ridge from Elkhead Basin**	
Ratings:	Summer Climb—Intermediate Ski Descent—Advanced	
	Snow Climb—Intermediate	
Season:	Summer, or Spring snow	
RT Data:	12 hours, 9 miles, 4,427' ↑	
Start:	Vicksburg Trailhead 9,640'	
1 Day from Rd:	Yes	
Map:	Missouri Mountain, pg. 73	
Photo:	pg. 82	

Almost every fourteener has an easy route—this is the one for Missouri Mountain. It's also a good snow climb during snow season and a fine ski descent (though you can't ski it from the summit). The summit of Missouri Mountain is not obvious from Elkhead Basin. Read route 1.4.9 for tips on identification.

Summer after snow melt-off: Follow route 1.4.1 from Vicksburg up to Elkhead Basin. From 12,600' in Elkhead Basin (where the basin steepens) climb easy ground directly W up the flank of Missouri's northwest ridge. Crest the ridge at an obvious saddle (13,690'), then follow the ridge S to the summit. Descend your ascent route.

Spring snow season: Use the summer route above and leave skis at the saddle (or lower if your ability dictates).

Safety notes: Descend your ascent route—not the couloirs dropping from the summit! Use standard sunrise for sunhit.

1.4.11	**Missouri Mountain—West Ridge from Lake Fork Creek**	
Ratings:	Summer Climb—Intermediate Ski Descent—Advanced	
	Snow Climb—Intermediate	
Season:	Summer/Spring	Winter
RT Data:	(from Cloyses Lake)	
	8 hours, 5 miles, 3,207' ↑	12 hours, 10 miles, 4,081' ↑
Start:	Rockdale Trailhead 9,986',	Rockdale Trailhead 9,986'
	or Cloyses Lake 4-wheel-drive Trailhead 10,860'	
1 Day from Rd:	Yes	
Maps:	Huron Peak, pg. 72; Missouri Mountain, pg. 73	
Photo:	pg. 84	

Summer after snow melt-off: With a 4-wheel-drive vehicle, this is an elegant way up Missouri Mountain. With 2-wheel-drive, you'll have to park near Rockdale and walk 2½ miles and 874 vertical feet of jeep road. In that case, a more aesthetic choice is to hike up Missouri Gulch and climb via the other routes in this chapter. Refer to section 1.5 for directions to Cloyses Lake and Rockdale trailheads.

Whether you drive or hike from Rockdale, from the Cloyses Lake Trailhead continue up the valley on the public trail east of Cloyses Lake. Obey private property signs (there may also be a sign indicating the trail to Missouri Mountain). While still near the lake, leave

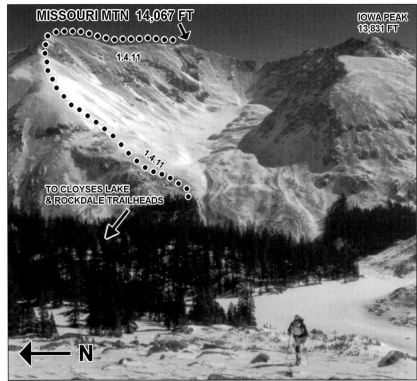

While climbing Huron Peak from Cloyses Lake, you get a good view of Missouri Mountain.

the main trail and head southeast up Missouri's west flanks. Before you reach the main drainage dropping from Missouri's west face, swing NE then climb E up a rib to point 13,930' on Missouri's northwest ridge. Follow the northwest ridge to the summit. Descend your ascent route.

Spring snow season: Use the summer route above, with variations as you seek snow for climbing or skiing.

Winter: This is probably the best route for a winter climb of Missouri Mountain. It's more likely to be blown clear of slide-prone snow, it's shorter, and you don't have the steep switchbacks of the Missouri Gulch Trail. You'll have to park at Rockdale, but the 2½ mile road to Cloyses lake is often packed by snowmobile.

Safety notes: You won't find an obvious trail up this route, so bring your navigation gear—and skill. Add 3 hours to standard sunrise for sunhit.

SECTION 1.5
Huron Peak (14,003')

Compared to nearby fourteeners, Huron Peak stands alone. To the east, the deep cleft of the Lake Fork drainage separates Huron from Missouri Mountain. Clear Creek forms a deep rift to the north and west. It's only to the south that Huron is attached to its fellow mountains. Here, the Continental Divide rears up into Ice Mountain and the spectacular Three Apostles. The view from Huron's summit includes a good angle on the Continental Divide, as well as an unobstructed western panorama of the stupendous Elk Mountains.

Huron is a good bet for hiking, skiing, and snow climbing. Several interesting snow couloirs split the East Face (1.5.3), while the West Face (1.5.2) provides "walk-ups" with mellow skiing during spring snow season. In the summer, these westerly routes make good first fourteeners.

ROADS AND TRAILHEADS

USGS Map: Winfield
USFS Forest Visitors Map: San Isabel NF

Clear Creek Reservoir Road

Drive US Highway 24 for 16 miles S from downtown Leadville or 14.5 miles N from Buena Vista (as in section 1.4 introduction) and turn W onto the well-signed Clear Creek Reservoir Road (Chaffee County 390).

Rockdale Trailhead, Cloyses Lake Trailhead

Drive 9.5 miles to the Rockdale townsite (9,986'). Identify Rockdale by the row of cabins just south of the road. Summer parking is abundant while snow season parking is poor. Your best bet during snow season is in a wide spot about 100 feet down the road from Rockdale. In summer with 4-wheel-drive, you can cross the creek S from Rockdale, then drive a jeep trail 2.5 miles to Cloyses Lake 4-wheel-drive parking (10,860'). Obey private property signs in this area.

South Fork of Lake Creek Trailhead

Drive the Clear Creek Reservoir Road 11 miles (from Highway 24) to the Winfield Townsite. Head S through Winfield, cross a bridge over Clear Creek, and continue ¼ mile to roadside parking (10,300') where the road becomes a 4-wheel-drive track. Hike or continue with 4-wheel-drive 1¾ miles (rough with mud bogs) to an obvious closure gate (10,560'). Call the Forest Service (see appendices) for current road information. In winter or early spring snow-closure is at Winfield, with melt-out to the closure gate occurring in late May. Don't mistake this trailhead for the North Fork of Clear Creek, which you reach by continuing straight W through Winfield.

1.5.1	**Huron Peak—Southwest Face from South Fork of Clear Creek**	
Ratings:	Summer Climb—Intermediate Ski Descent—Intermediate	
	Snow Climb—Intermediate	
Season:	Summer or Spring	Winter
RT Data:	8 hours, 10½ miles, 3,703' ↑	multi day, 11 or more miles, at least 3,777' ↑
Start:	South Fork Lake Creek Trailhead 10,300'	Winfield vicinity 10,226'
1 Day from Rd:	Yes, summer or spring	depends on road closure in winter
Map:	Huron Peak, pg. 72	

Though it lacks excitement, this route is a good beginner's climb. It's the most popular way up Huron and the best winter option.

Summer after melt-off: Drive to Winfield and the South Fork Lake Creek Trailhead (section introduction). Continue by foot or 4-wheel-drive up the jeep trail. Just past the road to the Banker Mine, you will come to the Forest Service road closure gate. Continue up the valley past the closure gate to the Hamilton Townsite. Hike E on a well-used trail that leads through Hamilton, then climbs E up Huron's rocky southwest shoulder. Continue climbing E, then at the 12,200 foot level swing NE to the summit. Descend your ascent route.

Spring snow season: This is the windward side of Huron Peak, so all routes may lack snow cover and be scree hikes. With snow cover, the gulch above the Hamilton Townsite can be a terrific ski descent.

Winter: Safe winter climbs are possible if you follow any one of the myriad ribs and ridges on this wind blasted side of Huron.

Safety notes: This side of Huron Peak is covered with scree. Be ready for more than a trail hike. Add 3 hours to standard sunrise for sunhit.

1.5.2	**Huron Peak—Direct West Face from South Fork of Clear Creek**	
Ratings:	Summer Climb—Intermediate Ski Descent—Intermediate	
	Snow Climb—Intermediate	
Season:	Summer or Spring	Winter
RT Data:	8 hours, 8¼ miles, 3,703' ↑	multi day, 9 or more miles, at least 3,777' ↑
Start:	South Fork Lake Creek Trailhead 10,300'	Winfield vicinity 10,226
1 Day from Rd:	Yes, summer or spring	depends on road closure in winter
Map:	Huron Peak, pg. 72	

This is the shorter-steeper-harder route for Huron Peak. It's efficient, but heavy use could cause undue erosion on the upper scree slopes. Since these slopes are frustrating at best, they are probably better as snow climbs during the spring snow season. For a summer climb, consider route 1.5.1, which is longer but slightly lower angled.

Summer after melt-off: Drive to Winfield and the South Fork Lake Creek Trailhead (section introduction). Continue by foot or 4-wheel-drive up the jeep trail. Just past the road to the Banker Mine, you will come to the Forest Service road closure gate. Continue up the old jeep trail past the closure gate for approximately ½ mile, then climb SE up a tundra covered flank to the basin between Huron and Browns Peak. Take a frustrating talus slope from the basin SE to Huron's summit. Use your map to be sure you're not climbing Browns Peak instead of Huron!

Spring snow season: With snow cover, this is highly recommended as a snow climb or ski descent.

Winter: Safe winter climbs are possible if you follow any one of the myriad ribs and ridges on this wind blasted side of Huron.

Safety notes: This side of Huron Peak is covered with scree. Be ready for more than a trail hike. Add 3 hours to standard sunrise for sunhit.

1.5.3	**Huron Peak—East Face from Lake Fork Creek**	
Ratings:	Summer Climb—Intermediate Ski Descent—Advanced	
	Snow Climb—Intermediate	
Season:	Summer, or Spring snow	
RT Data:	7 hours, 5 miles, 3,143' ↑	
Start:	Cloyses Lake 4-wheel-drive Trailhead 10,860' (or Rockdale Trailhead)	
1 Day from Rd:	Yes	
Map:	Huron Peak, pg. 72	
Photo:	pg. 88	

Summer after snow melt-off: This route is a fine summer hike that gets you away from the crowds. From Rockdale (see section introduction), follow an obvious road across Clear Creek, then up a switchback on the bank to the east of Lake Fork Creek. Continue up the road to a private land gate approximately ¼ mile before Cloyses Lake. To avoid trespassing, head to the W, cross the outlet area of Cloyses Lake, then follow the W shore of the lake to a point a few hundred yards before the Lois Lake drainage inlet.

From here, climb to Lois Lake via a stretch of hard bushwhacking. The trick is to link several open areas just to the north of Lois Lake Creek. At Lois Lake, you break out of timberline into a spectacular basin. Use your compass and map to identify Huron, which looks slightly mundane in comparison to the jagged aretes forming the south side of the basin. Once you are oriented, let the basin lead you to the pass (13,400') between Point 13,518' and Huron's summit. From the pass follow an easy ridge to the summit.

Spring snow season: This side of Huron Peak has better snow cover than the wind-scoured west face. Thus the skiing and snow climbing are more predictable. The mountain has a more alpine feel on the east side, with granite towers rising from an airy hanging valley.

Follow the summer directions above. In early spring the road to Cloyses Lake may be closed. If so, you'll need more time in the morning or a high bivouac. For advanced variations, climbers and skiers will find several terrific couloirs on the east face. You can get to these from the basin below the pass (13,400') between Point 13,518' and Huron's summit. For your descent, move down the south summit ridge a short way, and you'll reach several breaks that allow access to the couloirs.

Safety notes: During the spring season, alpine climber's should get the usual early morning start. Due to rockfall danger, summer climbers should stay out of the couloirs (stick with the summer route above). Use standard sunrise for sunhit.

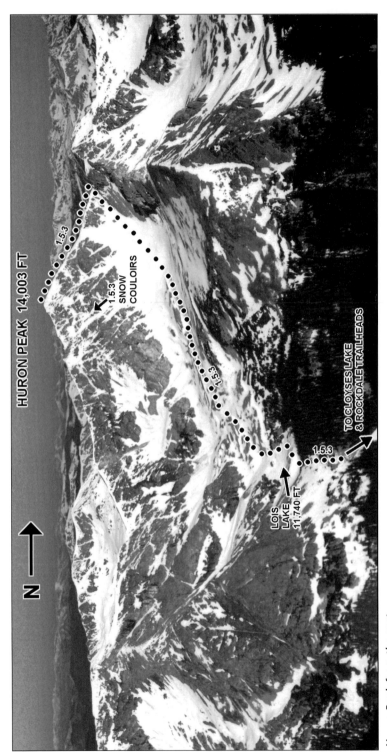

HURON PEAK 14,003 FT

N

1.5.3

1.5.3 SNOW COULOIRS

1.5.3

1.5.3

LOIS LAKE 11,740 FT

TO CLOYSES LAKE & ROCKDALE TRAILHEADS

Huron Peak from the east.

SECTION 1.6
Mount Harvard (14,420'), Mount Columbia (14,073')

Mount Harvard and Mount Columbia form the north end of a group of fourteeners in the Sawatch called the "Collegiate Peaks" or "Collegiates." Huge nondescript peaks like most of the other Sawatch, the Collegiates earned their moniker by virtue of the peaks' college names. The Collegiates have the dubious distinction of college mountaineering clubs erecting flags on their summits. The size of some of the flag poles makes you question the alumni's sanity and wonder at the sanctity of wilderness.

These are easy hikes and climbs with Columbia being a bit harder than Harvard. A jagged arete known as Rabbit Ridge connects the two peaks. Rabbit Ridge looks tempting from afar, but up close the Rabbits appear dead and rotten. That they are, and Rabbit Ridge is not recommended. To climb both peaks in a day, do Columbia first, then either drop back into upper Horn Fork and climb the South Ridge of Harvard (1.6.1) or take a high traverse north of Rabbit Ridge to Mt. Harvard, then descend Harvard's South Ridge (1.6.1) to Horn Fork Basin. Either way, this is a terribly long day.

During spring snow season, it's best to enjoy these Collegiates from a high camp in or near Horn Fork Basin. Even with snow to contend with, you can leave the North Cottonwood Creek Trailhead in the afternoon and be to the high camp before nightfall. The two peaks can be smooth winter climbs via their ridge routes, but access is arduous. During recent winters the Cottonwood Creek road has been plowed higher and the Kroenke Lake Trail is broken more often. But snow closure is still closer to Buena Vista than most mountaineers would like. During winter closure the North Cottonwood Creek road is a heavily used snowmobile trail, so consider mechanical access.

One caveat for your map reading: remember that the "Main Range Trail" as marked on your USGS maps is now part of the Colorado Trail (a new trail that crosses the state). As a result, the names Main Range Trail and Colorado Trail are often synonymous. To reduce confusion, this trail is termed the "Colorado/Main Range Trail" herein. The Colorado Trail is marked with small white triangles that say COLORADO TRAIL.

ROADS AND TRAILHEADS

USGS maps: Mount Harvard, Mount Yale, Harvard Lakes
USFS Visitors Map: San Isabel National Forest

North Cottonwood Creek Road
First, get your bearings in Buena Vista. A good landmark is the stoplight intersection at the south end of town, where U.S. Highway 24 and the Cottonwood Creek Road intersect. Another landmark is the Pizza Hut up at the north end of town—but who knows what could happen to a Pizza Hut!

Colorado/Main Range Trail Trailhead
At any rate, once you know Buena Vista, turn W off Highway 24 onto Chaffee County Road 350. This turn is across from the Pizza Hut and .4 miles north on Highway 24 (the main street of Buena Vista) from the aforementioned stoplight intersection. Take Road 350 two miles to a T intersection with a stop sign. Turn right (sign says N COTTONWOOD CREEK 1 MILE) and drive 1 mile to another T with a small sign that points left and says N COTTONWOOD CREEK. Take a left (this is Chaffee County Road 365). At 3.5 miles you'll hit the well signed Colorado/Main Range Trail Trailhead (9,440'). Signs here indicate the trail to Harvard Lakes.

North Cottonwood Creek Trailhead
For the North Cottonwood Creek Trailhead, continue up the road 5.4 miles to road's end and obvious parking (9,860').

North Cottonwood Creek Road

The North Cottonwood Creek Road opens in early May. Call the Forest Service (see directory) for up-to-date road information. In the winter the road is closed just 4 miles from Buena Vista. It's a popular snowmobile trail.

Three Elk Creek Trailhead

This is a good trailhead with a tangled access drive. Start with the directions above for the North Cottonwood Creek Trailhead. Drive Chaffee County 350 for 2 miles to the T intersection with County 361. Turn right onto Road 361, drive 3.8 miles, and take a left turn onto Chaffee County Road 368. Drive 368 for 1.2 miles W and turn left onto Road 368A. Drive .1 mile S on 368A and turn right onto unimproved Forest Service Road 368 (marked with a brown USFS road stake.) Drive up USFS road 368 for .8 miles (high clearance two-wheel-drive) to a signed trailhead at 9,260' in a logged area. The sign says THREE ELK CREEK and points left. Parking is obvious.

Pine Creek Trailhead (for Missouri Basin, see 1.4 introduction)

Frenchman Creek Trailhead

Drive Highway 24 N 7½ miles from central Buena Vista, or 27 miles S from oldtown Leadville, to a populated area known as Riverside (no sign). Turn west off the highway onto Chaffee County 386 (good county sign). Drive .3 miles, then turn right onto USFS Road 386. You can 2-wheel-drive 1.4 miles to a fork (9,290'). Park 2-wheel-drive here. Continue up the left fork (steep) by foot or 4-wheel-drive (several rough sections) 2¼ miles to the Collegiate Peaks Wilderness boundary at 10,800'. Sadly, Road 386 is closed from early winter to late spring, and thus only useful for summer access.

1.6.1	Mount Harvard—South Ridge	
Ratings:	Summer Climb—Intermediate	Snow Climb—Intermediate
Season:	Summer or Spring	Winter
RT Data:	10 hours, 12¼ miles, 4,554' ↑	multi day, depends on closure, 5,414' ↑
Start:	North Cottonwood Creek Trailhead 9,860'	North Cottonwood Creek Road closure 9,000'
1 Day from Rd:	Yes, in summer; high camp spring	winter, multi-day
Maps:	Mount Columbia, pg. 93; Mount Harvard, pg. 92	
Photo:	pg. 94	

Another classic fourteener hike or climb; if you're a peak bagger this is your route for Harvard.

Summer after snow melt-off: Though fit climbers can get this route in one day from the roadhead, Horn Fork Basin is a beautiful place for a wilderness high camp.

Drive the North Cottonwood Creek Road to the North Cottonwood Creek Trailhead. Hike the well-traveled trail W up North Cottonwood Creek for 1¾ miles to an obvious, well signed junction (10,360'). Take the right (N) fork, and follow a beaten pack trail 2 miles up into Horn Fork Basin. The trail gradually peters out in the vicinity of Bear Lake. Sheltered camping can be found at 11,500'; for better "alpine aesthetics" camp higher in Horn Fork Basin (see section introduction).

For the climb, continue to the upper apex of Horn Fork Basin, where an elegant tarn nestles beneath Harvard's north face (12,900'). Swing left (W) and climb scree (with faint trails) to a saddle (13,400') on Harvard's south ridge. Climb the ridge to the summit. You'll have to squirm over some small shelves and boulders. Descend your ascent route and take care so you don't add to the erosion problem in this area.

Winter: The summer route above uses an avalanche slope to crest Harvard's south ridge. To avoid this, start from the lower-angled area at 12,600' in the upper part of Horn Fork Basin. Use careful map reading to identify the rib that drops from point 13,598 on Harvard's south ridge. Use this rib for a safe line to the ridge, then follow the ridge to the summit. A few piles of boulders, combined with powder snow, can be strenuous. Descend the same route.

Safety notes: This is a popular route. Watch for rockfall from people above you. Use standard sunrise for sunhit.

1.6.2	**Mount Harvard—South Face Snow Route**		
Ratings:	Ski Descent—Intermediate		Snow Climb—Advanced
Season:	Spring snow		
RT Data:	10 hours, 12 miles, 4,554' ↑		
Start:	North Cottonwood Creek Trailhead 9,860'		
1 Day from Rd:	Yes, but high camp recommended		
Maps:	Mount Columbia, pg. 93; Mount Harvard, pg. 92		
Photo:	pg. 94		

This south facing route has good corn snow early in the spring. The view from the summit over Missouri Basin is heavenly—it makes you want to climb forever. This route can be done in a day—albeit a hard day with a painfully early start. For more civilized enjoyment, work from a high camp at about 11,500' in Horn Fork Basin.

Spring snow season: Drive the North Cottonwood Creek Road to the North Cottonwood Creek Trailhead (section introduction). Hike or ski (depending on snow cover) the trail W up North Cottonwood Creek for 1¾ miles to an obvious well signed junction (10,360'). Take the right (N) fork and follow a beaten pack trail 2 miles up into Horn Fork Basin. Sheltered camping can be found at 11,500', or for better "alpine aesthetics" bivouac near Bear Lake. From your camp follow the route of the pack trail as marked on the USGS Mount Harvard map up into Horn Fork Basin. At 12,400' elevation, where the trail turns left to Bear Lake, do a climbing traverse to the right into the beautiful amphitheater under the south face of Mount Harvard.

Trek into the apex of the amphitheater, then examine the south face of Harvard. You'll see several obvious lines of attack. For the best snow climbing or skiing take the gully to the right, the one with a small gendarme on the right hand side about half way up.

At the top of the gully traverse left onto a small summit snowfield. Climb the snowfield to a short gully on the summit ridge about 300 feet SE (R) of the summit. Climb this gully to the crest of the ridge, then follow the ridge to the summit. Descend your ascent route or the South Ridge route (1.6.1).

For a ski descent follow the northeast side of the summit ridge for about 400 feet to a convenient short gully that takes you back to the summit snowfield you climbed up. With sparse snow you may need to downclimb this section. From the snowfield ski your ascent route. The gully is between 30 and 36 degrees steep with one short headwall of 41 degrees.

Safety notes: Climb and ski this route only on frozen spring snow.
Sunhit on this southern exposure occurs several hours after sunrise; plan accordingly.

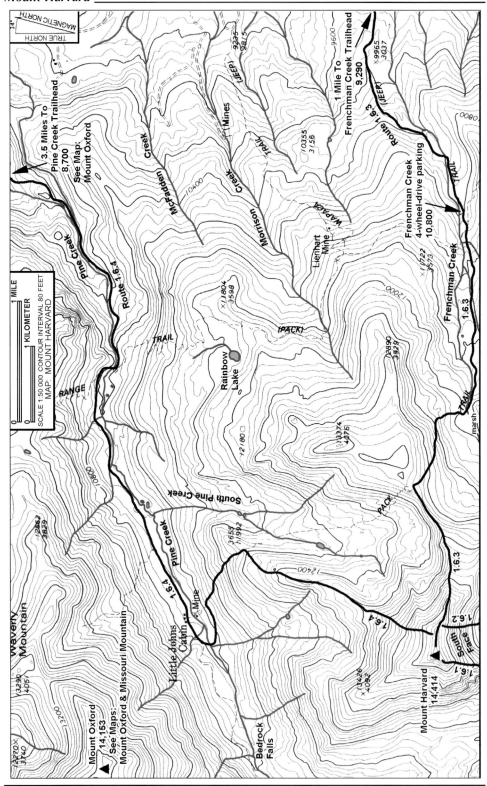

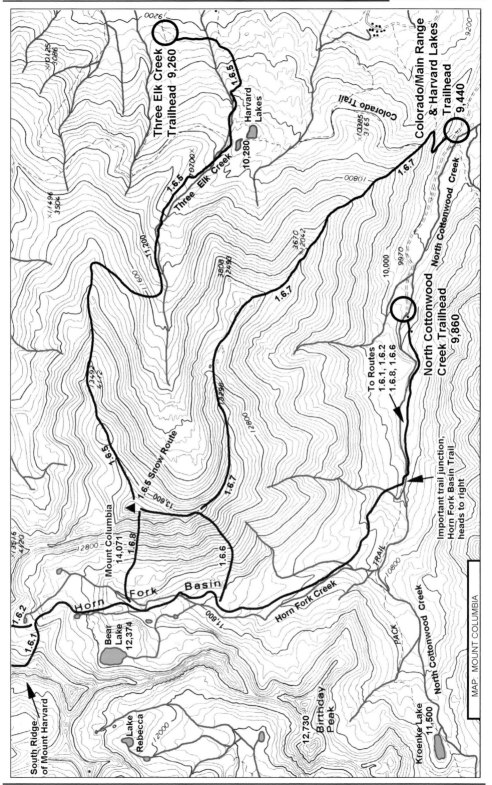

MOUNT COLUMBIA 14,071 FT

1.6.7

NORTH COTTONWOOD CREEK

MOUNT HARVARD 14,414 FT

1.6.8

HORN
FORK
BASIN

1.6.6

1.6.2

1.6.1

Spring skiing on the north side of Mount Yale, with a good view of Mount Harvard and Mount Columbia.

1.6.3	Mount Harvard—Mount Harvard Trail	
Ratings:	Summer Climb—Advanced	Snow Climb—Advanced
Season:	Summer (access road closed in spring)	
RT Data:	12 hours, 14 miles, 5,124' ↑	
Start:	Frenchman Creek Trailhead 9,290'	
1 Day from Rd:	Yes	
Map:	Mount Harvard, pg. 92	

This is the most aesthetic wilderness route for Mount Harvard.

Summer after snow melt-off: Park at the Frenchman Creek Trailhead or 4-wheel-drive to the wilderness road closure. Continue up the closed road. The road becomes a trail which leads to 13,000' on Harvard's east ridge. Climb the ridge 1½ miles to the summit. It's rocky but easy.

Safety notes: You'll find no unusual hazards on this climb. The route follows easy terrain and is rated Advanced considering its length and required navigation skills. Use standard sunrise for sunhit.

1.6.4	Mount Harvard from Missouri Basin	
Ratings:	Summer Climb—Novice	Ski Descent—Intermediate
	Snow Climb—Novice	
Season:	Summer, or Spring snow	
RT Data:	long day or overnight, 20 miles, 5,570' ↑	
Start:	Pine Creek Trailhead 8,850'	
1 Day from Rd:	Yes, in summer for the very fit;	
	skiers need high camp	
Map:	Mount Harvard, pg. 92	
Photo:	pg. 81	

Missouri Basin is an astonishing place. A vast high basin, rimmed with five fourteeners, it's been called "where God lives" by at least one pilgrim. This is a backpack trip—plan on a few days of climbing out of the basin to make it worth the work. While summer hikes and climbs out of the basin are recommended, it's too remote for most climbers' idea of a winter base-camp. Nonetheless, if you want a real winter expedition, give it a go.

If you plan on working from the higher reaches of Missouri Basin, a simple way there is to hike Missouri Gulch to Elkhead Pass, then drop into Missouri Basin from the pass. See Route 1.4.1 for directions to Elkhead Pass. If you're only goal is the north side of Harvard, it's just as efficient to reach Missouri Basin by hiking Pine Creek from U.S. 24 and the Pine Creek Trailhead (section introduction). The routes below are described as if you used the Pine Creek approach.

Summer after snow melt-off: Start from the Pine Creek Trailhead (section introduction) and trudge the long backpack to camp at about 10,800' in Pine Creek, just above a mining area known as Little Johns Cabin. This is about 2 miles downvalley from the real Missouri Basin, but it's your best stage for several routes up Harvard. From camp you have an average climb of 3,620 vertical feet. First, contour and intersect the trail that heads up South Pine Creek.

Follow this trail to another mining area on a ridge at 12,000'. Leave the trail here and climb SW up a mile of distinct ridge to Point 12,811'. From here continue up a less prominent, but no less obvious ridge, to the summit. Descend your ascent route.

Spring snow season: The route above makes a fine spring route, but with good snow cover you can take a more direct line up Harvard's north face drainage (to the west of the summer route described above). For the first 1,000 vertical feet, stay in open areas to either side of the drain. From 11,800' climb directly to the summit. You can ski or glissade your ascent route or descend the summer route.

Safety notes: If you're using the north drainage, take care to stay out of the narrow creek bed below timberline. Though Harvard has some easy hike routes, plenty of steep rocky areas can catch unwary climbers. While northern portions of this route get a late sunhit, you may climb on snow that gets sun at standard sunrise time.

1.6.5	Mount Columbia from Three Elk Creek	
Ratings:	Summer Climb—Intermediate Ski Descent—Intermediate	
	Snow Climb—Intermediate	
Season:	Summer or Spring	Winter
RT Data:	9 hours, 10 miles, 4,811' ↑	overnight, 10¼ miles, 4,921' ↑
Start:	Three Elk Creek Trailhead 9,260'	Three Elk Creek Trailhead 9,150'
1 Day from Rd:	Yes, summer or spring	No, winter
Map:	Mount Columbia, pg. 93	
Photos:	pgs. 97, 99	

You want more wilderness? Fewer people? Take this fine route. One party reported a sighting of 500 elk near the trailhead. The climb involves slightly less distance than the Columbia routes from North Cottonwood Creek, hence it's a better "one-dayer." You need superb orienteering skills for this route, since the trails are not so beaten. You can also reach this side of Columbia via Four Elk Creek, Frenchman Creek, or via the Colorado/Main Range Trail from the North Cottonwood Creek Road (1.6.7). In the latter case you pass by Harvard Lakes, as you will from the Three Elk Creek Trailhead. All other things being equal, the Three Elk Creek Trailhead is higher and a little closer, so it's a better choice. Hence, this description is written from that point of view. In winter, the Three Elk Creek Trailhead gets you closer via plowed roads.

Summer after snow melt-off: Drive to the Three Elk Creek Trailhead (section introduction). From your parking, leave the main jeep trail and traverse S on a logging road for several hundred yards. When the logging road swings right (W), continue traversing S (with a few small ups and downs) on a well-defined foot path marked with tree blazes and cairns. The trail intersects several other logging roads. Don't turn onto these; continue traversing S ¼ mile to cross Three Elk Creek in a miniature gorge. Climb S up out of the gorge for several hundred feet to intersect an old jeep trail (now a foot trail) that climbs W 1 mile to intersect the Colorado/Main-Range Trail at 10,270' just north of Harvard Lakes.

Don't take the Colorado/Main Range Trail. Instead, stay on the old jeep trail as it climbs 1½ miles W to timberline at about 11,300'. Swing N here and follow any likely looking route to the crest of Columbia's northeast ridge. Follow the long ridge 2 miles to the summit, contouring around several bumps. Return via the same route.

Spring snow season: Use the summer route above. For the best skiing and snow climbing attack the southeast face with a "directisima" from the summit.

Winter: Due to road closures, this can be a long winter trek. Plowing policy varies, however, so do a bit of automobile exploration if you're looking for a winter route up Columbia. At

MOUNT HARVARD 14,414 FT

MOUNT COLUMBIA 14,071 FT

1.6.5

1.6.5
SNOW
ROUTE

1.6.7

THREE ELK CREEK

1.6.5

HARVARD
LAKES

10,280 FT

SOUTHEAST RIDGE

1.6.7

TO COLORADO/MAIN RANGE
TRAILHEAD

TO THREE ELK
CREEK TRAILHEAD

Mount Columbia from the east, summer.

timberline in Three Elk Creek, contour N through light timber, then climb Columbia's northeast ridge to the summit. This ridge is long, with several false summits—but it's safe from avalanches.

Safety notes: Snow climbers and skiers should get an early start for this long, east facing route. Plan your day using standard sunrise time for sunhit.

1.6.6	**Mount Columbia—West Flank to South Ridge**	
Ratings:	Summer Climb—Intermediate	Snow Climb—Intermediate
Season:	Summer or Spring	Winter
RT Data:	11 hours, 10 miles, 4,211' ↑	Multi-day, 5,071' ↑
Start:	North Cottonwood Creek Trailhead 9,860'	North Cottonwood Creek Road closure 9,000'
1 Day from Rd:	Yes, with open road; with snow closure you'll need an overnight or snowmobile.	
Map:	Mount Columbia, pg. 93	
Photos:	pgs. 94, 99	

This flank and ridge route is one of the most convenient Collegiate climbs. Snow season sojourners should note that, because of windscour and a long section of ridge, this route is not a good summit ski descent. For the same reasons, however, it's a good winter route.

Summer after snow melt-off: From the North Cottonwood Creek Trailhead, (section introduction) hike pack trails 3¾ miles to 11,600' (timberline) in Horn Fork Basin. Leave the trail and make a climbing traverse SE ¼ mile to Columbia's lower flanks. You're next project is to climb directly up Columbia's west side to the south ridge. These slopes are covered with loose scree. In spring and early summer you can avoid some of the scree by snow climbing either of several gully systems. Later on, try to stay with a series of ribs that have less scree.

The climbing is easier—even fun—once you reach the crest of the south ridge (13,600'). Follow the ridge ¾ miles to the summit. Descend the same route. To avoid causing erosion by "scree running," descend the stable areas you (hopefully) found during your climb.

Spring snow season: Use the route above and stick with the gullies where possible.

Winter: Use the summer route. Windscoured ribs form a safe path to the south ridge. With your energy sapped by cold, stress, and the long approach, the scree can be painful. A pair of ski poles helps.

Safety notes: Carry an ice axe so that you can snow climb to avoid scree. The sun will hit the ridge crest around sunrise time (use table in Appendix 5). For sunhit add 2½ hours to standard sunrise.

1.6.7	**Mount Columbia—Southeast Ridge**
Ratings:	Summer Climb—Intermediate
Season:	Summer
RT Data:	11 hours, 12½ miles, 4,730' ↑
Start:	Colorado/Main Range (Harvard Lakes) Trailhead 9,440'
1 Day from Rd:	Yes
Map:	Mount Columbia, pg. 93
Photos:	pgs. 94, 99

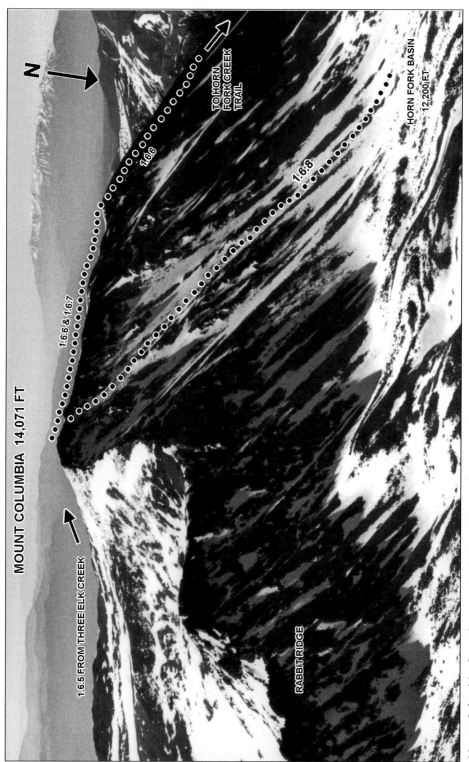

MOUNT COLUMBIA 14,071 FT

N

1.6.5 FROM THREE ELK CREEK

1.6.6 & 1.6.7

1.6.6

TO HORN FORK CREEK TRAIL

1.6.8

HORN FORK BASIN 12,200 FT

RABBIT RIDGE

Mount Columbia, from the summit of Mount Harvard.

Since the other summer route for Columbia involves steep and erosion prone scree, this has the potential of becoming the standard route. It's aesthetic, scenic—and long.

Summer after snow melt-off: Drive the North Cottonwood Creek Road to the Colorado/Main Range (Harvard Lakes) Trailhead. Hike the Harvard Lakes trail ½ mile to the timbered crest of Harvard's southeast ridge (9,880'). Stick with the trail for another ¼ mile along the ridge. When the trail swings N away from the ridge at 10,000', leave the trail and continue NW up the ridge. This is a critical juncture, since it's tempting to stay on the improved trail.

Once you're off the Harvard Lakes Trail and on the ridge, stick with it as it climbs NW for 2 miles over a small subpeak to a major saddle (12,600'). Follow the ridge from the saddle W 1½ miles to Point 13,544, then stay on the ridge as it swings north, joins route 1.6.6, and leads ¾ mile to the summit. The ridge gets rocky but it's all easy ground. Contour around as many of the bumps as you can. Descend your ascent route.

Safety notes: This is a *long* route. Beware of lightning and start early. Use standard sunrise for sunhit.

1.6.8	**Mount Columbia—West Face Snow Route**	
Ratings:	Ski Descent—Advanced	Snow Climb—Intermediate
Season:	Spring snow	
RT Data:	10 hours, 11½ miles, 4,211' ↑	
Start:	North Cottonwood Creek Trailhead 9,860'	
1 Day from Rd:	Yes, but high camp recommended	
Map:	Mount Columbia, pg. 93	
Photos:	pgs. 94, 99	

Spring snow season: This is a simple snow climb or ski route. Indeed, considering the tedium of the summer scree route described above, climbers who need to check Mount Columbia off their "Grand Slam" list should hit this route in the spring. If you're fit and like starting just after midnight, do the route in one day from the North Cottonwood Creek Trailhead. Climbers of more relaxed ilk should consider a high camp at 11,500' in Horn Fork Basin. In this case you have an easy climb of only 2,571 vertical feet.

Start at the North Cottonwood Creek Trailhead (road's end). Hike the beaten pack trail into Horn Fork Basin. With snow cover, try to stick with the pack trail route till timberline, since you need the trailcut to get through dense timber. Once in Horn Fork Basin, follow the drain to 12,000'.

Leave the drainage and climb E up a short headwall that leads to a lower angled area at the base of the west face of Mount Columbia. From here follow an obvious gully system that leads to a notch on the summit ridge a few hundred feet to the south of the summit. The gully gives you several detail choices; don't get too picky, they all work. Snow climbers can downclimb their ascent route. Skiers should pick a line that avoids passing directly above rock outcrops. Though the snow on this face is never steeper than about 40 degrees, if you fall it's good to have a few feet of snow for a self arrest before you fly into space.

Safety notes: Only climb or ski this route on frozen spring snow. When dry, rockfall danger is extreme. From a high camp, average climbers can start this west facing route about 2 hours before sunrise time. Climbers planning a one day ascent can take advantage of the late western sunhit but will still need an extremely early start.

2

SOUTHERN SAWATCH MOUNTAINS

Skiing the Angel of Shavano, winter.

USFS Forest Visitor Map:
San Isabel National Forest

Divided from the Northern Sawatch by the North Cottonwood Creek drainage and road, the Southern Sawatch mountains continue the massive nature of the Sawatch Peaks. While you'll find few technical rock climbs on the Southern Sawatch fourteeners, these peaks are all good hikes and climbs. For a technical challenge look to the snow and ice on some of the north faces in the late spring. This is a dry group of peaks since most storms drop the bulk of their moisture in a vast mountainous area to the northwest. The result is drier weather for summer climbs, but winter snow can be sparse. In spring, you'll find skiable routes, but snow will be sparser than in Colorado's other ranges.

Road access to the Southern Sawatch is excellent. On the east side of the range, where most climbs originate, U. S. Highway 285 and Colorado Highway 24 connect Leadville and Salida with good pavement. On the west side a network of gravel roads connects Pitkin, Cottonwood Pass and Taylor Pass. Most of these roads are navigable with high clearance two-wheel-drive. They're closed to auto traffic during snow season but provide good ski and snowmobile access.

A fit mountaineer can bag any Southern Sawatch fourteener in one day. Even so, you can find plenty of overnight wilderness adventures. For example, backpack to Kroenke Lake (2.1.1), then spend several days bagging Mount Yale, Mount Harvard, and Mount Columbia.

SECTION 2.1
Mount Yale (14,196')

Mount Yale is the southern most fourteener in the Collegiate group. Yale is a good hikers' mountain, with several easy routes on the west side (2.1.3). During spring, this side of the mountain also provides basic snow climbing and easy skiing. Experienced snow climbers and skiers should look at Yale's north and northwest faces (2.1.1), accessed from Kroenke Lake. If you study a map, you'll see an obvious summer route that takes Denny Gulch. Sadly, heavy use threatens a riparian area near this route, so it's not suggested for summer. It's okay to use Denny Gulch as a snow climb, but better snow routes exist. For these reasons the Denny Gulch route is not described here.

ROADS AND TRAILHEADS

USGS Maps: Buena Vista West, Mount Yale, Mount Harvard
USFS Forest Visitors Map: San Isabel National Forest

Cottonwood Pass Road, Avalanche Gulch Trailhead, Denny Creek Trailhead

Drive Highway 285 or Highway 24 to Buena Vista. From the stoplight at the south end of town, turn west on Main Street, which becomes the Cottonwood Pass Road. At 8.8 miles turn right into the huge paved parking area for the Avalanche Gulch Trailhead (9,340'). For the Denny Creek Trailhead continue up the Cottonwood Pass Road. At 12 miles from the stoplight turn right into an obvious parking area (a sign for 9,910' indicates DENNY CREEK Trailhead). Winter closure of Cottonwood Pass is at a gate a short distance past the Denny Creek Trailhead.

North Cottonwood Creek Trailhead, Harvard Lakes Trailhead, Silver Creek Trailhead (see 1.6 section introduction)

2.1.1	Mount Yale from Kroenke Lake	
Ratings:	Summer Climb—Intermediate Ski Descent—Intermediate	
	Snow Climb—Intermediate	
Season:	Summer, or Spring Snow	
RT Data:	overnight, 13 miles, 4,336' ↑	
Start:	North Cottonwood Creek Trailhead, 9.860'	
1 Day from Rd:	High camp recommended; possible for the super fit	
Maps:	Mount Yale, pg. 103; Mount Columbia, pg. 93	
Photo:	pg. 104	

For summer climbs, Mount Yale is slightly less accessible via this north side route and thus more of a wilderness escapade. During spring snow season, you'll find the best snow climbing and skiing on this (N) side of the mountain.

Summer after snow melt-off: While the fleet and fit can do this route in one day from the trailhead, a high camp at Kroenke Lake is recommended. Hike to Kroenke lake via four miles of well-marked trail from the North Cottonwood Creek Trailhead (see section introduction). From Kroenke Lake you have 2,676 vertical feet and about 2½ miles to the summit. The best summer hike route climbs the pack trail from the lake W ¼ mile to 12,000'. Swing SW off

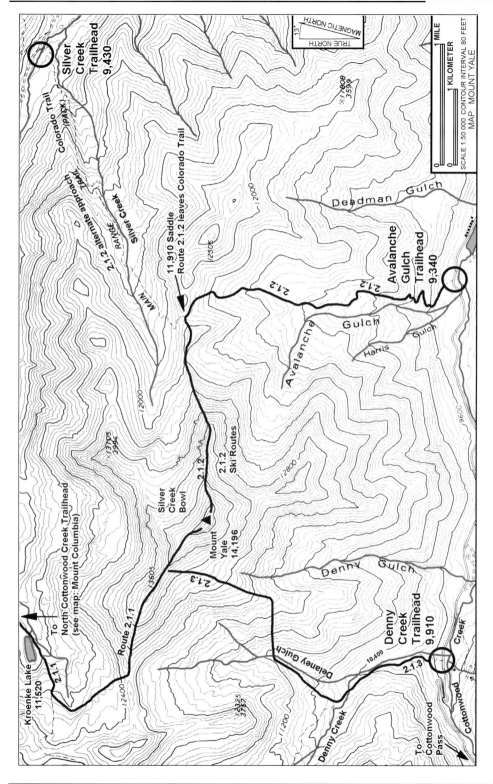

Mount Yale from the north, spring.

the trail here and climb through the basin S and SE to the crest of Mount Yale's long west ridge (12,560'). Follow the west ridge 1¾ miles to the summit.

Spring snow season: Innumerable snow climb and ski routes cover Mount Yale's northwest shoulder. The lines are obvious. For a true summit ski descent you'll probably need to drop off the summit to the northwest or southwest, then traverse (perhaps with a bit of climbing) back to a point where you can ski down to Kroenke Lake. The basin above Kroenke Lake has marvelous ski terrain.

Winter: Though this side (N) offers several avalanche-safe ridge routes, the approach up the valley to Kroenke Lake can be arduous, and you'll have to contend with the snow-closed roads from Buena Vista. Use the summer route above and pick a route to the ridge crest using lower-angled sections and ribs.

Safety notes: During summer, you'll find no hazards aside from ordinary weather concerns. With snow, all the gullies on this side (N) of Mount Yale are avalanche paths and should only be climbed and skied with a consolidated spring snowpack. Several ribs and ridges can be used for avalanche-safe routes, but approaches to these may cross slide terrain. The true northwest exposures above Kroenke Lake get a late sunhit, but exposures higher on the mountain may get sun at standard sunrise.

2.1.2	Mount Yale—East Ridge	
Ratings:	Summer Climb—Intermediate Ski Descent—Intermediate	
	Snow Climb—Intermediate	
Season:	Summer, or Spring Snow	Winter
RT Data:	14 hours, 9 miles, 4,856' ↑	multi-day, 9 miles, 4,856'↑
Start:	Avalanche Gulch Trailhead, 9,340'	
1 Day	Summer/Spring	Winter
from Rd:	Yes	long day
Map:	Mount Yale, pg. 103	
Photos:	pgs. 104, 106	

This is a fine ridge run that gives you a more alpine experience than hiking up the west side of Mount Yale. You can start the route from either of two trailheads for the Colorado Trail. For the northern approach, use the Silver Creek Trailhead on the North Cottonwood Creek Road (see below and section introduction). The Avalanche Gulch Trailhead (section introduction) provides access from the south. It's on the maintained Cottonwood Pass Road and thus provides winter and spring access. This description is written for the Avalanche Gulch approach.

If you're already in the North Cottonwood Creek drainage for climbs of Mount Harvard and Columbia, climbing Yale via Silver Creek is logical. The poorly marked Silver Creek Trailhead (9,430') is on the left (S) side of the North Cottonwood Creek Road .1 mile past the Harvard Lakes Trailhead (section introduction). Climbing the east ridge from Silver Creek is close to the same elevation and distance as that from Avalanche Gulch, but it might have a lower snow line during the spring snow season—better for skiing but harder for foot travel.

Summer after snow melt-off: Park at the Avalanche Gulch Trailhead. Find the start of the Colorado Trail on the north side of the parking lot, near the outhouse. Hike the steep and well-used Colorado Trail 3 miles to a saddle (11,910') on Yale's long east ridge. Leave the Colorado Trail, and hike/climb W along the ridge 2 miles to the summit. Most of the ridge is an easy hike, with a bit of boulder hopping and scrambling around several rocky points. A well-traveled trail is imprinted on most of the ridge, though it disappears where you need it most. The intimidating point is a jagged outcrop at 13,420'; pass this on the left (S) side. Descend your ascent route or traverse the peak by descending the Denny Creek route (2.1.3).

Spring snow season: Use the summer route above. For good skiing put your planks on

MOUNT YALE 14,196 FT

SILVER CREEK BOWL

ROUTE 2.1.2

AVALANCHE GULCH

N

A spring climb of Mount Yale's east ridge

at the summit and cut your mark in the Silver Creek Bowl (rated Advanced). A steeper ski run, rated Extreme because of a short steep section (which can be avoided) at the start, takes a beautiful line into Avalanche Gulch from about 13,700' on the ridge. If you ski Avalanche Gulch, stop your descent at about 11,200', then take a dropping traverse though timber E to the pack trail. Don't descend lower Avalanche Gulch; it becomes a steep-sided ravine choked with loose rocks, dirt, and deadfall.

Winter: This is a good winter route if wind or avalanche conditions make the Denny Creek (2.1.3) route unattractive. It is quite exposed, however, so keep an eye on the weather.

Safety notes: This route involves a long ridge run, so summer climbers should start early to avoid lightning. In winter, you can avoid slide terrain by following ridges or timber. Use standard sunrise for sunhit.

2.1.3	**Mount Yale via Denny Creek & Delaney Gulch**	
Ratings:	Summer Climb--Intermediate Ski Descent—Intermediate	
	Snow Climb—Intermediate	
Season:	Summer, or Spring Snow	Winter
RT Data:	7 hours, 6 miles, 4,286' ↑	10 hours, 6 miles, 4,286' ↑
Start:	Denny Creek Trailhead, 9,910'	
1 Day from Rd:	Yes	
Map:	Mount Yale, pg. 103	

Because of good access from the all-season, paved Cottonwood Pass Road, this side (S) of Mount Yale provides the most sensible routes for weekend mountaineers. As mentioned above, Denny Creek used to be a popular summer route but is not now recommended because of overuse. The Delaney Gulch route is slightly longer and involves a bit more bush-whacking, but it goes. Allow plenty of time for wandering through the forest!

Summer after snow melt-off: Park at the Denny Creek Trailhead (section introduction). Hike the well-defined Denny Creek Trail (it begins as a road) 1½ miles to 10,720' (after you cross Denny Creek). Cut NE off the trail here, head towards the summit of Mount Yale and do a climbing traverse into Delaney Gulch. Intersect the creek in a large open area (11,080'). Be careful on the traverse: if you go too low you'll have worse bushwhacking; too high and you'll have to thread your way through small cliff bands. Even if you find the best line, you will still have a small amount of bushwhacking through tight aspens.

Another route follows an unimproved trail that leaves the main trail at approximately 10,400', then takes a more direct line up the gut of Delaney Gulch. With heavier use, this will probably become the more popular alternative since the trail will become more obvious over time.

Either way, once you're in the open area at 11,800' in Delaney Gulch, travel to the upper end of the open area, then up through timber for a few hundred yards more, then choose a route NE up the headwall from 11,400' to 12,000', where you'll break timberline. From here follow ribs or gullies to the large basin to the northwest of the summit. Pick the best line for the conditions (snow or dry), ascend to a saddle on the summit ridge (13,490'), and follow the ridge ½ mile SE to the summit. The terrain from timberline to the summit allows any number of variations. Descend your ascent route.

Spring snow season: Use the summer route described above, with the higher elevation entrance into Delaney Gulch. Make logical variations for snow cover and avalanche hazard avoidance. For good skiing, stay in either arm of Delaney Gulch all the way to the summit ridge. Unless you must have an exact summit ski descent, leave your boards at the 13,490' saddle.

One strategy for a summit ski descent is to drop NE off the summit and ski Silver Creek Bowl, climb back to one of the saddles on the summit ridge, then ski Delaney Gulch. If conditions warrant, you can get a rewarding (rated Advanced) summit ski descent via a small couloir that drops down the south face a few hundred yards east of the summit. If you choose this route ski down to the 11,800' level in Denny Gulch, then climb back over the shoulder to the west and traverse back to your ascent route.

Winter: Use the summer route described above with the higher elevation entrance into Delaney Gulch. Above timberline, climb ribs and a shoulder to the right (S) of Delaney Gulch. This route can be done in reasonable safety with a winter snowpack, provided slide conditions are fairly stable and you climb ribs and shoulders. The Denny Creek Trail is likely to be broken to the point where you head up Delaney Gulch.

Safety notes: Summer climbers won't find any unusual hazards on this route, but they should take all normal precautions. People get lost in the timber after leaving the trail. Use your map, compass, and altimeter. Shelter from lightning would be impossible in the large basin above timberline. During snow season, while traversing into Delaney Gulch, be aware of the avalanche slopes on Point 12,325' and those slopes that dump from the east into the open area. Add 2 hours to standard sunrise for sunhit.

SECTION 2.2
Mount Princeton (14,197')

Mount Princeton, another huge Sawatch fourteener, separates the Chalk Creek and Cottonwood Creek drainages. Though of little interest to technical climbers, Princeton's flanks abound with easy hike routes and appealing snow gullies. The two routes below have the best access. If you're ambitious, explore Princeton's north face.

For winter climbing, Princeton offers accessible and safe ridges via the Merriam Creek route (2.2.1). Grouse Canyon makes a poor winter route unless avalanche conditions are perfectly safe.

Unfortunately, Princeton is situated at the intersection of 4 USGS 7.5 minute maps. The maps in this book should be adequate for navigating the routes described below. For more intricate navigation with the USGS maps, tape them together and cut off the parts you don't need.

ROADS AND TRAILHEADS

USGS Maps: Buena Vista West, Mount Antero, Mount Yale, Mount Antero
USFS Forest Visitors Map: San Isabel National Forest

Frontier Ranch Trailhead

For the Frontier Ranch Trailhead drive Highway 285 S from Buena Vista 8½ miles, or N from Salida 15 miles, to the well-signed Chaffee County Road 162 (known as the Chalk Creek Road).

Mount Princeton Road

Drive Road 162 for 4 miles west to the inviting Mount Princeton Hot Springs Resort. If you're tired of bivouacs, the Hot Springs Lodge is a good base for an early morning start on either route. At the Hot Springs Lodge, take a right (N) on Chaffee County 321 and drive 1.2 miles to a T intersection. A sign here points left (W) to Frontier Ranch and the Young Life Camp. Take a left onto the dirt road and drive just under a mile to the well-signed Frontier Ranch. At Frontier Ranch, look for a massive log gate with a sign for MOUNT PRINCETON TRAIL. This gate marks the start of a public access corridor through private land on the Mount Princeton

Road. If you're driving a low-clearance 2-wheel-drive vehicle, or the road is closed by snow, park in the obvious area near the gate (8,900'). With a dry road you can continue with high clearance 2-wheel-drive 3 miles to a saddle (10,820') near an antennae array. With 4-wheel-drive, you can drive the Mount Princeton Road above 11,000', but don't force it. Turnarounds and parking are scarce. The road opens to the antennae array sometime in early May.

Grouse Canyon Trailhead

To reach the Grouse Canyon Trailhead, continue past Mount Princeton Hot Springs on the Chalk Creek Road (Chaffee County Road 162). At 5.7 miles from the hot springs, take a right across a bridge and onto Chaffee County Road 292 (9.7 miles from Highway 285). Drive Road 292 for .4 mile to an unsigned and unimproved spur road that turns off to the right. Follow this spur a few hundred feet to 2-wheel-drive parking (9,100'). You can 4-wheel-drive a few hundred yards farther, but there's no parking. The Grouse Canyon Trailhead is unsigned, so follow the above directions exactly and use your maps.

All the trailheads in this area are near private land. Do not block roads and obey all signs.

2.2.1	Mount Princeton from Merriam Creek	
Ratings:	Summer Climb—Intermediate Ski Descent—Intermediate	
	Snow Climb—Intermediate	
Season:	Summer, or Spring Snow	Winter
RT Data:	8 hours, 6 miles, 3,377' ↑	11 hours, 7 miles, 5,297' ↑
Start:	Mount Princeton Road	Frontier Ranch Trailhead
1 Day	near antenna array, 10,820'	8,900'
from Rd:	Yes	
Map:	Mount Princeton, pg. 110	
Photo:	pg. 112	

In summer, with a 4-wheel-drive vehicle, you can pick your vertical for this route—it's the peak bagger's choice. Winter climbs are somewhat of a slog since you must foot travel the Mount Princeton Road. In spring, if you're lucky and plan carefully, you can enjoy a moderate snow climb, followed by a three or four thousand vertical foot ski descent.

Summer after snow melt-off: Drive to the Frontier Ranch Trailhead (section introduction), then walk or drive the Mount Princeton Road (depending on snow, your vehicle, and your choice in vertical). At about 4½ miles from Frontier Ranch, the road makes the last of a series of switchbacks and begins a long traverse across Princeton's east flank just below timberline. At the start of this traverse (11,800') take a right off the road onto a poorly-signed trail and hike this trail a short distance N to the crest of Princeton's east ridge. Stick with the trail as it continues past the ridge crest and climbs gradually through boulder fields and scree on the S side of Princeton's huge east amphitheater. About halfway through the amphitheater, at 12,680', leave the trail and climb left (S) 400 vertical feet to a saddle on Princeton's east ridge. Follow the ridge 1 mile to the summit. Descend your ascent route.

Spring snow season: From the Frontier Ranch Trailhead (section introduction) ski, walk, or drive, depending on snow and 4-wheel-drive capability, up the Mount Princeton Road. Make your first goal the radio towers next to the road at 10,820' (a good place to calibrate your altimeter). From here, follow the well-defined roadcut 1/4 mile W up the ridge. At this point, the road begins to switchback up to the north of the ridge. These switchbacks cross a fairly active avalanche path several times. In the case of avalanche danger, avoid slide paths by taking a more direct line up the ridge to timberline at 12,000'.

From timberline you have three options: during avalanche hazard you'll have to use the

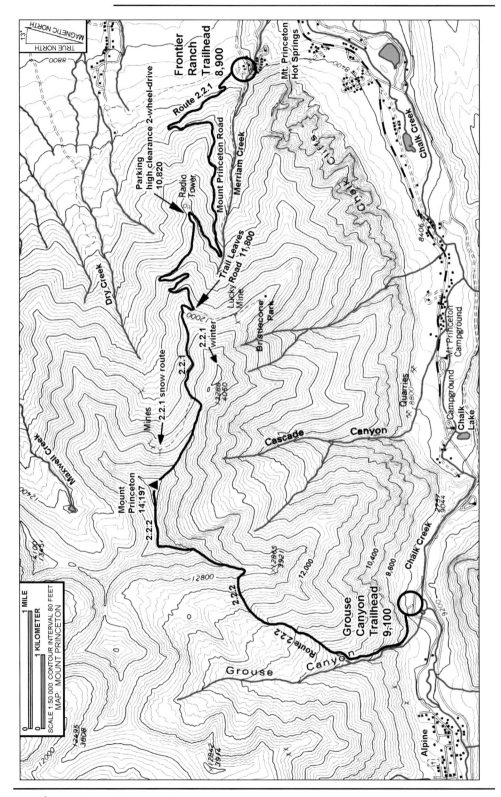

ridge the remainder of the way to the summit. This is a spectacular walk, but crawling over the boulders can wear you out (unless you luck into windpacked snow). Another option is to follow the long trail used by summer climbers that climbs gradually along the south side of Princeton's east amphitheater. This route is only useful at times with no avalanche danger. The remaining option is best suited for a spring snow climb or ski descent: take the road to the last switchback before it makes the long traverse (you'll be at timberline). Take a dropping traverse into the bowl, climb the lower-angled gut of the bowl, then ascend whichever snow gully looks best to the summit—they vary from year to year. Descend your ascent route.

Winter: To avoid avalanche danger, stick to the east ridge. This is safe, but requires a great deal of high altitude travel. During early winter, or after the mountain is windscoured, you may be able to use the summer trail described above.

Safety notes: Summer climbers should take the usual precautions, but no unusual hazards exist. During snow season, as with most fourteeners, Mount Princeton is surrounded by avalanche terrain but gives you a choice of relatively safe ridge routes. In addition, the Southern Sawatch's strong winds seem to always keep the snow cleared somewhere. If you choose to travel in the winter when the east bowl is snow loaded, forget all but the ridge route. Use standard sunrise for sunhit.

2.2.2	**Mount Princeton from Grouse Canyon**	
	Ratings:	Summer Climb—Advanced
	Season:	Summer or late spring after snow melt-off
	RT Data:	12 hours, 8 miles, 5,097' ↑
	Start:	Grouse Canyon Trailhead, 9,100'
	1 Day from Rd:	Yes
	Map:	Mount Princeton, pg. 110

Summer after snow melt-off: Mount Princeton's southern ramparts look impenetrable, and the rocky defile of Grouse Canyon looks, at best, like a brutal bushwhack. Yet Grouse Canyon hides a rough but passable trail that takes an elegant course next to the creek's mossy rocks, with the constant accompaniment of rushing water echoing off the canyon's rock walls. The trail soon breaks into a beautiful area of alpine bowls and ridges, then follows a classic non-technical ridge to the summit. Perhaps the best feature of this route is it's never crowded—it's all non-mechanized. Keep your eyes open for Bighorn Sheep, which look like white boulders from afar.

Park at the Grouse Canyon Trailhead (section introduction). Hike the 4-wheel-drive road up from the trailhead. At ¼ mile the road becomes a well-defined trail, which then intersects Grouse Creek at 9,440' just below the entrance to Grouse Canyon. Take care to stick with the trail, which is ill-defined at times, as it stays close to the creek and climbs ½ mile to the top of the canyon; a rocky gate at 9,800'. Continue paralleling the creek through a small open area. When paralleling the creek becomes improbable, climb directly to your right several hundred feet up the side of the drainage to intersect a well-worn trail through the aspen forest. You must find this trail; it follows the only feasible route.

Hike the trail as it stays above but parallel to Grouse Creek for ¼ mile, then gradually swings to the right and away from Grouse Creek. At 10,140' the trail enters a new drainage where a small stream fed by a spring enters Grouse Creek. The trail gets fainter and continues to swing right and away from Grouse Creek to parallel the right side of the smaller stream. Above the spring, the trail traverses into the dry gulch, then follows the apex of the gulch, which forms a natural trail tread to a talus field at 11,000'.

Despite several large cairns on the talus up to your right, break left from the gulch and

MOUNT PRINCETON 14,197 FT

DRY CREEK

2.2.1

2.2.1 SNOW ROUTE

PARKING AT RADIO TOWERS 10,820 FT

2.2.1 WINTER

2.2.1

MOUNT PRINCETON ROAD

FRONTIER RANCH TRAILHEAD 8,900 FT

CHALK CLIFFS

N

Mount Princeton from the east, late summer.

hike up a timber-studded ridge for a few hundred feet, then gradually trend to your right back into the gulch, where you'll find a fainter but, nonetheless, obvious trail tread.

Continue up the gulch to timberline (11,400'), then make a climbing traverse left to an obvious tundra and rock-covered rib. Climb the rib E to the summit ridge. Run the summit ridge ¾ mile to a false summit, then continue ¼ mile to the summit. Descend your ascent route or stash a car on the Mount Princeton Road to avoid a knee banger descent of Grouse Canyon. If you do descend Grouse Canyon, take care to stick with the creek until you're below the last of the canyon walls. If you leave the canyon too soon, you run the risk of getting cliffed.

SECTION 2.3
Mount Antero (14,269'), Mount Shavano (14,229'), Tabeguache Peak (14,155')

Mount Shavano and Tabeguache Peak are separated from Mount Antero by Browns Creek, but the three peaks are still close enough to be called siblings. Shavano and Tabeguache are connected by a short ridge and climbers usually hit both peaks at once. Both mountains yield good snow climbing and extreme skiing in several north face gullies. How do you pronounce "Tabeguache"? Easy: "tab-uh-wash." Put the accent on the first syllable.

While Mount Antero is a fine hike, most of the peak's slopes are of little interest to snow climbers. The exception is Antero's north face—an inaccessible wall approached via a low elevation couloir that is rarely in condition. Skiers will find plenty of spring ski terrain in the Baldwin Creek area. Mount Antero is known for its beautiful crystals of aquamarine, quartz, and topaz. Sadly, this has resulted in roads being gouged all over the mountain. One road ascends to 13,800'!

As luck would have it, Tabeguache and Shavano are located at the intersection of 4 USGS 7.5 minute maps. If you choose to purchase the full-sized maps, tape them together and trim the excess. The maps in this book should be adequate for most climbs.

ROADS AND TRAILHEADS

USGS Maps: Maysville, Garfield, St. Elmo, Mount Antero
USFS Forest Visitors Map: San Isabel National Forest

Chalk Creek Road
As well as accessing Mount Antero, Chalk Creek Road also accesses Mount Princeton and is covered in that section. To reach the Chalk Creek Road, drive 8.5 miles S on Highway 285 from Buena Vista or about 15 miles N from Salida. Turn west onto the well-signed Chalk Creek Road (Chaffee County 162).

Cascade Campground
Drive the Chalk Creek Road 9.1 miles from U.S. 285. The campground is well-signed and parking is obvious (8,800').

Poling off the summit for a spring ski descent of Mount Princeton's east face.

Baldwin Creek Jeep Trail.

Drive the Chalk Creek road 12 miles from Highway 285. Just past the town of Alpine, on the left (S) side of the road, you'll see the trailhead with a sign for Mount Antero. Parking is obvious (9,420'). With 4-wheel-drive you can continue up the jeep trail to the flanks of Mount Antero, perhaps parking at a road fork at 10,850'. In winter, the Chalk Creek Road is maintained past Alpine, but the Baldwin Creek Jeep Trail is closed and lightly used by snowmobiles.

Angel of Shavano Trailhead,

Drive Highway 285 S from Buena Vista, or N from Saguache, to Poncha Springs. At an obvious well-signed intersection, turn W onto Highway 50. Drive 6.5 miles on Highway 50 to Maysville, and take a right (N) on to Chaffee County Road 24 (sign here reads ANGEL OF SHAVANO C.G). Drive 3.7 miles on Road 24 to the Angel of Shavano Trailhead (9,187'), which is on the right (N) a short distance off the road. A sign near the Forest Service trailhead bulletin board indicates the Colorado Trail heading east and west. Don't let the name of this trailhead confuse—the Blank Gulch Trailhead is actually a better start for climbing the Angel of Shavano. Nonetheless, you can climb the Angel from the Angel of Shavano Trailhead by taking the Colorado Trail to the Blank Gulch Trailhead.

In winter, Road 24 is regularly snowplowed to the trailhead and campground nearby (2-wheel-drive is fine). You'll find plenty of parking at the plow turnaround.

Jennings Creek Trailhead

Continue 3½ miles past Angel of Shavano Trailhead (high clearance 2-wheel-drive) to obvious signs and parking (10,550'). The road from the Angel of Shavano Campground to the Jennings Creek Trailhead is closed in winter and early spring, with melt-out in mid May. In winter, this section of road is a well-used snowmobile route.

Blank Gulch Trailhead

Drive west on Highway 50 from Poncha Springs. At 1.8 miles turn right (N) on Chaffee County Road 250. Drive Road 250 (begins as pavement then soon becomes dirt) to the National Forest boundary at 6.6 miles from Poncha Springs. Enjoy views of Mount Shavano as you pass through the Shavano Wildlife Area. Fifty feet past the N.F. boundary, take a left fork (Road 252). Follow Road 252 as it swings left, loops through Placer Creek, then drops into Blank Gulch. Continue straight at an intersection at 8.1 miles, then turn left (towards Shavano) at 9.3 miles when you hit the Sawmill Gulch Road. Continue straight at the next intersection (9.5 miles). You are now sharing the road with the Colorado Trail. At 9.7 miles from Poncha Springs, bear right past a stone memorial. Park 2-wheel-drive vehicles at the memorial.

Continue up the road N past the memorial. At 9.8 miles pass through a cattle guard, then take the left fork just past the cattle guard. Continue several feet to a rough 4-wheel-drive hill. Walk (or bounce) fifty feet up the hill, then continue 400 feet up the road to the well-signed trailhead (9,880').

Browns Creek Road

Drive 12 miles S on Highway 285 from Buena Vista or 11.6 miles N from Poncha Springs. Turn west onto Chaffee County Road 270 (good sign). At 1.4 miles continue toward Mt. Antero on Road 272 (now the Browns Creek Road). At 3.3 miles take a left and follow Road 272 to the obvious trailhead area on the right (W) side of the road at 4.9 miles from Highway 285. The actual, well-signed trailhead is hidden several hundred feet W up a rough spur road that starts at the outhouse. You can park at the actual trailhead (8,960').

2.3.1	**Mount Antero—Direct North Face from Chalk Creek**	
Ratings:	Ski Descent—Extreme	Snow Climb—Extreme
Season:	Spring Snow	
RT Data:	8 hours, 6 miles, 5,469' ↑	
Start:	Cascade Campground Trailhead, 8,800'	
1 Day from Rd:	Yes	
Map:	Mount Antero, pg.116	
Photos:	pgs. 118, 119	

Spring or early summer snow: This route is perfect for a direct, early spring snow climb of Antero's North Face. The upper section provides thrilling skiing, but thus far no one has skied the entire route. If this line is possible on skis, it has one of greatest vertical drops in Colorado. To accomplish such a descent you'd need to attempt it after a heavy winter so the lower couloir would be filled in and skiable, and you'd have to be there early enough in the season so the snow would not be melted. Moreover, many nights at the 9,000' level are not cold enough to freeze the snowpack and make it safe from avalanches. Thus, you'd need an unseasonably cold night—and a very early start.

Park at Cascade Campground (see section introduction). As you enter the campground, note the two huge couloirs straight ahead. These are split by a rock rib—the right hand couloir is your route. From the upper portion of the campground loop road, climb through timber a bit east and south to the couloir. Ascend the couloir 2,400 vertical feet to 11,800' on Mount Antero's north ridge. The most expedient route continues 1½ miles up the ridge to the summit. Because of the low altitude of the couloir, and attendant warming of the snowpack, it might be safer to descend the Baldwin Creek Route (2.3.2). Bring snowshoes or skis if you expect snow in Baldwin Creek.

Another option, which yields a more exciting finish, is to take a slightly dropping traverse S from the ridge into the drainage below Antero's north face. Beware of cliff bands if you get too high on this traverse. Ascend the drainage to the base of the north face. The face offers a choice of several couloirs, all good climbing. If these couloirs are too steep for you, a more relaxed line drops from just to the north of the summit. Again, consider a descent of Baldwin Creek (2.3.2).

Safety notes: This route is very exposed to sun and weather, and the low elevation of the start makes it a problem to pick a night when the snow has a chance to freeze properly. Most of the drainages on this side of Mount Antero are full of cliff bands. Thus, only descend routes that you have checked during your ascent or descend Baldwin Creek (2.3.2). Use standard sunrise for sunhit.

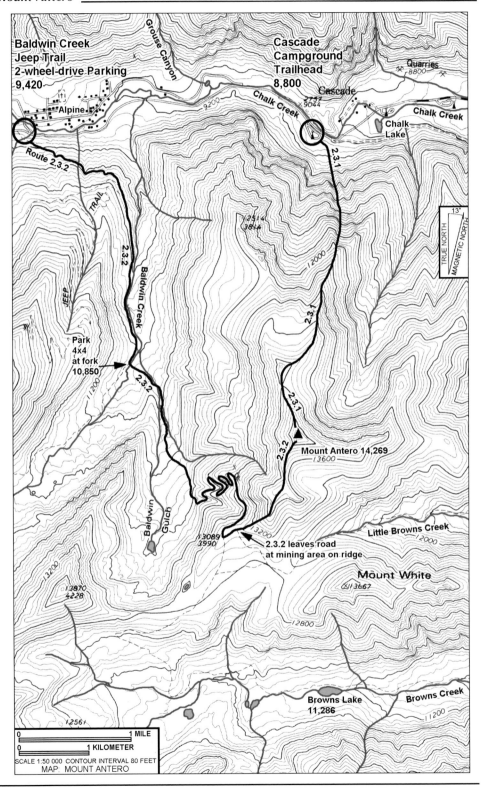

Baldwin Creek
Jeep Trail
2-wheel-drive Parking
9,420

Cascade
Campground
Trailhead
8,800

Quarries
8800

Alpine

Chalk Creek

Cascade
9044

Chalk Creek

Chalk
Lake

Route 2.3.2

TRAIL

2.3.2

JEEP

Baldwin Creek

12514
3846

12000

13°
TRUE NORTH
MAGNETIC NORTH

2.3.1

2.3.1

Park
4x4
at fork
10,850

2.3.2

11200

2.3.1

2.3.2

Mount Antero 14,269
13600

Baldwin Gulch

13089
3990

3200

Little Browns Creek
12000

2.3.2 leaves road
at mining area on ridge

Mount White
13667

13200

13870
4228

12800

Browns Lake
11,286

Browns Creek

11200

12561

0   1 MILE
0   1 KILOMETER
SCALE 1:50 000 CONTOUR INTERVAL 80 FEET
MAP: MOUNT ANTERO

2.3.2 Mount Antero via Baldwin Creek

Ratings:	Summer Climb—Novice		Ski Descent—Advanced
		Snow Climb—Novice	
Season:	Summer	Spring	Winter
RT Data:	5 hrs., 4¼ miles, 3,419'↑	9½ hrs., 10 miles, 4,849'↑	12 hrs., 10 miles, 4,849'↑
Start:	Baldwin Creek	Baldwin Creek	Baldwin Creek
1 Day	Jeep Trail 10,850'	Jeep Trail, snow 9,420'	Jeep Trail, snow 9,420'
from Rd:		Yes	
Map:		Mount Antero, pg. 116	
Photos:		pgs. 118, 119	

Enjoyable as a summer hike or climb, spring snow route, or winter challenge, this is a popular climb. Spring skiing on this side of Antero is superb. During any season, consider enjoying this area from a base camp at timberline. In addition to Mount Antero, Peak 13,870' to the southwest is a beautiful high thirteener with superb skiing and snow climbing.

Summer after snow melt-off: This is one of those peaks where use of a 4-wheel-drive vehicle can get you as close to the summit as you desire. Probably the best compromise between convenience—and still calling it a climb—is to 4-wheel-drive (rough) to a fork at 10,850' on the Baldwin Gulch Jeep Trail. The data block assumes that this was your approach. If you have 2-wheel-drive, park at the start of the Baldwin Creek Jeep Trail on the Chalk Creek Road (9,420') (see section introduction). In this case add about three hours to the summer round-trip estimate.

Depending on your transportation, hike or 4-wheel-drive up Baldwin Creek Jeep Trail 2¾ miles to its intersection with the Baldwin Gulch Jeep Trail at 10,850'. Use your altimeter and map to locate this intersection. Cross Baldwin Creek and hike up the Baldwin Gulch Jeep Trail 2½ miles to a mining area (13,200') on the bump ½ mile S of Mount Antero's summit. The jeep trail to this point swings wide around Antero's south ridge. At several points you'll be tempted to leave the trail and climb toward the summit. Avoid temptation; the trail avoids misery on loose scree. From the aforementioned bump, follow the south ridge to the summit. Descend your ascent route. Prevent erosion by resisting the temptation to scree run.

Spring snow season: Use the summer route above, or the more direct line of the winter route below. In spring try to connect a line on frozen snow to avoid unstable footing in the scree and boulders that cover this side of Mount Antero. If you're after a ski descent, pick a line of continuous snow that will take you down into the prominent gulch just to the north of the ascent route flank. One good bet for this is to drop down the ridge north from the summit for a few hundred feet, ski down the west side of Antero for about 1,100 feet, traverse S above Point 12,772', then drop in to the obvious gulch. If you choose this option be careful of the cliff bands directly west and below the summit.

Winter: Drive the Chalk Creek Road to parking at the Baldwin Creek Jeep Trail. Ski the summer route up the Baldwin Creek Jeep Trail then up the Baldwin Gulch Jeep Trail. Follow the Baldwin Gulch Jeep Trail (not obvious in winter) to a prominent lateral moraine at 11,720' (just before the trail begins a switchback climb of one of Antero's west flanks). Leave the trail here and climb directly up to Antero's south ridge.

Follow the south ridge to the summit, generally keeping to the east side to work your way around several rock outcroppings. Descent is via the same route.

Vary your route by the snow cover and avoid avalanche danger by following wind-scoured ribs. Winter climbers should note that residents of Alpine use the Baldwin Creek Jeep Trail for snowmobiling. Their packed route saves you from a hard trail break (and allows you to use a snowmobile if you're so inclined). Their use of the trail is irregular, however, so check it the day before your trip.

Mount Antero from the northeast, summer.

You get a good view of Mount Antero from the summit of Mount Princeton, spring.

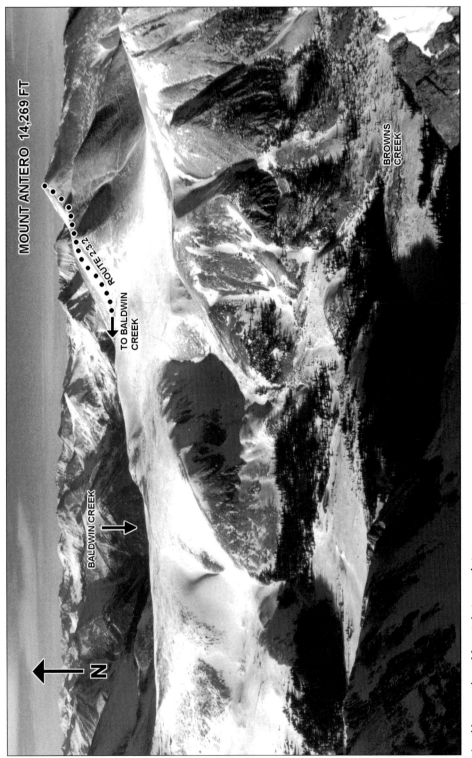

MOUNT ANTERO 14,269 FT

ROUTE 2.3.2

TO BALDWIN CREEK

BALDWIN CREEK

BROWNS CREEK

N

Looking north at Mount Antero, winter.

Safety notes: Summer hikers: Enjoy this as a novice climb, but take proper gear and start early. During snow season, because of high winds and less snow than many of Colorado's other mountain ranges, this side of Antero almost always gives you a choice of windscoured ribs for a safe ascent. Wind-transported snow, however, can cause slide danger on tempting leeward ski slopes. Add 2 hours to standard sunrise for approximate sunhit.

2.3.3	**Mount Shavano—Southeast Couloir**	
Ratings:	Ski Descent—Advanced	Snow Climb—Advanced
Season:	Summer or Spring Snow	
RT Data:	10 hours, 6½ miles, 5,522' ↑	
Start:	Angel of Shavano Trailhead, 9,187'	
1 Day from Rd:	Yes	
Maps:	Mount Shavano West, pg. 122; Mount Shavano East, pg. 123	
Photo:	pg. 125	

A tough climb that follows a direct couloir, this route is for experienced climbers with solid knees. Though it's done in summer, doing so causes erosion and is not recommended.

Spring or summer snow season: Drive to the Angle of Shavano Trailhead (section introduction). Climb through timber N from the trailhead for a few hundred yards, then trend NW. Cross one drainage, then hold a NW climbing traverse until you intersect a second drainage. Use this drainage to guide you up to timberline. Vary your exact route according to snow conditions and vegetation. Continue up the couloir to the ridge crest, then along the ridge ¼ mile to point 13,630'—a nice little false summit! Drop 250 vertical feet from Point 13,630' to a saddle between you and Shavano's summit. Climb from the saddle to the summit on easy ground. Return via the same route or descend the Angel of Shavano (2.3.4) and return to the trailhead via the Colorado Trail.

Safety notes: Try May or June for the best snow conditions. Remember, while the snow may be consolidated lower down, it could still be unstable several thousand feet higher in the couloir. This is less likely later in the season. Use standard sunrise for sunhit.

2.3.4	**Mount Shavano—The Angel Snowfield**	
Ratings:	Summer Climb—Intermediate Ski Descent—Intermediate	
	Snow Climb—Intermediate	
Season:	Summer/Spring	Winter
RT Data:	9 hours, 7 miles, 4,349' ↑	12 hours, 11 miles, 5,042' ↑
Start:	Blank Gulch Trailhead 9,880'	Angel of Shavano Trailhead 9,187'
1 Day from Rd:	Summer/Spring	Winter
	Yes	Yes; long day
Maps:	Mount Shavano West, pg. 122; Mount Shavano East, pg. 123	
Photo:	pg. 125	

During winters with enough snow, the vast snowfield on the east face of Mount Shavano takes on the appearance of a gigantic angel. The Angel of Shavano makes a fantastic ski descent, and it's a good snow climb for novices.

Summer after snow melt-off: The Angel Trail is a terrific hike. Park at or just below the Blank Creek Trailhead (section introduction). Hike west from the trailhead up a wide, well-trav-

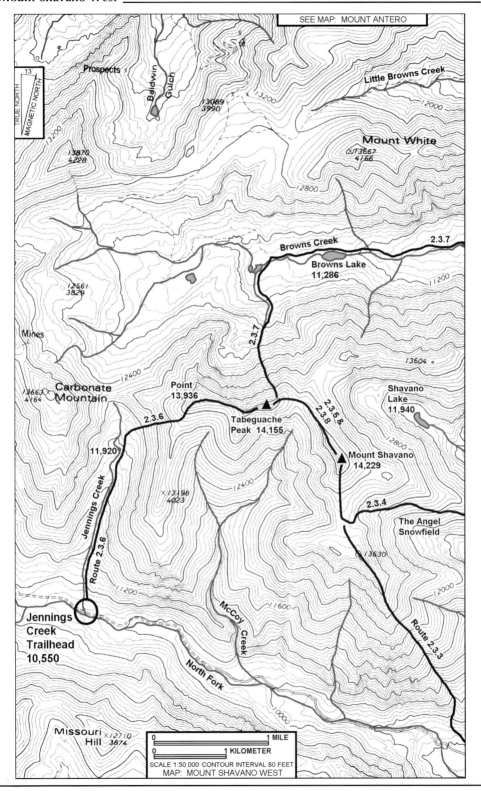

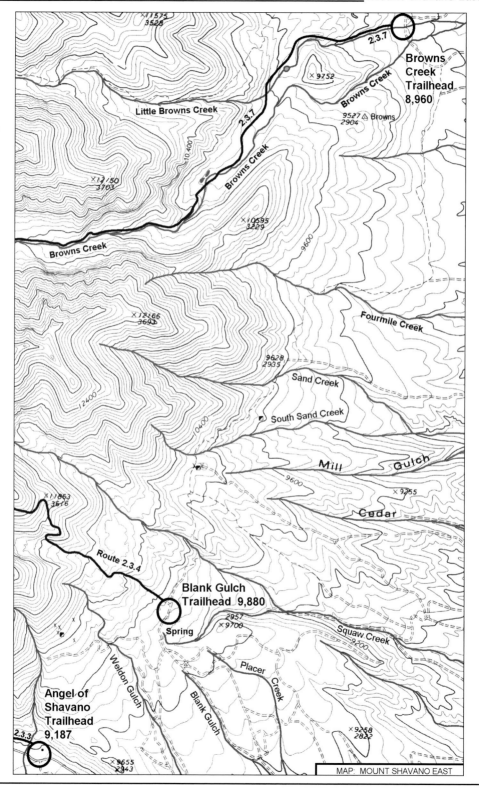

MAP: MOUNT SHAVANO EAST

eled trail through conifer and aspen. The trail leads to timberline, passes to the north of the Angel (the Angel may have flown away during a dry year), then climbs to a prominent saddle (13,390') at the base of the summit pyramid, ¾ mile from the summit. Follow the ridge from the saddle N to the summit. Descend your ascent route or glissade the Angel. The snow is fairly low-angled and very manageable, though a few steeper rolls could dump an unwary slider into the rocks.

Spring snow season: While you'll usually have good skiing on the Angel Snowfield, a summit ski descent of this windscoured peak is a rarity. To get to the Angel use the summer route above if you can reach the Blank Creek Trailhead. Otherwise start very early and use the Angel of Shavano Trailhead (see winter route below). For the best snow climb, ascend the Angel's right wing to the high saddle between point 13,617' and Shavano's summit. Follow the rocky east ridge to the summit.

Winter: In the winter, The Angel of Shavano is usually wind-hammered. If it's covered with deep sastrugi, that means it is probably safe enough to ski. Even so, beware the possibility of a deep, hard slab avalanche, and take normal precautions. You can climb several obvious ridges to avoid slide terrain.

Park at the Angel of Shavano Campground. From the campground, walk back down the road a few hundred feet to the well-signed Angel of Shavano Trailhead. This is also the trailhead for the Colorado Trail, a low altitude hiking route that spans Colorado between Denver and Durango.

From the trailhead, follow the Colorado Trail 2 miles E and N to its intersection with the Angel Trail at 9,880' elevation at the Blank Gulch Trailhead. This section of the Colorado Trail is fairly well-used for ski touring and is usually packed to this point (though that could be different during a heavy snow year). The Colorado Trail is not marked on the Maysville USGS 7.5 minute quadrangle map; see the map herein.

The Angel Trail is poorly marked from the start to about 10,100', and there is no definitive trailcut to follow. By staying to the right of a small but steep-sided gulch, you can stick with the general route of the trail. Above 10,100' the trail tread is mostly obvious and blazes are prevalent below timberline. To climb the Angel, follow the Angel Trail to 11,000', then climb directly up the drainage and up the body of the Angel, then up her right wing to the high saddle between point 13,617 and Shavano's summit. Follow the rocky east ridge to the summit.

For your descent, glissade or ski the Angel. It is fairly low-angled and very manageable, though a few steeper rolls could dump an unwary slider into the rocks. Other possibilities from the summit include skiing down the north face couloirs, then climbing back to the summit and descending the Angel, or skiing the spectacular gully that drops back almost to the campground from point 13,630' for ¾ mile S of the summit. Skiing this will net you 4,443 vertical feet in one swoop. If you decide to go for this, remember that the low elevation, SE facing portions of the gully melt out early in the spring, and the upper part may be blown clear of snow at any time. So plan an alternate route, and if you get to ski the gully, count yourself lucky.

Safety notes: Though this route follows a "trail" of sorts, summer climbers should still have at least one person in their party who can read a map. When your goal is a summit, obscure sections of trail are no place to learn orienteering. If you intend to climb or glissade the Angel, carry an ice axe and know how to use it. Snow season climbers should note that, other than ridges, all the terrain crossed by the routes above may be prone to avalanche. Consequently, the spring season is the best time to climb or ski the Angel. If you're in doubt, the ridge to the north of the Angel (Shavano's east ridge) makes a safer route. Even so, several pitches on the ridge could be dangerous. Use standard sunrise for sunhit.

MOUNT SHAVANO 14,229 FT

ANGEL OF SHAVANO SNOWFIELD

ALTERNATE RIDGE

ROUTE 2.3.3

ANGEL OF SHAVANO TRAILHEAD 9,187 FT

BLANK GULCH TRAILHEAD 9,880 FT

SQUAW CREEK

N

2.3.4

2.3.3

2.3.4

2.3.3

2.3.3

You get a good view of Mount Shavano when you drive to the Blank Gulch Trailhead.

2.3.5	**Mount Shavano via Tabeguache Peak**	
Ratings:	Summer Climb—Advanced Ski Descent—Intermediate	
	Snow Climb—Advanced	
Season:	Summer/Spring	Winter
RT Data:	14 hours, 10 miles, 4,873' ↑	overnight, 18 miles, 6,256'↑
Start:	Jennings Creek Trailhead 10,550'	Angel of Shavano Trailhead 9,187'
1 Day from Rd:	Yes, with Jennings Creek Trailhead; No, with road closure	
Map:	Mount Shavano West, pg. 122	

Summer, or spring snow season: Glance at the map, and you'll see that while this trip is feasible in one day from the Jennings Creek Trailhead, doing it from the Angel of Shavano Trailhead adds 4 miles and 1,363 vertical feet elevation. Thus, plan your trip for road melt-out in may; use a snowmobile early in the season or carry a sleeping bag.

Follow the Jennings Creek Route (2.3.6) to the summit of Mount Tabeguache. From the summit, descend the ridge E to an obvious saddle (13,720'), then slog up ½ mile more of ridge to Mount Shavano. Return via the same route.

Winter: Use the route described above and under the Jennings Creek Route (2.3.6) for Mount Tabeguache. You'll either need an overnight, lots of headlamp batteries, or a snowmobile for the jeep trail—or all of the above.

Safety notes: Whatever the season, allow plenty of time for this route. It's rated Advanced because of its length, while the skiing is rated intermediate because most skiers park their boards at timberline in Jennings Creek. Use standard sunrise for sunhit.

Though you can climb Tabeguache Peak from Mount Shavano (2.3.8), you can enjoy the mountain as a separate entity via several routes. The Jennings Creek routes are probably the most popular of these. All the terrain in this area is delightful for alpine hiking. Watch for Bighorn Sheep.

2.3.6	**Tabeguache Peak—Southwest/West Ridge from Jennings Creek**		
Ratings:	Summer Climb—Advanced Ski Descent—Advanced		
	Snow Climb—Intermediate		
Season:	Summer	Spring	Winter
RT Time:	10 hrs., 8 miles, 3,855'↑	12 hrs., 10 miles, 5,238'↑	multi-day, 10 miles, 5,238'↑
Start:	Jennings Creek Trailhead 10,550'	Angel of Shavano Campground 9,187'	Angel of Shavano Campground 9,187'
1 Day from Rd:	Summer Yes	Spring Depends on road closure	Winter No
Map:	Mount Shavano West, pg. 122		
Photos:	pg. 118		

Summer after snow melt-off: To climb Tabeguache via Jennings Creek, drive to the Jennings Creek Trailhead (section introduction). From the Jennings Creek Trailhead, bushwhack N up the east (R) side of Jennings Creek to 11,000', then follow either side of the drainage to a small tarn at 11,920'. Head N then E from the tarn and climb obvious gullies and scree slopes to Point 13,936'. One gully in particular, the longest and deepest, may provide solid snow climbing (early summer) that allows you to avoid nightmarish scree. Yet, no matter what your route, you'll still have discouraging scree slogging.

Once at Point 13,936', you still have some work ahead of you to get to Tabeguache's true summit. Stay on the ridge and hike just under ½ mile to the next point—a classic false summit. From here, you have about ¼ mile of gnarled ridge to the summit. In general, when the ridge becomes impassable because of dropoffs, drop a short distance to the right (S) and do a climbing traverse for a short distance below the ridge crest until easier ground takes you back onto the ridge. Stick with it to the summit.

Spring snow season: Tabeguache Peak is a hard fourteener to snow climb or ski in one day. You can climb it from Mount Shavano (2.3.4), but this entails quite a bit of scrambling there and back from Shavano's summit.

In detail: Follow the summer route described above to the small tarn at 11,920'. Head N then E from the tarn and climb obvious gullies and scree slopes to point 13,936'. One gully in particular, the longest and deepest, is attractive for climbing and skiing—provided the snow is stable.

Once at Point 13,936', you still have some work ahead of you to get to Tabeguache's true summit. Stay on the ridge and struggle just under ½ mile mile to the next point: a classic false summit. From here, take another stretch of gnarled ridge to the summit. In general, when the ridge becomes impassable because of dropoffs, drop a short distance to the right (S) and do a climbing traverse for a short distance below the ridge crest until easier ground takes you back onto the ridge. Gain the summit cone via a short south face. Snow climbers should descend their ascent route. Do not use McCoy Creek.

For a ski descent, you might be tempted to climb Tabeguache from Shavano, then ski down McCoy Gulch, which looks mighty inviting at the top. Be forewarned, McCoy Creek cliffs off around 11,000', and several people have been rescued after being stranded in this inhospitable place. However, an aesthetic ski descent off Tabeguache is possible by climbing via Jennings Creek, then skiing southeast off the summit to 12,600' in the east branch of McCoy Creek. At this point, instead of descending farther, traverse W, climb several hundred vertical feet over a saddle, then ski into the Jennings Creek Drainage. Join up with your ascent route in Jennings Creek. Only expert navigators should wander in this area.

Winter: Use the summer route described above. Allow plenty of time for postholing along the high ridge.

Safety notes: For winter ascents, one advantage of climbing this side of Tabeguache is it is often blown almost clear of snow, creating minimal avalanche problems. Yet even when the mountain is scoured, you can find snow in the gullies. If such snow is windpacked, beware of hard slab avalanche potential. Because March is the heaviest snow month in Colorado, the climbing and skiing on Tabeguache is usually better in April, May, and June. Of course, if you have no transport for the North Fork Road, the requisite alpine start can be a problem. If this is the case, you may need a high camp for safe travel. For sunhit add 2 hours to standard sunrise.

2.3.7	**Tabeguache Peak—North Face**	
Ratings:	Ski Descent—Extreme	Snow Climb—Advanced
Season:	Spring Snow	
RT Data:	overnight, 14 miles, 5,195' ↑	
Start:	Browns Creek Trailhead, 8,960'	
1 Day from Rd:	No	
Maps:	Mount Shavano West, pg. 122; Mount Shavano East, pg. 123	

Extreme ski mountaineers recommend this spectacular couloir route. It's also a good snow climb and avoids the scree and long ridges of other routes. With the long approach, this trip is hard to do in one day; a high camp is recommended.

Spring snow season: Drive to the Browns Creek Trailhead (section introduction). Spend a leisurely day hiking 5½ miles up the Browns Creek Trail to high camp at Browns Lake (11,286'). When you leave the trailhead, pay attention to signs and your map. The trailhead is actually located on Little Browns Creek, while the drainage you want to climb is the main Browns Creek. The trail you want reaches the correct drainage by first climbing Little Browns Creek for 1½ miles, then jogging left (S) on the Colorado Trail to intersect the true Browns Creek and Browns Lake Trail.

While you can reach the Browns Creek drainage via the Baldwin Creek Jeep Trail (see section introduction), most of the jeep trail remains closed by snow during early spring.

From Browns Lake, continue up the drainage to several small lakes at 11,400'. Swing S here and climb the drainage up the north face of Tabeguache Peak. This becomes a major couloir that leads to the ridge near the summit. Descend your ascent route. Snow climbers or skiers who want an easier descent can walk the ridge W from the summit and descend lower-angled slopes NW from point 13,936' into Browns Creek. Snow cover may vary on this face, so no matter which route you have in mind, examine it carefully from Browns Creek.

Safety notes: This is a more serious climb or ski than other routes in this section. You must be expert with ice axe and crampons, and skiers should be capable of "no fall" skiing. A high camp will allow a reasonable starting time—usually just several hours before sunrise. For sunhit add 3 hours to standard sunrise.

2.3.8	Tabeguache Peak via Mount Shavano	
Ratings:	Summer Climb—Advanced Ski Descent—Intermediate	
	Snow Climb—Advanced	
Season:	Summer / Spring	Winter
RT Data:	10 hours, 9 miles, 5,293' ↑	overnight, 13 miles, 6,006'↑
Start:	Blank Gulch Trailhead 9,880'	Angel of Shavano Trailhead 9,187'
1 Day from Rd:	Summer/ Spring Yes	Winter; Yes, long day from Angel of Shavano Campground
Map:	Mount Shavano West, pg. 122	

Aggressive peak baggers use this route for their Tabeguache/Shavano hit.

Summer, or spring snow season: Drive to the Blank Gulch Trailhead (spring climbers should check for road closure). Climb Mount Shavano via the Angel of Shavano route (2.3.4). From the summit of Mount Shavano descend the ridge NW to the main saddle between you and Tabeguache. Climb the ridge from the saddle 435 vertical feet to the summit of Mount Tabeguache. Return via your ascent route—including the slog back to Shavano's summit.

Winter: Follow the winter route for the Angel of Shavano (2.3.4). Continue to Tabeguache via the route described above.

Safety notes: This is a tough day, but you'll bag two peaks for the effort. Use standard sunrise for sunhit.

Spring skiing in Mount Evans' Summit Lake Bowl.

3

MOSQUITO AND FRONT RANGES

USFS Forest Visitor Maps: San Isabel National Forest, Pike National Forest, Roosevelt National Forest

The Mosquito and Front Ranges, being close to front range cities, e.g. Denver and Boulder and Colorado Springs, are popular with Colorado's eastern slope mountaineers. Some of the easier peaks have European style crowds every weekend of the summer, and even winter mountaineers bump into their brethren.

The two ranges are twined enough to treat them as one chapter. The Front Range can be viewed as all the mountains bordering Colorado's eastern plains. At the its north end, the range begins in the vicinity of Longs Peak. Extending south for about 240 miles, the Front Range ends at the mountainous area south of Pikes Peak and northwest of Walsenburg. (Due to space limits, Pikes Peak will be covered in the second volume of this guide).

The Mosquito Range is connected to the Front Range by the mountains around Hoosier Pass. It deserves status as a separate range because of its separation from the Front Range by South Park, a spectacular high basin to the east of Fairplay. South Park is crossed by U.S. Highway 24, a superb scenic drive.

Summer climbing and hiking on these mountains is fabulous. Each peak boasts an easy summit walk-up. Thus, most of these peaks are good "first fourteeners." More ambitious climbers can enjoy optional alpine rambles, but other than the technical climbs on Longs Peak, technical climbers should look elsewhere.

If any category fits the Mosquito and Front Range fourteeners, they could be called skiers' mountains. Along with terrific road access, you'll find plenty of intermediate and advanced ski routes, and more novice routes than in any other group of fourteeners. Snow climbers will find that most of the routes on these peaks are "snow hikes" rather than climbs. Even so, expert snow climbers can find a few challenging lines, such as the north and west faces of Mount Democrat, Mount Evans' north face couloirs, and routes on Longs Peak.

Due to good access and plenty easy ridge routes, winter climbs on the Mosquito and Front Range peaks are popular. Quandary Peak and Mount Bierstadt are so accessible that they get countless winter ascents via their enjoyable and safe ridge routes.

Another distinction of the Front Range is that Pikes Peak and Mount Evans have roads to their summits. These roads open early enough in the spring to allow snow climbers and skiers easy access to terrain that would take an extra day to approach on foot. Some mountaineers might scoff at the notion of driving to the top of a mountain, then skiing it—or climbing it—then driving down. But the pragmatic approach is the most popular. That is, with transportation available, many people use it. Mount Evans is a long trip after the road closes for the winter. And Longs Peak is often a multi-day day trip in the winter, though it can be done in one long day. All the other peaks in these ranges have open roads so close by that you can climb them in one day during any season.

The weather in the two ranges is average Colorado. The only consistent difference is, compared to the Elks and Northern Sawatch, the Mosquito Range and Front Range get less snow. This happens because major mountain ranges to the west suck most of the moisture out of most storms, which move from the west or northwest. That, combined with windscouring, can cause some awfully dry mountainsides. If you find your intended route has too little snow to enjoy—take heart. Usually the wind has blanketed one or two exposures with snow, so consider other routes. Also, thin snow can be quite climbable and skiable, as long as it is well compacted by the wind or sun.

SECTION 3.1
Mount Sherman (14,036'), Mount Lincoln (14,286'), Mount Bross (14,172'), Mount Democrat (14,148').

Mounts Sherman, Democrat, Bross and Lincoln are located in the Mosquito Range. This spine of high peaks separates the Arkansas River Valley from South Park and the foothills west of Denver. Connected closely by high ridges, Democrat, Bross, and Lincoln can be climbed in the same day—a peak bagger's dream. Such a "triple bagger" is standard for people checking peaks off their list. For the best snow climbing or skiing, however, take each peak from lower down.

Mount Sherman has a flat summit and easy slopes that make a popular family climb. As a testament to this, Sherman is perhaps the only fourteener that's had a plane land high on its slopes—with survivors.

Mount Lincoln and Mount Bross are separated by a ridge with a bump known as Cameron Point. Not long ago, Cameron Point was counted as a separate fourteener and called Mount Cameron. Doing so has fallen into disfavor. Once you clamber over Cameron Point enroute to Mount Lincoln or Mount Bross, you'll see why. Calling it a separate fourteener is like calling a town-house a mansion.

Mount Lincoln and Mount Bross offer several unique attractions. One is a bicycle route that connects the two peaks. This option is only for fit, expert riders, but it's highly recommended. The bicycle route starts at the Dolly Varden Creek Trailhead, then climbs the road (start with route 3.1.7) around the east side of Mount Bross to the Bross/Cameron saddle. A rough road leads from the saddle to Bross' summit. After Bross, the road leads around the north side of Mount Lincoln (with a short walk to touch the summit) then down Quartzville Creek via the Quartzville Creek Jeep Trail. While aerobic gods could ride the total loop back to the Dolly Varden Creek Trailhead, mortals should stash a vehicle on Roberts Road (see trailheads).

The other attraction is ice climbing on several frozen waterfalls which form below Lincoln Amphitheater (3.1.5). These are climbable from late fall until the winter avalanche season and are quite popular.

ROADS AND TRAILHEADS

USGS MAPS: Alma, Climax, Mount Sherman, Fairplay West
USFS Forest Visitors Map: San Isabel National Forest

Buckskin Creek Road and Kite Lake Trailhead

Follow Highway 9 from Fairplay or Frisco to the small town of Alma. Locate the post office in the center of Alma. Across the highway from the Post Office, find a dirt road next to the Alma Fire House and Mining Museum (You may find a sign pointing to kite lake but don't count on it). Turn W off Highway 9 onto this road. Past several houses and a few hundred yards up the dirt road you'll see a partly hidden sign on the right that identifies the road as Park County 8, a.k.a. the Buckskin Creek Road. Drive the Buckskin Creek Road 5.7 miles to parking at Kite Lake campground (12,020'). The last switchback to the lake is rough, but passable in all but the lowest clearance passenger cars. During snow season, snow closure is about three miles from Alma (depending on mining activity). In winter the closed portion of the Buckskin Creek Road is packed by snowmobiles.

Dolly Varden Gulch Trailhead

Follow the directions above for the Buckskin Creek Road. From Alma, drive the Buckskin Creek Road 2.7 miles and turn right (N) onto the Windy Ridge Road. Drive the Windy Ridge Road 3.1 miles to a mining area at 11,340'. Parking is obvious in the vicinity of an old mine tipple. With high clearance 2-wheel-drive, you can continue N from the mining area .6 mile up Forest Service Road 415 to parking at the Windy Ridge Bristlecone Pine Scenic Area (11,600'). With 4-wheel-drive you can continue up Road 415 as high as you please on the side of Mount Bross. Winter snow closure is on the Buckskin Creek Road.

Subdivision Road (Moose Creek) and Roberts Road Trailheads

While you can reach the following trailheads from the north via Highway 9, for simplicity they are described from the south on Highway 9, starting at the town of Alma. If you're new to the area, but coming from the north, it's not much extra distance to drive to Alma, then double back using the directions below.

To reach the Subdivision (Moose Creek) Trailhead, drive Highway 9 to Alma. From the Alma Post Office, drive 2 miles N on Highway 9, and turn left (W) onto Park County Road 4. Drive Road 4 across the river .4 mile, then take a left on Park County Road 6. Drive .3 mile S on Road 6 and turn right on the Quartzville Road, which climbs 2.3 miles to its high-point at a curve south (11,140'). During spring snow season, parking will be at the plow turn, possibly below the 11,140' high-point.

For the Roberts Road Trailhead, follow the directions above to Park County Road 6. Turn right on Road 6, drive 1.7 miles, and take a left on Roberts Road. Drive Roberts Road up steep switchbacks. At 1.8 miles from Road 6, look carefully for a right turn onto USFS Road 437, the Quartzville Creek Jeep Trail. This turnoff is poorly signed but obvious. Obey private property signs, but don't let such signs confuse you. Park just off Roberts Road on the side of Road 437 (11,350'). With 4-wheel-drive you can continue up the Quartzville Creek Jeep Trail. Expert 4-wheel-drive enthusiasts can drive the rough trail to the summits of Mount Lincoln and Mount Bross. It's possible to bicycle up the road, but it's better used as a descent after a bicycle climb of smoother Road 415 (see Dolly Varden Creek Trailhead). Snowplowing of Roberts Road varies. If people are occupying their homes in winter, the road may be completely plowed to its connection with the Quartzville Road near Moose Creek. During other years, snow closure may be at the first switchback (10,900').

Montgomery Reservoir Trailhead

If you're coming from southern Colorado, take Colorado State Highway 9 to Alma. Drive 4.5 miles N from Alma on Highway 9, then turn left (W) on to Park County Road 4. Drive Road 4 down .9 mile to a fork at Montgomery Reservoir. Take the right fork (the left leads to the spillway) and continue on rougher road 1 mile to parking at 10,960' at the southwest end of the reservoir, near a creek gauging station, slightly downhill from a huge old stamping mill.

If you're coming from central Colorado, drive to Hoosier Pass on Highway 9, then continue S on Highway 9. Look for a right (W) turn onto Park County Road 4 just 1 mile from the Hoosier Pass Summit. From there use the directions above.

In winter, the plow turns around at the road near the spillway. An extreme 4-wheel-drive road leads up the valley from the trailhead. Unless you're out for recreational 4-wheeling, park at the trailhead and walk the road. Route descriptions from this trailhead are written assuming you do so.

Colorado Highway 91 (Fremont Pass)

Drive N on Highway 91 for 12 miles from Leadville or S for 9 miles from Interstate Highway 70 to the lower portion of a sharp curve about ¼ mile down the road on the south side of Fremont Pass. Park out of the way on the side of the highway (11,040'). The best parking is a short distance down the valley from the industrial buildings of the Climax Mine.

Iowa Gulch Trailhead

To reach the Iowa Gulch Trailhead, you follow the poorly signed and confusing Iowa Gulch Road (Lake County Road #2) from Leadville. Though this road is hard to find, it provides good year-round access to Mount Sherman and surrounding peaks.

The route that follows is described as if you were driving S out of Leadville on Harrison Avenue (Highway 91). Just as you leave downtown Leadville (Stringtown is down the road) you'll see a black slag heap on your left, with Elm Street to your right. Take a left here on unsigned East Monroe Street and follow it a short distance up the hill to South Toledo Street. Take a right onto South Toledo, which becomes Lake County 2 and passes numerous technicolor slime pits and abandoned mines. At 4 miles from Harrison Avenue, take an obvious left fork (the right fork leads to an obvious active mine). Snow closure is usually at this fork (11,120'); after melt-off you can drive a few miles farther to a closure gate at 11,600'.

Leavick Trailhead

Drive Colorado State Highway 9 or U.S. Highway 285 to Fairplay. From the Fairplay Hotel, drive S on Highway 285. At 1.7 miles from Fairplay turn right (W) on to the well-signed Fourmile Creek Road. After melt-off you can 2-wheel-drive 9.5 miles to the Leavick townsite and residential area (11,250'). Depending on road conditions, you can can motor several miles past Leavick with 4-wheel-drive or possibly high clearance 2-wheel-drive, but do so at your own risk. During snow season, snow closure is usually near Leavick. The road from snowclosure is often packed by snowmobile.

3.1.1 Mount Sherman—South Ridge from Iowa Gulch

Ratings:	Summer Climb—Novice	Ski Descent—Novice
	Snow Climb—Novice	
Season:	Summer/Spring	Winter
RT Data:	6 hours, 5 miles, 2,436' ↑	8 hours, 5 miles, 2,916' ↑
Start:	Iowa Gulch Trailhead 11,600'	Iowa Gulch Trailhead 11,120'
1 Day from Rd:	Yes	
Map:	Mount Sherman, pg.134	
Photo:	pg.135	

This excellent alpine tour is the shortest route on Mt. Sherman—summer or winter. If you're from Colorado's Eastern Slope cities, the route's shorter length is canceled by a much longer drive.

Summer after snow melt-off: Park at the Iowa Gulch Road Trailhead, near the huge basin below Sherman's west face. Hike the road a short distance into the basin. Leave the road, contour SE into the basin, then climb the obvious gulch separating Mount Sheridan from Mount Sherman. From the saddle (13,160') at the top of the gulch, follow Sherman's South Ridge to the summit. For descent use your ascent route.

Spring Snow Season: Skiers and snow climbers can use the summer route above. For good skiing, drop into the Hilltop Mine bowl, climb back to the 13,160' saddle, then follow your ascent route back to your car.

Winter: Sherman is a fine winter climb via the South Ridge. Use the summer route above, with parking at snow closure in Iowa Gulch.

Safety notes: This is an easy, accessible route that attracts many novice climbers. Such tyros should still carry proper equipment, and study their map. In winter, the gulch next to Mount Sheridan is exposed to several slide paths on the north face of Mount Sheridan. You can lessen your exposure to these by following rock ribs a few hundred feet north of the gulch. Many other parts of this route are threatened by avalanches; thus, you should only climb here during times of lesser risk. You can avoid the Sheridan Peak avalanche slopes by climbing from Fourmile Creek and Leavick (3.1.2). For sunhit, add several hours to standard sunrise.

3.1.2 Mount Sherman from Fourmile Creek (Leavick)

Ratings:	Summer Climb—Novice	Ski Descent—Intermediate
	Snow Climb—Intermediate	
Season:	Summer/Spring	Winter
RT Data:	6 hours, 8 miles, 2,786' ↑	overnight, 2,786' ↑ (depends on closure)
Start:	Leavick Trailhead 11,250'	Leavick Trailhead 11,250'
1 Day	Summer	Winter
from Rd:	Yes; Depends on snow closure	
Map:	Mount Sherman, pg.134	
Photo:	pg.137	

Summer after snow melt-off: Drive to the Leavick Trailhead (section introduction). Park your car near Leavick or farther up the road with 4-wheel-drive. After parking, simply

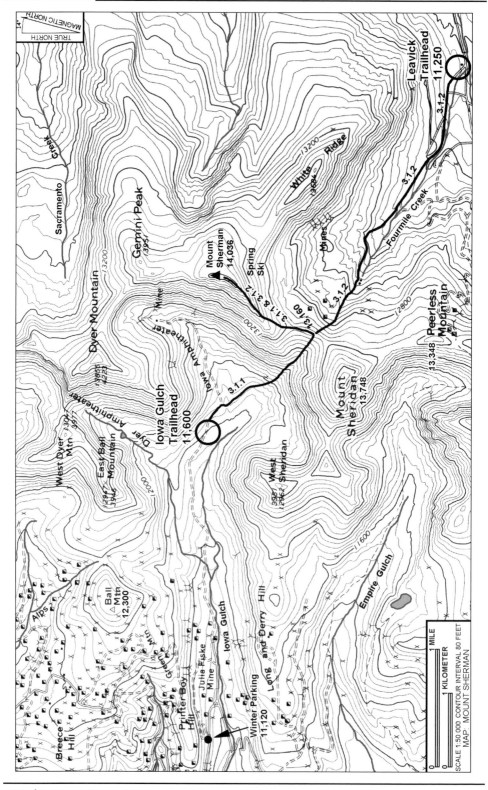

MOUNT SHERIDAN 13,748 FT

SHERIDAN SADDLE 13,160 FT

WHITE RIDGE 13,684 FT

3.1.1

MOUNT SHERMAN 14,036 FT

3.1.1

3.1.1

N

IOWA AMPHITHEATER

IOWA GULCH

ROUTE 3.1.1

SUMMER PARKING 11,600 FT

WINTER PARKING 11,120 FT

Mount Sherman from the west, fall.

hike the road NW up the Fourmile Creek drainage to the Hilltop Mine site at 12,890'. From here climb 270 vertical feet NW to an obvious saddle (13,160'), then climb Mount Sherman's south ridge another mile and 876 vertical feet to the summit. The summit is a huge low-angled area. At least one party has wondered if they were really there. Descent is via the same route or the following variation: a more direct summer climb heads N and NE from the Hilltop Mine site and ascends broad slopes of scree and tundra to the summit.

Spring snow season: Use either route described above. You'll find plenty of terrific skiing. Novice snow climbers will enjoy crampon wandering up the low-angled slopes.

Winter: It's a long slog from snow closure on the Fourmile Creek Road to Mount Sherman's summit. Take care with cornices and avalanche danger when you climb to the 13,160' saddle from the Hilltop Mine site.

Safety notes: Whatever the season, with low visibility it's possible to get lost on Mount Sherman's huge summit dome. Carry map, compass, and altimeter. If you're on spring snow, remember that these east facing routes get early sun.

3.1.3	Mount Lincoln—The Russian Couloir	
Ratings:	Ski Descent—Advanced	Snow Climb—Advanced
Season:	Spring Snow	
RT Data:	7 hours, 7 miles, 3,146' ↑	
Start:	Subdivision Road (Moose Creek) 11,140'	
1 Day from Rd:	Yes	
Map:	Mount Democrat East, pg.139	
Photos:	pgs.141, 145, 147	

This treasure is short and sweet. It is a nice beginner's snow climb or a good "entry level" steep ski descent. Experienced skiers can take an optional extreme start. For added spice, a thrilling "narrows" completes the descent.

Spring snow season: Park at the Subdivision Road (Moose Creek) Trailhead (section introduction), then follow the snowcovered road N to the Robert's Road Trailhead (section introduction). If this road is open, drive to the Roberts Road Trailhead. From the Roberts Road Trailhead, climb the Quartzville Creek Jeep Trail into the apex of the Cameron Amphitheater. The Russian Couloir is the obvious narrow cleft to the left (W) of the Russia Mine shack, underneath Lincoln's mundane summit. Climb the couloir. Descend on skis or downclimb one of Lincoln's ridge routes (3.1.10 or 3.1.4).

For a ski descent, you can avoid the steep couloir entrance on the west side of Lincoln's summit. To do so, ski E off the summit a short distance, then ski back into the couloir by traversing above the precarious looking mine shack.

Safety notes: This west facing couloir should only be climbed or skied on frozen spring snow. Summer climbing is not recommended due to rockfall.

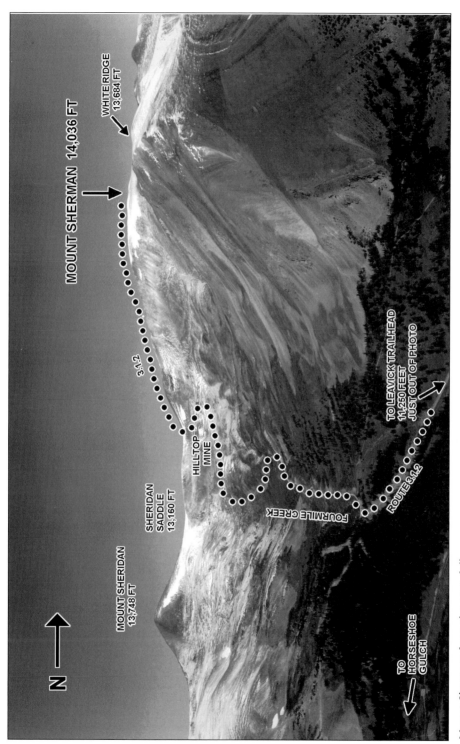

Mount Sherman from the east, fall.

WHITE RIDGE
13,684 FT

MOUNT SHERMAN 14,036 FT

3.1.2

TO LEAVICK TRAILHEAD
11,250 FEET
JUST OUT OF PHOTO

ROUTE 3.1.2

FOURMILE CREEK

HILLTOP
MINE

SHERIDAN
SADDLE
13,160 FT

MOUNT SHERIDAN
13,748 FT

N

TO
HORSESHOE
GULCH

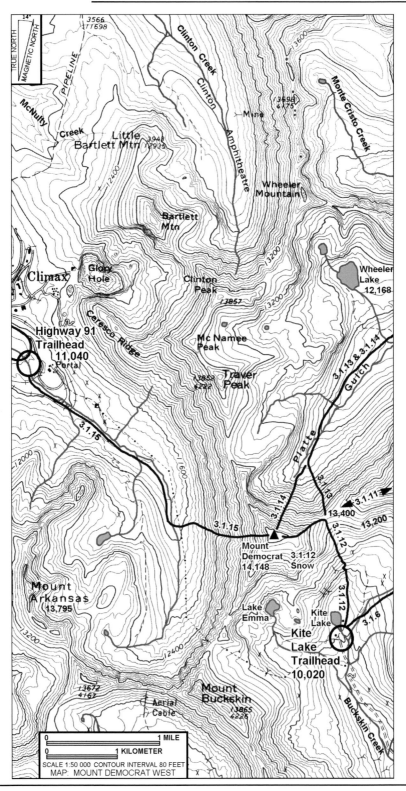

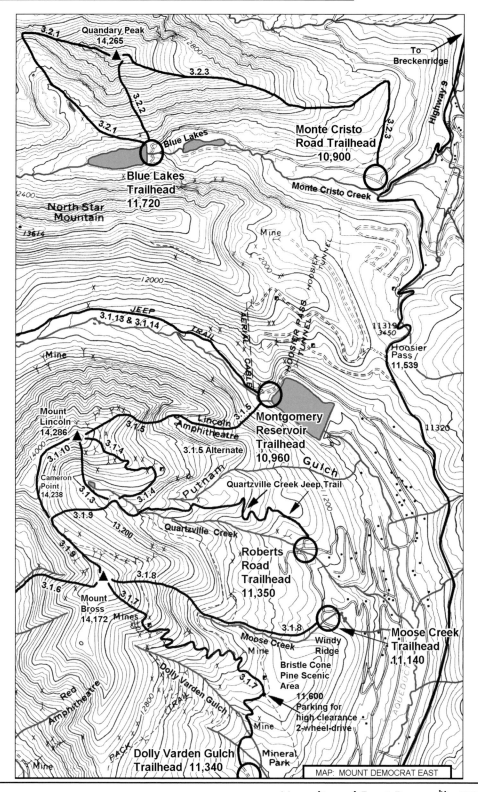

MAP: MOUNT DEMOCRAT EAST

3.1.4	**Mount Lincoln—East Ridge**		
Ratings:	Summer Climb—Novice		Snow Climb—Novice
Season:	Summer/Spring		Winter
RT Data:	8 hours, 7 miles, 2,936' ↑		12 hours, 13 miles, 3,146' ↑
Start:	Roberts Road Trailhead 11,350'		Subdivision Road (Moose Creek) Trailhead 11,140'
1 Day from Rd:	Yes		
Map:	Mount Democrat East, pg. 139		
Photo:	pg. 141		

Summer after snow melt-off: Park at the Roberts Road Trailhead. Hike up the Quartzville Creek Jeep Trail 2¼ miles to a fork at 13,000'. Take the right fork and follow the road up onto the ridge. Continue up the road to 13,600'. Leave the road and hike directly to the summit (if you stay on the road, it will lead you on a traverse around the north side of the peak).

Spring snow season: Spring snowcover varies on this route.

Winter: Use the summer route, with variations to avoid avalanche slopes. One such variation gains the ridge at the 12,600' level. You be the judge.

Safety notes: Yes, this is easy—remember, you're on a mountain. Use standard sunrise for sunhit.

3.1.5	**Mount Lincoln—Lincoln Amphitheater**		
Ratings:	Summer Climb—Advanced Ski Descent—Advanced Snow Climb—Intermediate		
Season:	Summer/Spring		Winter
RT Data:	8 hours, 6 miles, 3,326' ↑		14 hours, 6 miles, 3,326' ↑
Start:	Montgomery Reservoir 10,960'		
1 Day from Rd:	Yes		
Map:	Mount Democrat East, pg. 139		
Photos:	pgs. 142, 145		
Notes:	Lincoln has some fine early winter ice climbing.		

While this huge hanging valley is certainly an awesome ski descent, it would be a boorish slog for all but the most devoted snow climbers.

Spring snow season: Park at the Montgomery Reservoir Trailhead (section introduction). Pick your way up the steep 500 vertical foot headwall that guards the entrance to the Amphitheater. This headwall looks worse than it is. If in doubt, work the right side of the stream course and don't hesitate to make traverses to look for the best line. You can study the headwall from the trailhead. If you're willing to forgo the "directisima," another alternative is to avoid the entire headwall by climbing the flank well to the left (S), then traversing right (N) at 11,800' into the beginning of the Amphitheater. Take care where you traverse, since you'll encounter steeper ground if you traverse too high or low. Above the headwall the route follows an obvious path of least resistance to Lincoln's summit.

An even better option, depending on snow cover, might be to avoid the entire lower

Mount Lincoln from Mount Bross, summer.

Amphitheater entirely. To do so start from Montgomery Reservoir; start your climb farther to the SE and ascend the right (N) arm of Putnam Gulch.

Descend your ascent route or descend the Quartzville Creek drainage from Cameron Point.

Winter: The Lincoln Amphitheater has been climbed in the winter during very stable avalanche conditions, but still with risk. Because there are so many safe ridge alternatives, it's not recommended for winter climbing. Ice climbers, however, will enjoy several frozen waterfalls on the Amphitheater headwall (see section introduction).

Safety notes: During summer, the lower portion of this route might be more of a bushwhack scramble than many climbers prefer. Skiers and snow climbers should plan for an early sunhit.

3.1.6	**Mount Bross from Kite Lake**		
	Ratings:	Summer Climb—Novice	Ski Descent—Intermediate
		Snow Climb—Novice	
	Season:	Summer, or Spring snow	
	RT Data:	3 miles, 6 hours, 2,152' ↑	
	Start:	Kite Lake Trailhead (summer) 12,020'	
	1 Day from Rd:	Yes	
	Maps:	Mount Democrat West, pg. 138; Mount Democrat East, pg. 139	

Use this route for a direct line to the summit of Mount Bross.

Summer after snow melt-off: Park at the Kite Lake Trailhead (see section introduction)

From Kite Lake climb E and a bit N over scree and tundra into the drainage dropping from Bross' summit. When the terrain steepens at 12,600', trend right (S) and follow a rib to the summit. Descend your ascent route. It's tempting to run the scree during your descent, but doing so causes irreparable erosion. Perhaps the best descent is to follow Bross' north ridge to Cameron Point, drop from Cameron W to the Democrat/Cameron saddle, then hike S down the basin to Kite Lake. To avoid causing erosion near Kite Lake, descend the more gradual trail to the east of a trail that drops directly to the lake.

Spring snow season: Use the summer route above. This side of Bross rarely has good snow cover. Nonetheless, what spring snow you do find will add spice to the route. On lean snow years, the gully system farther to the south, which drains below Kite Lake, might hold more snow.

Safety notes: Add 3 hours to standard sunrise for sunhit.

Lincoln Amphitheater from Montgomery Reservoir, winter.

3.1.7	**Mount Bross—East Flank**	
Ratings	Summer Climb—Novice	Ski Descent—Novice
	Snow Climb—Novice	
Season:	Summer / Spring	Winter
RT Data:	5 hours, 6 miles, 2,812' ↑	14 hours, 12 miles, 3,092' ↑
Start:	Dolly Varden Gulch Trailhead	Windy Ridge Road
	11,340'	11,080'
1 Day from Rd:	Yes	
Map:	Mount Democrat East, pg. 139	

Mount Bross' East Flank is one of the most casual fourteener routes in Colorado; enjoy it during any season! See the section introduction for information on bicycling this route, which is highly recommended.

Summer after snow melt-off: Drive to the Dolly Varden Gulch Trailhead. From parking in the mining area, follow USFS Road 415 from the north end of the mining area, then N and E up several switchbacks ½ mile to the Bristlecone Pine Scenic Area on Windy Ridge. Continue on the road up to 13,000', just below the decrepit structures of the Dolly Varden Mine. Leave the road and hike directly up through the mining area (avoid posted property) until you intersect the road again at 13,400'. Hike the road a few hundred yards N, then leave the road again and climb scree and tundra up the shoulder NW then N to the summit. You might see several white plastic claim markers above the road. These are near the best route but could be removed at any time.

Descend your ascent route. If you cut switchbacks, do so only when you will not cause erosion.

Spring snow season: Use the summer route above. This flank is wind-blasted, but skiers might find snow in Dolly Varden Gulch.

Winter: Drive the Buckskin Gulch Road to the turnoff for the Windy Ridge Road. Ski, snowshoe, or snowmobile the Windy Gulch Road to the Dolly Varden Gulch Trailhead, then use the summer route. Using the Subdivision Road (Moose Creek) Trailhead might get you closer to Windy Ridge, depending on snow plowing. Recon them both the day before your climb.

Safety notes: Use standard sunrise for sunhit. Stay away from mine shafts and structures.

3.1.8	**Mount Bross—Moose Creek Gulch**	
Ratings:	Ski Descent—Advanced	Snow Climb—Intermediate
Season:	Spring Snow	
RT Data:	6 hours, 5 miles, 3,032' ↑	
Start:	Subdivision (Moose Creek) Trailhead, 11,140'	
1 Day from Rd:	Yes	
Map:	Mount Democrat East, pg.139	
Photo:	pg.145	

Do you like fun snow climbs or ski descents with big vertical? In either case, put this route at the top of your list.

Spring snow season: Park at the Subdivision (Moose Creek) Trailhead (see section introduction). Climb Moose Creek to 12,200', then climb the obvious snow gully on the west face of Mount Bross. Descend your ascent route.

Safety notes: This route should only be climbed on frozen spring snow. It has the usual unreliable, early-thawing snowpack you find on eastern exposures, so plan your ascent so you're skiing or downclimbing at first sunhit—which will be near standard sunrise.

3.1.9	**Mount Bross via Quartzville Creek**		
Ratings:	Summer Climb—Novice	Ski Descent—Intermediate	
		Snow Climb—Novice	
Season:	Summer	Spring	Winter
RT Data:	8 hrs., 7 miles, 2,822' ↑	9 hrs., 8 miles, 3,032' ↑	12 hrs., 8 miles, 3,032' ↑
Start:	Roberts Road Trailhead	Subdivision (Moose Creek) Trailhead	
	11,350'	11,140'	
1 Day from Rd:	Yes		
Map:	Mount Democrat East, pg. 139		
Photos:	pgs. 141, 145		

Summer after melt-off: Drive to the Roberts Road Trailhead (see section introduction). Walk the Quartzville Creek Jeep Trail to 13,000'. Quit the road and climb west up easy ground to the Bross/Cameron saddle (13,880'). Follow the ridge ½ mile SE to the summit. Return via the same route.

Spring snow season: Use the summer route above, but start at the Subdivision Road (Moose Creek) Trailhead and traverse N a mile on snowcovered road to the Roberts Road Trailhead. Ski or glissade Cameron Amphitheater.

Safety notes: Use standard sunrise for sunhit.

3.1.10	**Mount Lincoln & Mount Bross via Quartzville Creek**		
Ratings:	Summer Climb—Novice	Ski Descent—Intermediate	
		Snow Climb—Novice	
Season:	Summer	Spring	Winter
RT Data	9 hrs., 8½ miles, 2,936' ↑	9 hrs., 9½ miles, 2,936' ↑	14 hrs., 9½ miles, 3,146'↑
Start:	Roberts Road Trailhead	Subdivision Road (Moose Creek)	
	11,350'	11,140'	
1 Day from Rd:	Yes		
Map:	Mount Democrat East, pg. 139		
Photos:	pgs. 141, 145, 147		

This is the standard all-season, peak bagger's route for Lincoln and Bross. Fit climbers can also hit Mount Democrat via a connecting ridge. During spring snow season, you'll find plenty of terrific skiing leading up to the summit ridge. Winter climbers might opt for ridge

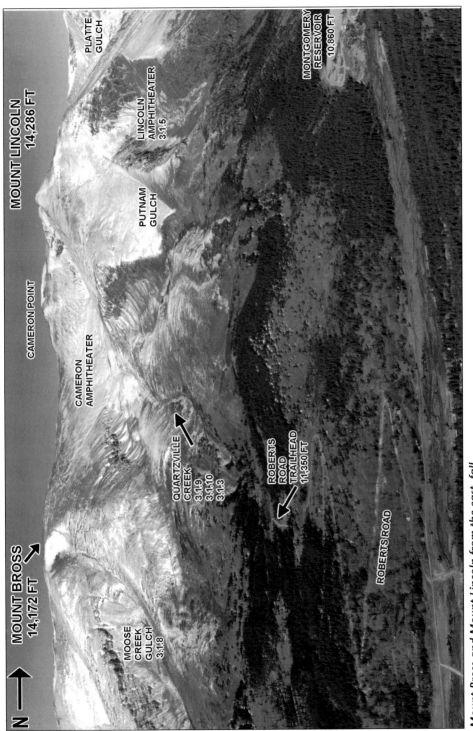

MOUNT LINCOLN
14,286 FT

PLATTE
GULCH

LINCOLN
AMPHITHEATER
3.1.5

PUTNAM
GULCH

MONTGOMERY
RESERVOIR
10,860 FT

CAMERON POINT

CAMERON
AMPHITHEATER

QUARTZVILLE
CREEK
3.1.9
3.1.10
3.1.3

ROBERTS
ROAD
TRAILHEAD
11,350 FT

ROBERTS ROAD

MOUNT BROSS
14,172 FT

MOOSE
CREEK
GULCH
3.1.8

N

Mount Bross and Mount Lincoln from the east, fall.

routes with more windscour, such as Windy Ridge (3.1.7). A network of rough jeep trails laces the summit of Mount Bross. These are tough for motorized vehicles but make Bross a fine goal for hardcore bicycle riders.

Summer after melt-off: Take Roberts Road to the Roberts Road Trailhead (see section introduction). Walk the Quartzville Creek Jeep Trail to 13,000'. Quit the road and climb west up easy ground to the Bross/Cameron saddle (13,880'). Follow the ridge ½ mile SE to the summit. Play touch football or throw your Frisbee on the height, then take an easy ridge hike NW one mile over Cameron Point, then ½ mile NE to Lincoln's summit. For your descent, backtrack to Cameron Point, drop down easy ground into the Cameron Amphitheater, and walk the jeep trail back to your car.

Spring snow season: Use the Subdivision Road (Moose Creek) Trailhead (section introduction). From the curve at the upper end of the subdivision road, traverse N on an obvious main road (probably snowcovered, but drive if it's plowed) ½ mile to Quartzville Creek. Cross the creek, then locate Roberts Road Trailhead (section introduction) and the Quartzville Creek Jeep Trail.

Follow the jeep trail to the Cameron Amphitheater. Gain the ridge connecting Bross and Lincoln by ascending to the Bross/Cameron saddle (13,880'). Use this ridge to gain either summit. If you opt for Lincoln, you'll pick up another 100 vertical feet or so as you nip over Cameron Point. You can contour around the right (E) side of Cameron Point, but this involves a snow traverse that can take as much energy as going over the top. Bross is a straight shot ½ mile SE from the saddle.

Descend via the same route—or ski the Lincoln Amphitheater off Lincoln (3.1.5) or Moose Creek Gulch (3.1.8) off Mount Bross.

Winter: Use the spring route. Take care with slide terrain when you gain the Lincoln/Bross ridge.

Safety notes: While wandering the ridge between these two peaks, take the usual precautions for lightning and other weather dangers. Use standard sunrise for sunhit.

3.1.11	**Mount Lincoln & Mount Bross from Kite Lake**	
Ratings:	Summer Climb—Intermediate Ski Descent—Advanced	
	Snow Climb—Intermediate	
Season:	Summer, or Spring Snow	
RT Data:	8 hours, 5 miles, 2,666' ↑	
Start:	Kite Lake Trailhead (summer) 12,020'	
1 Day from Rd:	Yes	
Maps:	Mount Democrat West, pg. 138; Mount Democrat East, pg. 139	
Photos:	pgs. 141, 145, 147	

Choices, choices. While most peak baggers try for the "three bagger" of Democrat, Lincoln, and Bross, this "two bagger" is a good choice in marginal weather—or with a body that's not as fit as you'd like.

Your choices: Climb up the direct route to Bross (3.1.6), traverse to Lincoln, then return via the Democrat/Cameron saddle, or do the opposite. The former avoids running down the scree on the west face of Bross; scree running causes undue erosion. To avoid scree running, climb up the direct route and descend via the saddle. This description is written for the latter choice.

Summer after snow melt-off: Drive to the Kite Lake Trailhead (see section introduction). Climb Mount Bross direct from Kite Lake (3.1.6). Descend the ridge NW from Mount Bross, climb to within 200 vertical feet of Cameron Point, then contour the east side of

In Cameron Amphitheater, spring.

Cameron Point to the Cameron/Lincoln saddle. Use a roadcut if snow cover allows. Continue along the ridge NE to Mount Lincoln. Return to Cameron, then descend the ridge W to the Democrat/Cameron saddle. Leave the ridge and descend the basin to Kite Lake.

Spring snow season: Use the summer route described above, perhaps in the opposite direction if the west face of Bross looks like a good ski descent or glissade.

Safety notes: Beware of cliff areas on the south face of Cameron Point—don't try any short cuts. Add several hours to standard sunrise for sunhit.

3.1.12	**Mount Democrat from Kite Lake**		
Ratings:	Summer Climb—Intermediate	Ski Descent—Intermediate	
	Snow Climb—Intermediate		
Season:	Summer	Spring	Winter
RT Data	4 hours, 2½ miles,	13 hours, 14 miles,	multi-day, 14 miles,
	2,128' ↑	3,148' ↑	3,148'↑
Start:	Kite Lake Trailhead 12,020'	Buckskin Creek Road (snow closure) 11,000'	
1 Day	Summer	Spring	Winter
from Rd:	Yes	Fit groups	No
Map:	Mount Democrat West, pg. 138		

A high trailhead and well-traveled trail make this one of the easiest summer fourteener routes. It's crowded for the same reasons—climb it during the week. This summit is often combined with ascents of Mount Lincoln and Mount Bross. Such a triptych is hard (even with the high trailhead), but puts three checks on your list.

Summer after melt-off: Park at the Kite Lake Trailhead (see section introduction). Take a moment to examine the trails leading up into the basin from the lake. One trail follows a direct line to a mining area N of the lake. Another trail swings NE from the lake and takes a more gradual route to the upper basin. Using the direct trail causes erosion, while the more gradual line saves your legs—and the land.

At any rate, from 12,400' in upper Kite Lake Basin, climb a well-worn trail N then NW to the main saddle (13,400') on Democrat's northeast ridge. Climb the ridge 748 vertical feet on easy terrain to the summit. Descend your ascent route.

Spring snow season: From the Buckskin Creek snow closure (section introduction) continue up the valley for about 3.5 miles to Kite Lake at 12,000'. From the lake climb the beautiful snow face that rises from the north end of the lake to the summit of Democrat. You'll have to traverse around several cliff bands, so examine the face as you approach it. For even easier snow climbing, use the summer route described above.

For a ski descent, the face route is spectacular spring conditions. Take care skiing above the cliff bands. The ridge route also is a good ski with adequate snow cover.

Winter: You might find a route safe from avalanches by ascending various rock ribs up to the 13,400' saddle, then up the ridge to the summit. This is the leeward side of the mountain, however, so be ready for intense judgment calls.

Safety notes: Summer climbers, especially those hitting more than one summit, should plan their trudge so they'll be off the ridges by noon. This side of Democrat faces southeast, consequently the snow matures early in the spring, and by the same token becomes danger-ous earlier on spring days. In the winter all this is potential avalanche terrain and should only be climbed and skied at the most stable times. Use standard sunrise for sunhit.

3.1.13 Mount Democrat—North Flank

Ratings:	Summer Climb—Intermediate Ski Descent—Advanced
	Snow Climb—Intermediate
Season:	Summer or Spring Snow
RT Data:	8 hours, 10 miles, 3,188' ↑
Start:	Montgomery Reservoir 10,960'
1 Day from Rd:	Yes
Maps:	Mount Democrat West and East, pgs. 138-139
Photo:	pg. 150

Summer after snow melt-off: Park 2-wheel-drive at the Montgomery Reservoir Trailhead (section introduction). Hike the 4-wheel-drive road 2½ miles up Platte Gulch to 11,680'. Leave the main jeep trail and follow faint roads and trails leading SW up Platte Gulch another 1¼ miles to 12,300' at the head of the gulch. Swing to the left (S), and climb a scree face to the Democrat/Cameron saddle (13,400'). Take the ridge W from the saddle to the summit. Descend your ascent route.

Spring snow season: Use the summer route described above. With good snow cover, this can be a decent snow climb or ski trip.

Safety notes: While most parties should be able to do this route in one day, it includes several hours of valley travel. Plan accordingly. Use standard sunrise for sunhit, since the summit ridge faces east.

3.1.14 Mount Democrat—North Face Snow Route

Ratings:	Ski Descent—Extreme Snow Climb—Advanced
Season:	Spring or Summer Snow
RT Data:	9 hours, 10 miles, 3,188' ↑
Start:	Montgomery Reservoir 10,960'
1 Day from Rd:	Yes for the very fit; high camp recommended
Maps:	Mount Democrat West, pg. 138; Mount Democrat West, pg. 139
Photo:	pg. 150

The North Face of Mount Democrat has several excellent snow gullies. These gullies provide good climbing but to date no ski descents have been recorded.

Summer or spring snow season: For snow climbing, a high camp in Platte Gulch is recommended. From the Montgomery Reservoir Trailhead (section introduction), ski or walk 4 miles (about 1,700 vertical feet) up Platte Gulch to the base of the North Face. The best couloir is the farthest one to the right (W) side of the North Face. If you try a ski descent, do so early enough in the spring to allow you to ski most of Platte Gulch; this is an outstanding cruise. On your way up Platte Gulch, check out the north side of Mount Lincoln; it has several excellent gullies that might inspire your return.

An alternate approach uses the Kite Lake Trailhead (after the road opens in late spring). You climb to the Democrat/Cameron saddle from Kite Lake, descend N into Platte Gulch, then climb the face.

A rare view of Mount Democrat's north face, fall.

Safety notes: To mitigate rockfall danger, only climb these couloirs when they contain enough snow to cover loose rock. This north face gets a late sunhit. From a high camp you need only start a few hours before sunrise.

3.1.15	**Mount Democrat—West Face Snow Route & Ski Route**	
Ratings:	Ski Descent—Extreme	Snow Climb—Advanced
Season:	Spring Snow	
RT Data:	5 hours, 6 miles, 3,108' ↑	
Start:	Colorado Highway 91 Trailhead 11,040'	
1 Day from Rd:	Yes	
Map:	Mount Democrat West, pg. 138	
Photo:	pg. 152	

Casual access is the key to this classic snow climb and rewarding ski descent.

Spring or early summer snow season: From the Highway 91 Trailhead (section introduction), follow the right (W) side of the drainage between Mount Democrat and Mount Arkansas 1¾ miles to 11,520'. Here you'll be directly across from Democrat's grand West Face. Cross the valley, then climb the apron at the base of the face. Do a climbing traverse to the right into a gully system that takes you to a small saddle a few hundred feet N of the summit. Descend your ascent route or the Kite Lake route (3.1.12) if you can arrange a ride.

Other than a small section between the saddle mentioned above and the summit, the snow on this route is never steeper than 45 degrees. The skiing is rated Extreme because you cut above several cliff bands. These cliffs also make the climbing more dangerous than the angle alone would suggest.

Safety notes: Climb this route early in the morning on compacted spring or early summer snow. Due to rockfall, this route is not safe without snow. Use a sunhit time for a northwest exposure.

3.1.16	**The Three Banger—Mounts Democrat, Lincoln & Bross**
Ratings:	See routes 3.1.7, 3.1.8 and 3.1.12
Season:	Summer or Late Spring
RT Data:	12 hours, 7½ miles, 3,540' ↑
Start:	Kite Lake Trailhead (summer) 12,020'
1 Day from Rd:	Yes
Maps:	Mount Democrat West, pg. 138 ; Mount Democrat East, pg. 139

Three in a day. Yes! In summer or late spring, the best start for this route is the Kite Lake Trailhead. Earlier in the spring, if the road to the Kite Lake Trailhead is closed by snow, use the Subdivision Road Trailhead and start your Three Banger with the Mount Bross East Flank route (3.1.7), or Moose Creek Gulch route (3.1.8).

Summer after snow melt-off: From the Kite Lake Trailhead, climb route (3.1.12) to the summit of Mount Democrat, then descend back to the 13,400' Democrat/Cameron saddle. From the saddle climb ¼ mile E along the ridge to "Mount" Cameron (14,238'), which from this side does feel like a mountain. Next, stroll the easy ridge N then NE ½ mile to the summit

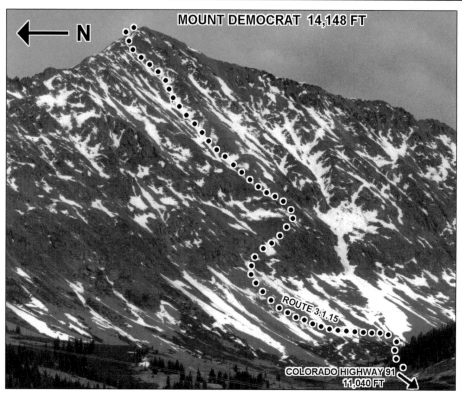

Mount Democrat's interesting west face, late spring.

of Mount Lincoln (14,286'). Reverse back to Cameron, contour around the east side of Cameron, then drop south to the Bross/Cameron saddle (13,880'). From the saddle, force your legs 292 vertical feet to the huge summit of Mount Bross.

It's possible to descend directly to Kite Lake from the summit of Mount Bross', this might be your best option if lightning threatens. A better, "greener" route, which causes less erosion, is to retrace your steps down to the Bross/Cameron saddle. From the saddle, slog back up most of the way to the "summit" of Cameron Point, contour left (W) near the summit and intersect the Democrat/Cameron ridge. Descend the ridge and retrace your steps down to Kite Lake.

Spring snow season: Use the summer route, but check out the west face of Mount Bross from Kite Lake. With good snow cover it makes a decent glissade or ski descent—but it's often windscoured.

Safety notes: Beware of cliffs on the south face of Cameron Point. Do not take short cuts; start early to avoid lightning.

SECTION 3.2
Quandary Peak (14,265')

You want a plain old-fashioned hike, a winter ascent, a snow climb or ski descent? Quandary Peak has them all. Access is a snap, and though the standard route is a cruise, you still get that feeling on the summit that only a fourteener can give you. Indeed, along with Mount Bierstadt, Quandary Peak is one of the two best winter "starter" fourteeners. It's also on the list of best summer fourteener climbs and spring snow routes. For good views of Quandary (and Mount Lincoln and Bross) drive to Hoosier Pass (see below).

ROADS AND TRAILHEADS

USGS Maps: Breckenridge
USFS Forest Visitors Map: Pike National Forest or Arapaho National Forest

Monte Cristo Road Trailhead

Drive Colorado State Highway 9 N from Fairplay over Hoosier Pass or S from Breckenridge to the obvious Monte Cristo Creek switchback on the N side of Hoosier Pass at 10,807'. This switchback is 2.2 miles from the summit of Hoosier Pass, 14.3 miles from the Fairplay Hotel in Fairplay, and 8.2 miles from central Breckenridge. It's easily identified by many private homes just to the west of the road.

At the lower (N) portion of the switchback, turn W onto the Monte Cristo Road, a dirt road that follows the north side of Monte Cristo Creek. Unreliable signs may indicate ROAD NUMBER 850, BLUE LAKES ROAD OR MONTE CRISTO ROAD. For the Monte Cristo Road Trailhead, drive the Monte Cristo Road .5 mile from Highway 9 and park where another road turns off to the right (N), at 10,900'. In winter and early spring, drive to snow closure, most likely about ¼ mile from Highway 9. Snow season parking is obvious, but snow closure will vary due to housing development.

Blue Lakes Trailhead

For the Blue Lakes Trailhead, drive the Monte Cristo Road (usually opens in May), upvalley 2 miles to Monte Cristo Reservoir (also called Blue Lakes). Park at 11,720' near the spillway.

3.2.1	Quandary Peak—West Ridge		
Ratings:	Summer Climb—Advanced		Snow Climb—Advanced
Season:	Summer/Spring		Spring Snow
RT Data:	6 hours, 4½ miles, 2,545' ↑		8 hours, 8½ miles, 3,365' ↑
Start:	Blue Lakes Trailhead 11,720'		Monte Cristo Road Trailhead 10,900'
1 Day from Rd:	Yes		
Map:	Mount Democrat East, pg. 139		
Photo:	pg. 155		

Summer after snow melt-off: Drive to the Blue Lakes Trailhead. From parking, start hiking up a trail on the north side of the reservoir. Stick with the trail as it swings right (NW) and climbs into a spectacular gulch. Persevere to the saddle at the head of the gulch (13,360'). The trail peters out below the saddle, but the route is obvious.

Climb E on the ridge from the saddle. It's easygoing to 14,040', where you have to amble around several towers to make the last ¼ mile to the summit. Descend your ascent route or descend the east ridge (3.2.3) for an aesthetic traverse. In the latter case, walk back up the Monte Cristo Road to your car.

Spring snow season: Park at the Monte Cristo Road Trailhead, walk or ski up the road to Blue Lakes, then use the summer route above. If you park low, it makes even more sense to descend the east ridge. Carrying skis is not recommended because of the rough terrain near the summit. For the best skiing, leave your skis at the 13,360' saddle, descend your ascent route, then ski the gulch back to Blue Lakes.

Safety notes: Though you don't need a rope on this route, a stumble could have dire consequences. Since portions of the approach face east, use standard sunrise for sunhit.

3.2.2	**Quandary Peak—South Gully (Cristo Couloir)**	
Ratings:	Ski Descent—Advanced	Snow Climb—Intermediate
Season:	Spring Snow	
RT Data:	7 hours, 6 miles, 3,365 vertical' ↑	
Start:	Monte Cristo Road Trailhead 10,900'	
1 Day from Rd:	Yes	
Map:	Mount Democrat East, pg. 139	
Photos:	pgs. 155, 156	

This classic ski should be a goal for every mountaineer. While still snowcovered, the route also makes a good glissade descent for summer climbers, but care is required—it may be icy. To prevent erosion and avoid rockfall danger, don't use this route when it's dry.

Spring snow season: Since it's south facing, the snow in the Cristo Couloir starts the spring melt-freeze compaction early in the season. Thus, this route can be safe and enjoyable as early as April. Naturally, this will vary from year to year—and from storm to storm. The snow usually lasts to the end of May, but may be patchy by then. A popular way to ski the Cristo Gully is via ascent by Quandary's east ridge (3.2.3). This breaks the "climb it first" rule, but replaces the two mile walk up the Monte Cristo Road with a more aesthetic jaunt. If the road is driveable, climbing up the gully would certainly be your best choice.

To climb the Cristo Couloir drive or foot travel (depending on snow closure) the Monte Cristo Road (section introduction)-Blue Lakes Trailhead (section introduction). The couloir begins a few hundred feet N up from the Blue Lake Reservoir dam. The route is obvious. For a ski descent follow your ascent route with natural variation to avoid rocky areas. To find the couloir from the summit, drop down the fall line south of the summit—you'll be automatically sucked into the gully. If in doubt, trend slightly to skier's left for several hundred vertical feet, then work back to skier's right. If the Monte Cristo Road has hard snow, the ski from the dam to your car only takes about 10 minutes.

Safety notes: The Cristo Gully is only safe with compacted snow. If you use the Monte Cristo Road for egress during late morning, be aware that several major avalanche paths threaten from the S side of Quandary's east ridge. If you have any doubt about these you'd be better off in the middle of the valley—though you will still be exposed. Access is so easy that many novice backcountry skiers attempt this route as their first mountain ski descent. Several of these people have nearly died after falling down the route. Indeed, it's close to the parking lot, but that doesn't make it any safer! Remember how easy it is to take a slide on compacted spring snow. Add about an hour to standard sunrise for sunhit

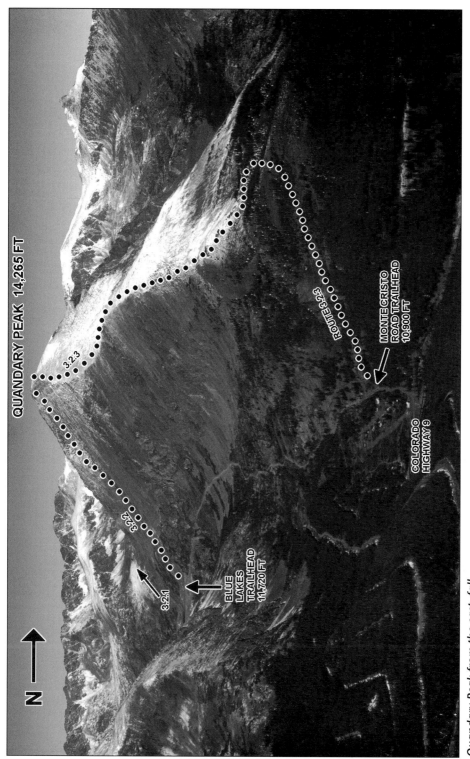

QUANDARY PEAK 14,265 FT

3.2.3

3.2.3

3.2.2

ROUTE 3.2.3

MONTE CRISTO
ROAD TRAILHEAD
10,900 FT

COLORADO
HIGHWAY 9

BLUE
LAKES
TRAILHEAD
11,720 FT

3.2.1

N

Quandary Peak from the east, fall.

You get a good view of Quandary Peak from the highway, early spring.

3.2.3	Quandary Peak—East Ridge		
Ratings:	Summer Climb—Novice		Ski Descent—Novice
		Snow Climb—Novice	
Season:	Summer /Spring		Winter
RT Data:	6½ hours, 6 miles, 3,365' ↑		8 hours, 6 miles, 3,365' ↑
Start:	Monte Cristo Road Trailhead 10,900'		
1 Day from Rd:	Yes		
Map:	Mount Democrat East, pg. 139		
Photo:	pg. 156		

Summer after snow melt-off: Though the angle of this climb is less than most four-teeners (maximum 38 degrees) it can still be tough—especially if you're working off winter fat. Park at the Monte Cristo Trailhead (see introduction). Climb ½ mile N through sparse timber to the broad ridge crest. Use an old road where convenient but don't hesitate to leave the road for a steeper, more efficient climb. Avoid posted land. Once on the ridge swing W and follow it 2 miles to the summit. The best trail follows the actual ridge crest on the S (left) edge of the greater ridge, which could be better termed a "flank." The actual summit is a few hundred feet west along the summit crest. Descend via the same route, or in early summer experts can glissade the south face down to the Monte Cristo Reservoir (see route 3.2.2). You must have an ice axe (and know how to use it) for this option.

Spring snow season: Skiers, this is one of the best. In general, follow the summer route above. Park at snow closure on the Monte Cristo Road (see section introduction). While you climb N from parking to ridge crest, the snowcovered roads and trails can be confusing. Don't fret, simply use whatever trails or roads that lead you up and north. With firm spring snow for travel your exact route is not critical. Take care to skirt any posted land.

Once you're on the ridge follow it 2 miles west to the summit. The actual summit is a few hundred feet west along the summit crest. Descend the same route, or experts can descend Cristo Couloir (route 3.2.2) for spice. On skis, after you reverse the summit crest, enjoy any of the classic lines on the broad face leading down to the higher of two "shelves" on the ridge. Below here stick closer to the ridge crest (skier's right), and be sure to catch your route back down to parking. Skiers in the learning stages should leave their skis at the step below the upper face.

Winter: Use the route described above. Most of the ridge can be climbed on skis with skins and ski crampons, but you might have to posthole a few steep sections. Snowshoes work well for non-skiers, but use those with a claw under your foot. Descend your ascent route.

Safety Notes: While Quandary's East Ridge is one of the gentler fourteener routes, you can stray over cliffs to either side—especially with poor visibility. In winter, most of the ridge is safe from avalanches, but slides could happen on the steep sections above the two lower-angled steps. Enjoy skiing the tempting face east of the summit (above the second step)—but only with low slide danger. If you choose to glissade for your descent, be conservative. Use standard sunrise for sunhit time.

SECTION 3.3
Grays Peak (14,270'), Torreys Peak(14,267')

Ever popular Grays and Torreys Peaks are located less than a mile apart on the same ridge, with just enough drop, distance and aesthetics between them to qualify as separate mountains. In the summer, you can bag both peaks in a day via several easy hike routes. The Northeast Ridge (3.3.5) of Torreys is a terrific semi-technical climb and challenging winter route. Skiers and snow climbers will enjoy the mellow west slopes of both peaks and the challenging couloirs on the northwest and northeast faces of Torreys. The classic winter tour of these peaks is done via route (3.3.2) from Chihuahua Gulch. Aggressive mountaineers should put route (3.3.7), the high ridge from Loveland Pass, on their "must do" list. This is certainly one of the best high-routes in Colorado.

[handwritten: 15 July 2005 w/ Greg Loy - up via trail to Grays, down to saddle (nice trail), up Torreys. Descent via Kelso Ridge.]

ROADS AND TRAILHEADS

USGS Maps: Montezuma, Grays Peak, Loveland Pass *[handwritten: 6:37 RT ↓ scary 4ᵗʰ Cl.]*
USFS Forest Visitors Map: Pike National Forest

Drive Interstate 70 E from Vail Pass or W from Eisenhower Tunnel to the Dillon exit (number 205). Leave Interstate 70 here and drive SE through Dillon on U.S. Highway 6 (the Loveland Pass Road). At 5.7 miles from the exit you will reach a stoplight with the Keystone Ski Resort on the right. Stay on Highway 6 through the stoplight; continue 1.7 miles on Highway 6 and turn right at signs for NORTH PEAK and MONTEZUMA ROAD.

After you turn right, take an immediate hard left to stay on the Montezuma Road. If you miss this left turn (many people do), you'll end up in a maze of parking lots. In this case simply backtrack to the turn.

Peru Creek Road
From your turn off Highway 6, drive the Montezuma Road 4.9 miles to the obvious Peru Creek Road turnoff on the left (N) side of the road. This is 14.3 miles from Interstate 70. The Peru Creek Road can be identified by a large parking area, possible signs, and by the green Forest Service road closure gate (10,004'). During snow season, the road is closed here (hence the parking area) and the Peru Creek Road is a popular ski and snowmobile route.

Chihuahua Gulch Trailhead
In summer, drive up the Peru Creek Road 2.1 miles to the Chihuahua Gulch Trailhead (10,440'). This is simply a wide part of the road near the start of the Chihuahua Gulch Jeep Trail. Signs here are poor, but with adroit odometer use you'll have no trouble. For Horseshoe Basin, continue up the Peru Creek Road (high clearance 2-wheel-drive) 1.7 miles to a chewed up mining area at 10,880'. If you're certain of your vehicle's capability, you can continue with high clearance 2-wheel-drive .8 mile to parking at the Shoe Basin Mine (11,100'). You can 4-wheel-drive higher into Horseshoe Basin. A good 4-wheel-drive trailhead option is to park near a mine turnoff at 11,690', 17.7 miles from Interstate 70. Though you can push somewhat higher, it's hardly worth the wear on your vehicle.

Grizzly Gulch Trailheads
Drive Interstate 70 E from Eisenhower Tunnel or W from Georgetown to the Bakerville exit (number 221). Follow the obvious public road S through the Bakerville area. Enjoy a view of Grays Peak up to the right. This road soon becomes the Quayle Creek—Stevens Gulch Road; it's steep but passable with a passenger car. For Grizzly Gulch take the first obvious right turn 1 mile from Bakerville, then drive .3 miles to the start of the Grizzly Gulch jeep trail

on the right just before a group of decrepit buildings (10,320'). Park at the start of the jeep trail, just off the main road. In summer you can can 4-wheel-drive this jeep trail several miles up Grizzly Gulch.

Stevens Gulch

For Stevens Gulch don't take the Grizzly Gulch turn at 1 mile from Bakerville. Instead, stay on the Stevens Gulch Road and drive 2.8 miles from Bakerville to an improved trailhead parking area on the left side of the road (11,230').

The best time to ski and snow climb Grays and Torreys from Stevens Gulch is just after snow on the Stevens Gulch Road melts out to timberline—usually in mid-June. If you hit it right you can ski back to your car door. In winter the Stevens Gulch Road is usually packed by snowmobiles and thus an easy route for ski or machine. Earlier in the spring, the north side of Torreys (via Grizzly Gulch) is slightly closer to parking.

Loveland Pass Trailhead

Before the Eisenhower Tunnel was completed in 1973, Loveland Pass was one of the main auto routes over Colorado's Continental Divide. It was windy and avalanche-prone in the winter, a grinding hill climb in any season—and quite scenic. Fortunately, the pass remains open year-round as an alternate route to the tunnel. Terrific alpine hiking and ski touring abound. Indeed, Loveland Pass gives you some of the best alpine access in Colorado.

To reach Loveland Pass from the west side of the Continental Divide, take exit 205 (Dillon) off Interstate 70. From the east, exit I-70 near the Loveland Ski area just below the Eisenhower Tunnel. Both exits are obvious. Park near the signs atop the pass (11,990').

3.3.1	Grays and Torreys Peaks via trail from Stevens Gulch	
Ratings:	Summer Climb—Intermediate Ski Descent—Intermediate Snow Climb—Intermediate	
Season:	Summer	Spring snow
RT Data:	6½ hours, 6 miles, 3,950' ↑	9½ hours, 9 miles, 4,630' ↑
Start:	Stevens Gulch Trailhead 11,230 '	Stevens Gulch Road snow closure 10,200'
1 Day from Rd:	Yes	
Maps:	Grays Peak North, pg. 160; Grays Peak South, pg. 161	
Photo:	pg. 167	

Certainly one of the easiest fourteener climbs (the trail is an old road and horse track) this hike route is popular with Colorado's eastern slope residents. It is the standard "bagger" route for Grays, so if crowds are not your game, climb any of the other routes described here. Because of good road access, spring and early summer skiing on this route are highly recommended.

Summer after snow melt-off: Drive to the Stevens Gulch Trailhead. Before you leave your car, examine your map and the basin above you. Notice that the obvious basin to the southwest is not your destination! What you're headed for is the smaller basin west of the large basin, separated by a rib that extends from the north side of Grays Peak. The trick, especially in poor weather, is to be sure you head up the subsidiary drainage leading to the smaller basin. The summer trail, known as the Grays Peak Trail, is fairly obvious. Nonetheless, a sidetrack leads to a mining area in the larger basin and could trap the unwary tourist.

After you have the map figured, hike up the road from the trailhead several hundred feet, then take a right (SW) and cross the creek. Just after crossing the creek, swing harder to

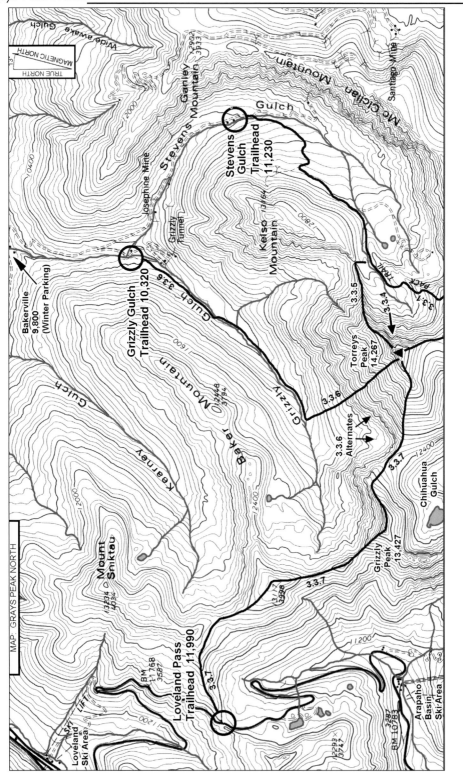

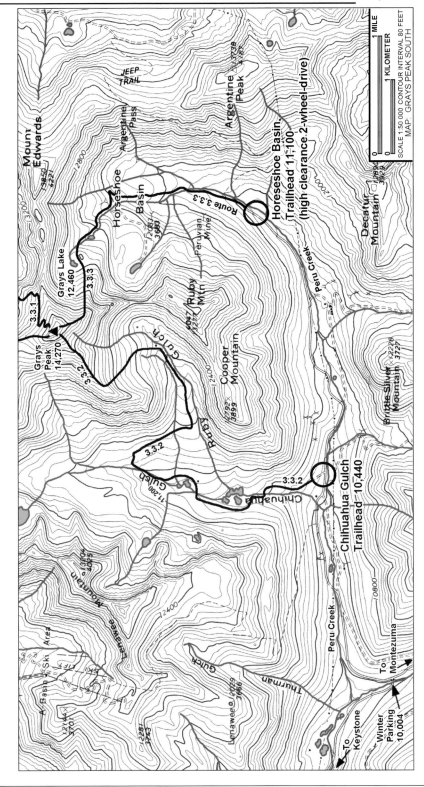

the right (W) and hike up a short hill to signs and a road closure gate. This is where the Grays Peak Trail really begins.

Continue SW two miles into the aforementioned basin. Stay on the trail as it climbs up the north rib of Grays Peak from 12,800' to 13,600', traverses out onto the rocky north face of Grays, then switchbacks to the summit. From the summit of Grays, follow an easy ridge N down to the Grays/Torreys saddle (13,707') then continue up the ridge N 560 vertical feet to the summit of Torreys Peak.

For your descent drop back to the Grays/Torreys saddle, climb about 350 vertical feet back toward the summit of Grays, traverse to the trail, then descend the trail. If that sounds like too much work, in early summer it's possible to find a snow route E down from the saddle into the basin. To do so, start from a point on the saddle closer to Grays Peak. Take care here with steep terrain and patchy snow. With no snow, "screeing" down these slopes causes erosion and makes ugly ruts. Your descent route is a test of how "green" you really are.

Spring snow season: Use the summer route above, with variations to find climbable or skiable snow. If you want to ski both peaks, head for the Grays/Torreys saddle. Climb Torreys first, ski the ridge back down to the saddle, climb the ridge to Grays, then enjoy the awesome run from Grays into the bowl below the saddle. Skiers will find plenty of optional slopes in this area, and due to the excellent access it is highly recommended. Of particular note for both snow climbers and skiers are several couloirs that drop from the ridge connecting Grays Peak and Mount Edwards. These are known as "The Remarkables"—which they are.

Safety notes: If you're new to the fourteeners, don't let the fact that this is a "hike" route be cause for a lack of concern. Lightning, foul weather, and altitude can cause trouble—no matter how easy the walk. It's possible to dislodge rocks on the north face of Grays. Keep this in mind with climbers above or below you. Snow climbers and skiers: Much of this terrain is east facing, so start your climb several hours before standard sunrise time.

3.3.2	Grays and Torreys Peaks from Chihuahua Gulch	
Ratings:	Summer Climb—Intermediate	Ski Descent—Novice
	Snow Climb—Novice	
Season:	Summer/Spring	Winter
RT Data:	10 hours, 9 miles, 4,393' ↑	12 hours, 13 miles, 4,829' ↑
Start:	Chihuahua Gulch Trailhead 10,440'	Peru Creek Road snow closure 10,004'
1 Day from Rd:	Yes	
Maps:	Grays Peak North, pg. 160; Grays Peak South, pg. 161	
Photo:	pg. 164	

Summer after snow melt-off: A simple, aesthetic hike, this route will bag you two fourteener summits. If you're a nonconformist who wants just one summit, use this route to summit Grays, then reverse down Ruby Gulch.

From the Chihuahua Gulch Trailhead, hike the Chihuahua Gulch Jeep Road to 11,200' at the end of a meadow. If the actual road route is vague, cross to the right (NE) side of the creek. The crux here is to get on the Ruby Gulch Jeep Trail, which continues up the valley at the edge of the forest right (NE) of the creek, then makes a long switchback in to Ruby Gulch. Follow the Ruby Gulch Jeep Trail to its end at 12,130' in Ruby Gulch. Next, head NW up the basin to 13,140' on Grays' southwest ridge. Take the ridge to the summit.

From the summit of Grays, hike N down to the Grays/Torreys saddle (13,707'), then nip up the ridge to the summit of Torreys Peak. Descend Torreys' stupendous west ridge 1,667 vertical feet down to the Torreys/Grizzly saddle (12,600'). Leave the ridge and drop down easy ground S into Chihuahua Gulch, then hike the gulch back to your car. During your return, skip the long switchback on the jeep trail by heading down the fallline from 11,600'. If your knees are begging for mercy, stick to the road.

Spring snow season: Though the summer route above can be used for a snow ascent, the following is more direct. In late spring, use the Chihuahua Gulch Trailhead. Earlier in the season, you'll have to park at the Peru Creek Road snow closure and ski or snowshoe the Peru Creek Road to what you wish was the trailhead. Either way, follow the Chihuahua Gulch Road up to the marshy flat area at 10,925'. Here, switchback up through sparse timber into Ruby Gulch. Follow shoulders just to the left (W) of Ruby Gulch to the summit of Grays Peak.

From the summit of Grays, hike N down to the Grays/Torreys saddle (13,707'), then nip up the ridge 563 vertical feet to the summit of Torreys Peak. From the summit of Torreys ski or glissade a spectacular system of wide couloirs SW back into Chihuahua Gulch, then follow Chihuahua Gulch back down to the Peru Creek Road to your car. Ruby Gulch also makes a fine ski descent from the summit of Grays Peak (rated intermediate).

Winter: A winter climb of this route can be reasonably safe from avalanche hazard—provided you use windscoured or low-angled terrain for your route. On some occasions in winter the couloirs will be filled with wind-compacted snow. This can yield excellent skiing but evaluate the possibility of hard slab avalanche danger. To avoid descending unknown terrain, consider backtracking over Grays and descending your ascent route. This adds vertical but eliminates guesswork.

Safety notes: Summer climbers should remember that though this route is a "hike," parts do not use defined trails. Remember your map, altimeter, and compass. For the safest snow season climbing, do this route during the spring season. Remember that you are doing two summits, so get an extra early start to avoid the late morning thaw. Plan for an eastern exposure sunhit, so start any snow work several hours before sunrise.

3.3.3	**Grays Peak from Horseshoe Basin**	
Ratings:	Summer Climb—Intermediate	
Season:	Summer or Spring Snow	
RT Data:	Summer: 5 hours, 4½ miles, 3,170' ↑	
Start:	Summer: Horseshoe Basin Trailhead 11,100'	
1 Day from Rd:	Yes	
Map:	Grays Peak South, pg. 161	
Photo:	pg. 165	

Another less populated route because of a longer drive from the Denver area, this is a fine trip. It's short (and shorter still with 4-wheel-drive), and you won't see many people. The route is only recommended for summer because of the long approach when the Peru Creek Road is closed by snow. If that doesn't bother you, have at it in any season.

Summer after snow melt-off: Park at the Horseshoe Basin Trailhead. Hike up the jeep trail to its intersection with the Grays Lake drainage at 12,070'. Climb from the road NW for ¼ mile up to Grays Lake, a good place for a break. Swing W from the lake over easy ground to the east shoulder of Gray's south ridge. Take the summit via this ridge, and descend your ascent route.

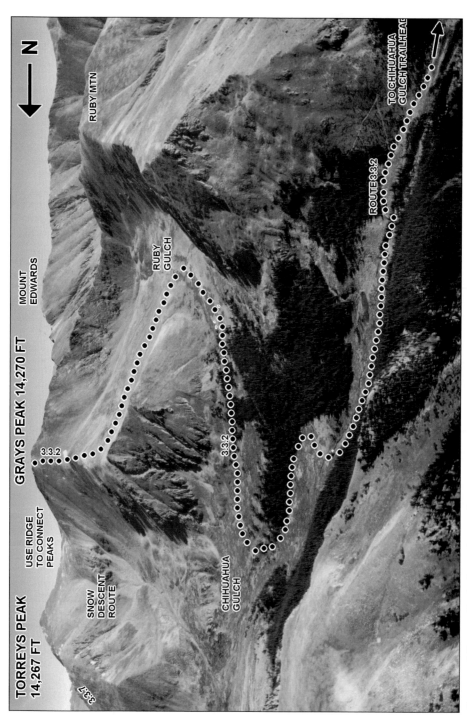

Grays and Torreys Peaks from the southwest, summer.

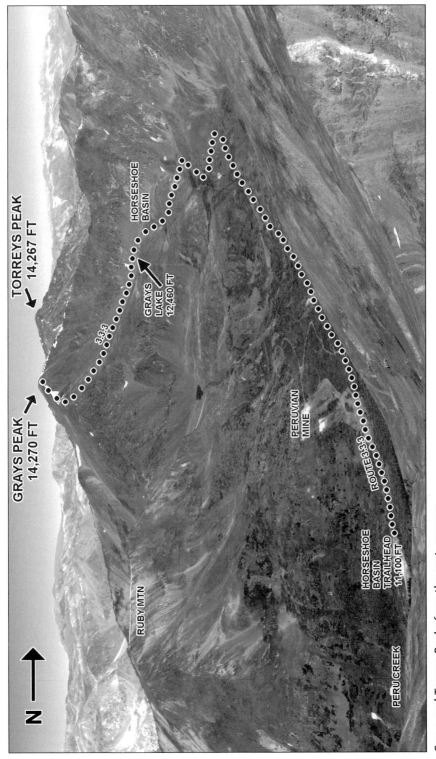

N

TORREYS PEAK
14,267 FT

GRAYS PEAK
14,270 FT

HORSESHOE
BASIN

GRAYS
LAKE
12,460 FT

3.3.3

RUBY MTN

PERUVIAN
MINE

ROUTE 3.3.3

HORSESHOE
BASIN
TRAILHEAD
11,100 FT

PERU CREEK

Grays and Torreys Peaks from the east, summer.

3.3.4	**Torreys Peak—Dead Dog Couloir from Stevens Gulch**	
Ratings:	Ski Descent—Extreme	Snow Climb—Advanced
Season:	Summer	Spring Snow
RT Data:	5½ hours, 6 miles, 3,037' ↑	8½ hours, 9½ miles, 4,067' ↑
Start:	Stevens Gulch Trailhead 11,230'	Stevens Gulch Road snow closure 10,200'
1 Day from Rd:	Yes	
Map:	Grays Peak North, pg. 160	
Photo:	pg. 167	

Spring or early summer snow season: Follow the Grays Peak Trail (see route 3.3.1) to 12,400' in the north basin between Grays and Torreys Peaks. Dead Dog Couloir is the deeply notched gully dropping from the right (N) side of the Torreys' summit. Climb W up the basin to the base of the couloir, then climb the couloir to the ridge crest just right (N) of the summit (maximum angle 45 degrees). Ski the gully if you have your Extreme card. If not follow Torreys' south ridge down to the Grays/Torreys saddle (13,707'), then glissade with care (or downclimb) to the basin.

Another ski descent or snow climb takes a directisima up Torreys' east face to the summit. This is rated Extreme as well and is harder than Dead Dog Couloir. Due to its unprotected eastern aspect, the snow is likely to be rotten and sparse.

Safety notes: Start early. And remember, "if you intend to ski it, climb it first." While the upper part of Dead Dog Couloir is shaded from early morning sun, much of the route gets hit at sunrise or shortly after. Start several hours before standard sunrise time.

3.3.5	**Torreys Peak—Northeast (Kelso) Ridge from Stevens Gulch**	
Ratings:	Summer Climb—Advanced	Ski Descent—Intermediate
	Snow Climb—Advanced	
Season:	Summer/Spring	
RT Data:	6 hours, 5½ miles, 3,037' ↑	
Start:	Stevens Gulch Trailhead 11,230'	
1 Day from Rd:	Yes	
Map:	Grays Peak North, pg. 160	
Photo:	pg. 167	

This classic ridge climb is a hand and foot scramble. Expert rock climbers may forego a rope, but many people belay several steep sections.

Summer after snow melt-off: Follow route (3.3.1) to 12,300' in the basin below the east face of Torreys Peak. Swing right (N) and climb about 100 vertical feet to the obvious Torreys/Kelso saddle. Now the fun begins.

From the saddle climb the ridge towards Torreys Peak. Stick to the ridge, with obvious variations and a few sections of trail. The crux is a steep section from 13,800' to the summit. Take this head-on for the classic challenge (you may need a rope). Stick to the ridge the remainder of the way to the summit and enjoy a section of knife ridge. Descend S from the summit to the Grays/Torreys saddle. Take a dropping traverse SE from the saddle to intersect the Grays Peak pack trail. Take the trail back to your car in Stevens Gulch.

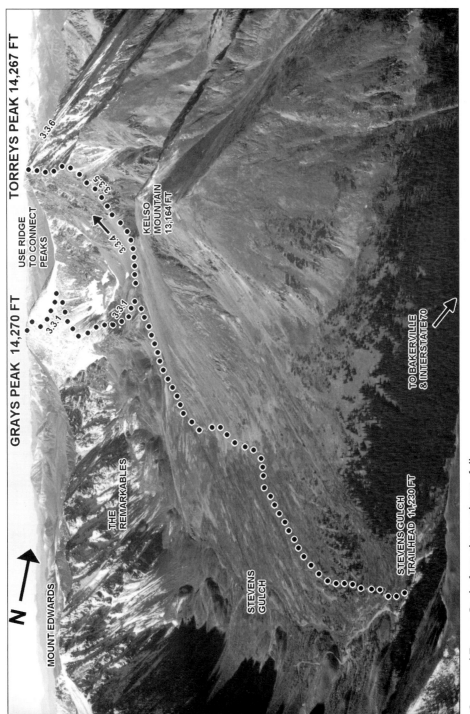

Grays and Torreys Peaks from the northeast, fall.

Spring snow season: Use the route above, get an early start, and bring your axe and crampons. Below the steep crux, you can traverse left into Dead Dog Couloir (3.3.4) and climb the couloir to regain the ridge just below the summit. For your descent, enjoy the glissade into Stevens Gulch from the Grays/Torreys saddle. Skis are useful for the approach but leave them in the basin. Having skis on your pack would be dangerous while scrambling up this steep ridge.

Winter: While this route has certainly had winter ascents, avalanche terrain and steep snow-covered rock make it a challenge.

Safety notes: Beware of rockfall from climbers above you. Carry and know how to use a rope and a small selection of hardware. Use standard sunrise for sunhit.

3.3.6	Torreys Peak Northwest Face from Grizzly Gulch	
Ratings:	Ski Descent—Advanced	Snow Climb—Intermediate
Season:	Summer	Spring Snow
RT Data:	7½ hours, 7 miles, 3,947' ↑	9 hours, 8 miles, 4,067' ↑
Start:	Grizzly Gulch Trailhead 10,320'	Stevens Gulch Road snow closure 10,200'
1 Day from Rd:	Yes	
Map:	Grays Peak North, pg. 160	
Photos:	pgs. 167, 169	

Spring snow season: Known to many skiers as the "Big-ol-strip-o-snow," this is one of the most beautiful ski runs in Colorado and makes a nice snow climb as well. It's a good route for aspiring extreme skiers, as it starts with a thrilling steep section. Park at snow closure on the Stevens Gulch Road and walk or ski to the Grizzly Gulch Road; take the Grizzly Gulch Road to the Grizzly Gulch Trailhead. Later in the spring you may be able to drive to the Grizzly Gulch Trailhead. Either way, ski or walk the Grizzly Gulch Road, depending on snow cover, up Grizzly Gulch to an avalanche path at 11,200'. From here follow an obvious couloir 3,067 vertical feet up the Northwest Face of Torreys Peak to the summit.

You have several choices for descent. The most direct line drops northwest after you descend W down the summit ridge for a short distance. In theory it's the route you climbed. If you found this couloir had sections without snow, descend the ridge west about 300 vertical feet and 1⁄8 mile to the top of a wider, lower-angled couloir. Ski this to the same point where you climbed out of Grizzly Gulch. Another alternative is to take route (3.3.2) into Chihuahua Gulch.

Safety Notes: This route follows a major avalanche path; therefore, it should only be climbed and skied at the most stable times—preferably on compacted spring snow. The route has a northwest aspect, so the snow will mature later in the season, usually in June but possibly late May. Sunhit is late as well. Since this route is close to being rated Extreme, skiers should be capable of "no falls" descents. While climbing Grizzly Gulch you might notice the deep-cut couloir that drops down the true north face. Though tempting, this line is hard to find from the summit and often has patchy snow. It is not recommended as a ski, but given good conditions it's an appealing snow climb.

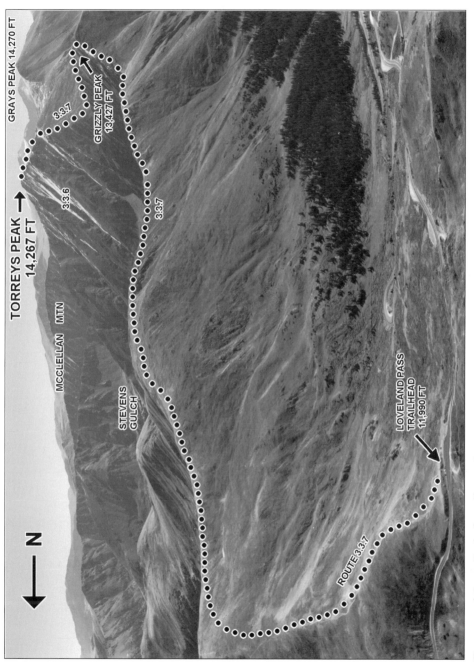

GRAYS PEAK 14,270 FT

GRIZZLY PEAK 13,427 FT

3.3.7

3.3.6

3.3.7

TORREYS PEAK 14,267 FT

MCCLELLAN MTN

STEVENS GULCH

LOVELAND PASS TRAILHEAD 11,990 FT

ROUTE 3.3.7

N

Torreys and Grays Peaks from the west, summer.

3.3.7	**Torreys Peak from Loveland Pass**	
Ratings:	Summer Climb—Advanced Ski Descent—Advanced	
	Snow Climb—Advanced	
Season:	Summer or Spring Snow	
RT Data:	11 hours, 8½ miles, 4,405' ↑	
Start:	Loveland Pass 11,990'	
1 Day from Rd:	Yes	
Map:	Grays Peak North, pg. 160	
Photo:	pg. 169	

Because of terrific all-season access to a high trailhead, this is one of the finest high tours in Colorado. Though long on miles, it's a technically easy summer trip. In spring, skiers will spend most of their day walking, but oh what a day! The route follows a high ridge that snakes over two 13,000 foot peaks with one or two fourteeners as your goal. Whatever the season, reversing this route is beyond most people's ken. Thus, the best strategy is to use two cars. Leave one on the Stevens Gulch Road (see Bakerville Trailhead) or at the Chihuahua Gulch Trailhead and use the other to reach Loveland Pass.

Summer after snow melt-off: Drive to the summit of Loveland Pass (11,990'). From parking, hike east up an obvious ridge ¼ mile towards a prominent bump. Save a little effort by traversing several hundred feet around the right (S) side of this bump, intersecting a saddle on the ridge S of the bump. Stick to the ridge as it swings S and leads you over a "thirteener," then on to the summit of Grizzly Peak, a worthy goal itself. Drop down the east ridge of Grizzly Peak to a major saddle (12,600'), then slug it out E up an obvious ridge 1,667 vertical feet to the summit of Torreys Peak.

Descend the south ridge of Torreys to the major saddle separating you from Grays Peak. To hit another fourteener, scramble 563 vertical feet S to the top of Grays Peak. Descend the Grays Peak Trail (starts on the northeast face of Grays, see route 3.3.1) to your car in Stevens Gulch. Early season climbers can glissade a good snow pitch from the Grays/Torreys saddle—but you'll wish you had something better than boots for carving turns!

Spring snow season: Use the summer route above. Don't hesitate to don skis at the top of Grizzly Peak and make a few turns to the saddle. If the climb from the saddle to Torreys looks too tough for tired legs, it's possible to ski from the saddle N into Grizzly Gulch or S into Chihuahua Gulch. In the former case, simply descend Grizzly Gulch to the Stevens Gulch Road. If you parked high you may have to walk back up the road to your car. In the case of Chihuahua, you'd hopefully have a car stashed on the Peru Creek Road (see Chihuahua Gulch Trailhead). Hitchhiking back to Loveland Pass is not recommended.

You have several options for ski routes off Grays and Torreys Peaks—your reward for that long ridge! A simple and safe option, since the snow will likely be thawed by the time you ski it, is to avoid steeper runs by descending the ridge to the saddle between Grays and Torreys, then skiing from the saddle into Stevens Gulch. For more options see the other routes in this section. For example, a good route would take the Torreys Peak ski descent into Chihuahua Gulch, then down to a car placed at the Peru Creek Trailhead. In this case, you'd ski firmer snow because of a later sunhit.

Safety notes: Whatever your season, your safety consideration with this route is its time consuming length. In summer, beware of lightning. During spring snow season, remember, your final descent routes are likely to be east facing and thawed by the time you hit them. Take care with cliff areas along the north side of the ridge. For sunhit, use standard sunrise because of the varied exposures.

SECTION 3.4
Mount Evans (14,264'), Mount Bierstadt (14,060')

Mount Evans and Mount Bierstadt are closely connected by a ridge, yet these are two very different peaks. Mount Evans is one of two fourteeners in Colorado that have improved roads to the summit, while Bierstadt is more of a classic arete, though it has a mellow route on the Guanella Pass side. Both peaks have excellent hikes/climbs and ski descents. Driving the Mount Evans road to a high starting point can be restful after a spring of hard climbing. After the road is open, you can make a casual ascent via bicycle, foot, roller skates—whatever! You can customize such ascents for your physical ability by picking your starting point. Mount Bierstadt is named after Albert Bierstadt, a famous painter of western landscapes. While both Mount Evans and Mount Bierstadt were probably first climbed by Indians or miners, Bierstadt made early ascents of both peaks. Pioneer Colorado climber Carl Blaurock and companions made a ski descent of Mount Bierstadt on New Year's Day, 1934.

Good alpine hiking is possible all over the east side of Mount Evans. Purists can choose where to park to make an "official" 3,000 vertical foot climb. If you're not that picky, a good compromise is to park near Summit Lake (12,830') and climb from there. A longer route with a bit more vertical gain takes the Northwest and West Ridges (3.4.3)—a pleasant alpine ramble from Summit Lake. For a longer climb, you can do the West Ridge from Guanella Pass (3.4.4).

The two peaks connect via a jagged arete known as the Sawtooth Ridge. While not a technical climb, "The Sawtooth" involves scrambling on ledges with plenty of abyss below you. Expert climbers on their "Grand Slam" quest can start from the summit of either peak and run The Sawtooth both directions (see routes 3.4.5, 3.4.10). This option is aesthetic and begets enough vertical for most people's summit claims. If the Sawtooth is too sharp for your taste, it takes about the same amount of work to climb Evans from Summit Lake, then drive around and climb Bierstadt from Guanella Pass.

ROADS AND TRAILHEADS

USGS Maps: Mt. Evans (winter: Harris Park, Idaho Springs)
USFS Forest Visitors Map: Arapaho National Forest

Mount Evans Road (State Highway 103)
The spectacular Mount Evans Road, the highest paved road in the United States, is closed in the winter. Around Memorial Day it opens to the alpine region of Summit Lake (12,830'), high enough to be useful for mountaineers. Soon after that it opens for the full 28 miles and 6,724 vertical feet to parking a few feet below the 14,264' summit of Mount Evans. To reach the Mount Evans Road, follow Interstate 70 to exit 240 on the west side of Idaho Springs. Turn off the interstate at the exit and follow the signs to the Mount Evans Highway. For information about road conditions call the Forest Service (see directory) or stop by the Forest Service headquarters at the start of the road, just after you turn off Interstate 70. Winter closure is at 10,900', 8 miles down the road from Summit Lake.

Summit Lake Trailhead
The Summit Lake Trailhead (12,830') is not signed, it's just a turnout at Summit Lake high on the Mount Evans Highway. To reach the trailhead, drive the Mount Evans Highway (Colorado Highway 103) 13 miles from Interstate Highway 70 to Echo Lake. Continue past Echo Lake to the intersection of Highway 103 with the Mount Evans Road. Head up the Mount Evans Road. At 23 miles from Interstate 70 you'll reach obvious Summit Lake nestled in the Summit Lake Bowl beneath Mount Evans' north face. Park at a picnic area on the north side of the Lake, or during the week park on the roadside near the lake outlet.

Epaulet Saddle Trailhead

For the Epaulet Saddle Trailhead, continue up the Mount Evans Road 2.2 miles from Summit Lake and park before a switchback (13,300').

Guanella Pass Road

Guanella Pass is open all year, and yields a bounty of skiing, winter climbing, and summer alpine hiking. Drive W from Denver (or E from Loveland Pass) on Interstate 70. Turn off at Georgetown. Follow a well-signed route through Georgetown to the Guanella Pass Road, which begins as paved switchbacks near the south end of town. The road soon becomes a dirt 2-wheel-drive road. It's 11 miles from Georgetown to Guanella Pass (11,669') and takes about a half hour to drive. Parking at the pass is obvious, either at the pass summit or slightly to the north of the true summit (11,650'). You can also get to the Guanella Pass road via a well-signed turnoff near the town of Grant, on Highway 285 between Denver and Fairplay.

Scott Gomer Creek Trailhead

For the Scott Gomer Creek Trailhead, drive the Guanella Pass Road 7.3 miles S from Guanella Pass or 12.3 miles from Grant to Burning Bear Campground (9,610').

3.4.1	Mount Evans—Northeast Ridge	
Ratings:	Summer Climb—Novice	Ski Descent—Novice
	Snow Climb—Novice	
Season:	Summer/Spring	Winter
RT Data:	3 hours, 2 miles, 1,434' ↑	overnight, 20 miles, 3,364' ↑
Start:	Summit Lake Trailhead 12,830'	Mount Evans Highway snow closure 10,900'
1 Day	Summer	Winter
from Rd:	Yes	No
Map:	Mount Evans North, pg. 175	

An easy hike, this is a popular and logical route for Mount Evans. Erosion will become a problem if it gains popularity. If this concerns you, climb the Northwest Ridge (3.4.3) instead. If you're out to climb every fourteener, either route will shorten your list in good fashion.

Summer, or spring snow season: Drive the Mount Evans Road to the Summit Lake Trailhead. Walk to the lake outlet and enjoy the alpine feel of the high cirque. Take a climbing traverse SE over patches of tundra and talus up the broad Northeast Ridge (more of a flank at this point). At about 13,000' swing SW (left) and wander ½ mile to the summit. If jarring descents are painful, beg a ride back down to your car.

Winter: Park at snow closure on the Mount Evans Highway. Ski or snowshoe to your base camp, then climb the summer route. If the summer route looks avalanche-prone, try heading SE on Summit Lake Flats, then climbing the general route of the road.

Safety notes: This is another short "easy" fourteener route—and one that catches many would-be climbers with their trousers around their ankles. Hitch your pants up and bring the proper gear, food, and water. Be aware of lightning danger and give yourself plenty of time. The average athlete should be able to do this in 2 hours or less, but don't underestimate the effect of altitude, and remember the time a human-powered descent will take. Subtract 1 hour from standard sunrise for sunhit.

3.4.2 Mount Evans—Summit Lake Bowl

Ratings:	Ski Descent—Advanced Snow Climb—Intermediate
Season:	Spring or Summer Snow
RT Data:	3 hours, 2 miles, 1,434' ↑
Start:	Summit Lake Trailhead 12,830'
1 Day from Rd:	Yes
Map:	Mount Evans North, pg. 175

Spring or summer snow seasons: Summit Lake Bowl yields fantastic snow climbs and thrilling ski descents. You can work with almost any exposure and level of difficulty. For an easy, fun day with lots of skiing, take two vehicles up the Mount Evans Road. Park one on the sharp curve (12,834') next to the Summit Lake outlet, then use car shuttles to the summit. Purists can park near Summit Lake and climb one of the Summit Lake couloirs to Mount Evans' summit.

Skiers and snowboarders often drive to the summit then hit the bowl. For the most most popular run, walk the rocky ridge west from the summit for several hundred yards to the first likely looking descent. This starts out narrow and steep, but widens into a swooping snowfield. For more adventure, continue along the ridge for ¼ mile and pick an east facing couloir. "Extremists" may want to hike farther and tackle the radical couloir that drops from the saddle near Mount Spalding. Whatever your choice, ski down to Summit Lake and follow the south shore to the road.

Intermediate and novice skiers can find good runs near the upper part of the road on the east face of the peak (not Summit Lake Bowl). Or just enjoy the lower-angled slopes around Summit Lake.

Safety Notes: Just because you can drive a car to the summit, don't forget the usual precautions. With snow cover, all the slopes in Summit Lake Bowl are exposed to avalanche danger. These are only safe with compacted spring snow. Don't ski past noon. Add one hour to standard sunrise for sunhit. Several inexperienced people have died on these snowfields. If you're descending from the summit, remember that you must walk W along the summit ridge to reach the safer couloir—dropping directly from the summit places you in a steep dangerous area.

3.4.3 Mount Evans—Northwest Ridge from Summit Lake

Ratings:	Summer Climb—Intermediate Snow Climb—Intermediate
Season:	Summer, or Spring Snow
RT Data:	6 hours, 5 miles, 1,918' ↑
Start:	Summit Lake Trailhead 12,830'
1 Day from Rd:	Yes
Map:	Mount Evans North, pg. 175

A classic ridge-run, use this as practice for the harder peaks.

Summer, or spring snow season: Park at the Summit Lake parking area near the outhouse. Walk N to the saddle near the north tip of the lake (12,876'). Head W up an easy ridge to the summit of Mount Spalding (13,842'). Drop S from Spalding to a saddle, then amble up Mt Evans' rocky northwest ridge for a "mile-in-the-sky" to the summit. For the most solitude descend your ascent route. For a nice loop, descend the Northeast Ridge (3.4.1) down to the Summit Lake outlet. If you do so, take care as you descend not to wander into a cliff area to your left (N).

Safety notes: The last mile of ridge can take longer than you expect. Use standard sunrise for sunhit.

3.4.4	**Mount Evans West Ridge from Guanella Pass**	
Ratings:	Summer Climb—Intermediate Ski Descent—Intermediate	
	Snow Climb—Novice	
Season:	Summer/Spring	Winter
RT Data:	8 hours, 10 miles, 3,150' ↑	9½ hours, 10 miles, 3,150' ↑
Start:	Guanella Pass Trailhead 11,650'	
1 Day from Rd:	Yes	
Map:	Mount Evans North, pg. 175	
Photo:	pg. 177	

One thing about Mount Evans in the summer: you'll see people almost everywhere! This route from Guanella Pass avoids the crowds of "gasoline climbers" on the east side of the mountain. It's long on miles but involves less elevation than most fourteener climbs. It's a fine choice in any season and is most always stripped of snow by the winds.

Summer after snow melt-off: Drive to Guanella Pass (section introduction), leave your car, and strike E towards the drainage that splits the southwest slope of Gray Wolf Mountain; this is the upper part of Scott Gomer Creek. Climb the slopes to the left (N) of Scott Gomer Creek to about 12,600' elevation. Begin a long (about 1½ mile) climbing traverse S to the saddle between the Sawtooth Ride and Mount Evans. Climb E from the saddle to Evans' northwest ridge, then follow the ridge to the summit. Descend your ascent route.

Winter: Follow the summer route described above—it's also the standard winter route for Mount Evans. It is long, tedious, windscoured, and has been termed everything from boring to death defying—depending on the weather. The route involves a great amount of high altitude mileage and could be hard to safely descend in low visibility due to the cliffs below Mt. Spalding. Depending on snow cover, it can be better for avalanche safety to gain Evans' northwest ridge sooner via a more direct line up Mount Spalding.

Safety notes: While rated Novice as a summer route, this is one of the harder of such routes due to its length and lack of a defined trail or ridge for navigation. In winter, this side of Mount Evans is usually windscoured; if so you'll only encounter isolated pockets of slide danger. You can avoid all these with studious route finding. Be careful of gullies dropping from the northwest ridge into Summit and Abyss Lakes. Be prepared for high winds. Use a sunhit for west facing terrain.

3.4.5	**Mount Evans from Mount Bierstadt via Sawtooth Ridge**
Ratings:	Summer Climb—Advanced
Season:	Summer
RT Data:	11 hours, 12 miles, 2,714' ↑
Start:	Guanella Pass Trailhead 11,650'
1 Day from Rd:	Yes
Map:	Mount Evans North, pg. 175
Photo:	pg. 177

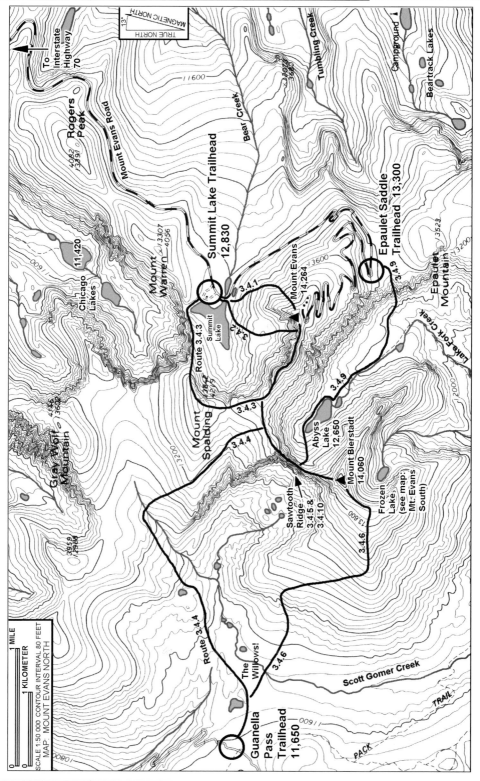

This exciting route loops over the famous Sawtooth Ridge to Mount Evans. While not a technical climb, the ridge involves plenty of scrambling.

Summer after melt-off: Park at the Guanella Pass Trailhead, and climb Mount Bierstadt via its West Flank (3.4.6). Drop down the north summit ridge to the saddle below the Sawtooth. Don't worry, the ridge ahead looks harder than it really is. Dance with several small pinnacles to another, smaller saddle, continue on the east side of the ridge for a few hundred feet, then climb to the ridge crest. The key here is to switch and work ledges on the the west side of the ridge. These ledges lead up to the low-angled slopes of Mount Evans.

With the Sawtooth behind you, hike ½ mile E along a saddle to Evans' West Ridge. Take the ridge to the summit, and drop back to Guanella Pass via Evans' West Ridge (3.4.4).

Safety notes: Though this is not a technical climb, carry a light-weight rope and small amount of hardware in case you get into trouble. You should be comfortable with steep rock and exposure. If you find yourself on steep rock which requires roped climbing, you are off route and should backtrack. Allow plenty of time. This route is much harder with snow or wet.

3.4.6	**Mount Bierstadt West Flank from Guanella Pass**	
Ratings:	Summer Climb—Novice Ski Descent—Intermediate	
	Snow Climb—Novice	
Season:	Summer/Spring	Winter
RT Time:	4 hours, 4½ miles, 2,410' ↑	6 hours, 4½ miles, 2,410' ↑
Start:	Guanella Pass Trailhead 11,650'	
1 Day from Rd:	Yes	
Map:	Mount Evans North, pg. 175	
Photo:	pg. 177	

Looking for your first fourteener? This "bagger's" route up Mount Bierstadt is one of the best. Also, during spring snow season it's a marvelous ski tour or beginner snow climb. Novice winter climbers will also enjoy it, while expert winter mountaineers can use it as an early winter shakedown.

Summer after snow melt-off: Park at Guanella Pass (section introduction), and head SE across "Guanella Flats." A trail of sorts threads through gradually thickening willows, which become a grunt near Scott Gomer Creek. Persevere (start with long pants) and cross Scott Gomer Creek. Once across the creek, the climb steepens to an obvious headwall at the 11,800' level. Take the headwall via a climbing traverse to the left, then angle southeast again across a broad low-angled shoulder, which gradually steepens and leads you to the southwest summit ridge. Follow the ridge to the summit and descend your ascent route.

Spring snow season: Use the summer route above, with slight variations for better snow cover. With a full winter's snowpack, the notorious willow thickets will not be a problem. Take care not to punch a leg into snow-covered boulders on the southwest summit ridge. Descend your ascent route. Though skiing from the summit may be sparse, it's likely that you'll have a terrific ski descent from the summit ridge to the "Guanella Flats" (which are longer on your return than they appear). As an alternative, expert level skiers can ski into Bierstadt's north bowl via several interesting gullies that start at the 13,000' level.

Winter: Use the summer and spring routes above.

Safety notes: If you're tackling your first "teener," don't let the "hike" nature of this climb lull you into false security. You need proper clothing, and you must time your ascent to avoid afternoon electrical storms. Winter climbers should note that, though this is one of the safer and easier winter fourteener climbs, it still should only be done when the general slide hazard is rated as low above timberline. Take care with small slopes on the lower headwall and with cornices on the summit ridge (remember that many deaths occur when people are

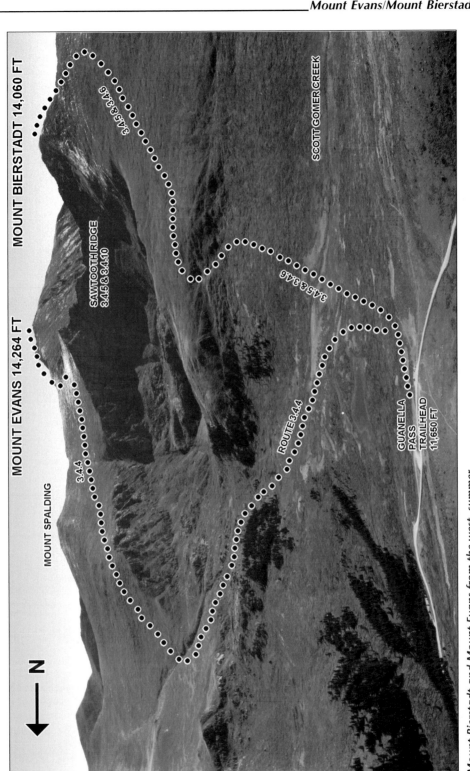

MOUNT BIERSTADT 14,060 FT

MOUNT EVANS 14,264 FT

SCOTT GOMER CREEK

SAWTOOTH RIDGE
3.4.5 & 3.4.10

3.4.5 & 3.4.6

3.4.5 & 3.4.6

MOUNT SPALDING

3.4.4

ROUTE 3.4.4

GUANELLA
PASS
TRAILHEAD
11,650 FT

N

Mount Bierstadt and Mount Evans from the west, summer.

caught in small avalanches on slopes they deemed innocuous). Since you're not following a ridge on the lower part of the route, navigation is hard in poor visibility. Carry your map, compass, and altimeter, and be familiar with their use! Add three hours to standard sunrise for sunhit.

3.4.7	**Mount Bierstadt Snow Route from Frozen Lake**	
Ratings:	Ski Descent—Advanced	Snow Climb—Advanced
Season:	Spring Snow	
RT Data:	overnight, 14½ miles, 4,450' ↑	
Start:	Scott Gomer Creek Trailhead 9,610'	
1 Day from Rd:	No	
Map:	Mount Evans South, pg. 180	

The tiny cirque around Frozen Lake yields a bounty of skiing and snow climbing. You'll have to slog a long backpack approach—but that gives you solitude.

Spring snow season: Park at the Scott Gomer Creek Trailhead. Backpack up the Scott Gomer Creek Trail 3/4 miles to a major fork at 10,400'. Continue NE on the Abyss Lake Trail about a mile to camp near timberline. From your high camp, continue up the Abyss Trail to 11,800', just to the east of a small lake. Leave the trail and cut W to the lake (11,730'). From the lake head W to the Frozen Lake drainage, then follow the general route of the drainage to Frozen Lake (12,950'). Climb N from Frozen Lake to Bierstadt's summit (several lines are possible). Descend your ascent route.

The Frozen Lake drainage leads through a steep rocky area just below Frozen Lake. With sparse snowcover, you might find a better route by leaving the drainage at 12,100', then climbing a direct line to Frozen Lake.

Safety notes: While the skiing and snow climbing in the Frozen Lake cirque gets a late sunhit (sunrise plus 3 hours), portions of the lower route are threatened by east facing snow slopes. Start early. Portions of this route are steep (at or just over 45 degrees). Beware of cliff bands below Frozen Lake.

3.4.8	**Mount Bierstadt from Abyss Lake**	
Ratings:	Summer Climb—Advanced	Snow Climb—Advanced
Season:	Summer	Late Spring Snow
RT Data:	14 hours, 16½ miles, 4,450' ↑	overnight, 16½ miles, 4,450' ↑
Start:	Scott Gomer Creek Trailhead 9,610'	
1 Day from Rd:	Summer	Spring
	Yes	No
Map:	Mount Evans South, pg. 180	

This is the wilderness route for Mount Bierstadt. Casual climbers should backpack to a high camp, perhaps at Abyss Lake, or near timberline. Experienced animals can run the whole route in one day. You can do the upper part of this route from the Mount Evans Highway. If this option becomes popular, crowds on the upper route might negate any solitude you expect from the long approach.

Summer after snow melt-off: Park at the Scott Gomer Creek Trailhead. Hike the Abyss Lake Trail to Abyss Lake. From the northwest tip of the Lake, climb W up rocky slopes to the

Sawtooth Saddle (13,360'). From the saddle, take Bierstadt's north ridge to the summit. Descend your ascent route. If you're on a one day ascent, consider descending (route 3.4.6) to Guanella Pass, where you'd have a vehicle stashed for your return down the road to the Scott Gomer Creek Trailhead.

Spring snow season: Use the summer route above. Snow climbers should consider using a high camp.

Safety notes: While this route has no hand-and-foot climbing, it's length and nearby cliffs dictate an Advanced rating. Use standard sunrise for sunhit.

3.4.9	**Mount Bierstadt from Mount Evans via Abyss Lake**		
Ratings:	Summer Climb—Intermediate		Ski Descent—Advanced
	Snow Climb—Intermediate		
Season:	Summer or Late Spring Snow		
RT Data:	7 hours, 6 miles, 2,760' ↑		
Start:	Epaulet Saddle Trailhead, 13,300'		
1 Day from Rd:	Yes		
Map:	Mount Evans North, pg. 175		

Many Europeans enjoy this sort of alpine ramble. You never drop below timberline, the views are outstanding, and the terrain varies from alpine tundra to a satisfying summit ridge.

Summer after snow melt-off: Drive the Mount Evans Highway to the Epaulet Saddle Trailhead at 13,300', just to the N of the broad saddle between Mount Evans and Epaulet Mountain. From parking at the switchback, walk S down to the saddle. Drop W off the saddle down a scree-filled couloir that leads into the Abyss Lake drainage. Contour NW through the drainage and intersect the Abyss Lake Trail at about 12,320'. Hike the trail up to Abyss Lake (12,650'). From the lake, follow route (3.4.8) to the summit of Mount Bierstadt. Descend your ascent route. As an alternative descent, perhaps the best way to finish this route is to descend Mount Bierstadt to Guanella Pass (3.4.6). Have a friend pick you up there. This latter option avoids ascending the scree back to the Evans/Epaulet saddle.

Late spring snow season: After the Mount Evans Highway opens, use the summer route described above. Consider skiing. With good conditions, you could ski from the Evans/Epaulet saddle into the Abyss Lake drainage, climb Bierstadt, then ski the grand west flank of Bierstadt down to your car. Such a trip would be a memorable "raid blanc."

Safety notes: Road access is good for this route, but don't let that lull you into a late start. The Evans/Epaulet saddle is a good place for lightning strikes. Use standard sunrise for sunhit. Carry an ice axe during all but late summer season.

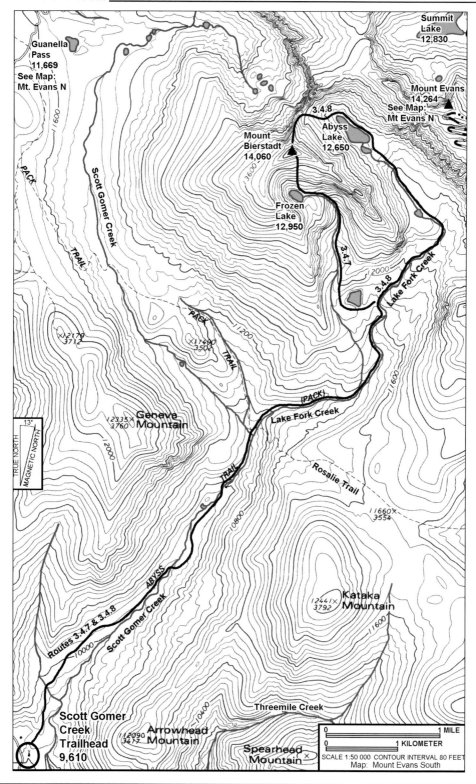

3.4.10 Mount Bierstadt from Mount Evans via Sawtooth Ridge

Ratings:	Summer Climb—Advanced
Season:	Summer
RT Data:	6 hours, 4 miles, 1,730' ↑
Start:	Mount Evans summit parking 14,230'
1 Day from Rd:	Yes
Map:	Mount Evans North, pg. 175
Photo:	pg. 177

For another alpine tour of Bierstadt, but one with more technical challenge, climb the peak from Mount Evans via the Sawtooth Ridge. You can cut-and-paste several versions of this route. The simplest, but technically hardest option, is to park at the summit of Mount Evans, traverse the Sawtooth Ridge to Mount Bierstadt, then reverse the Sawtooth Ridge. After this effort, even though you parked at the Mount Evans summit, you'll probably feel good about checking both peaks off your list—that ridge is a lot of work! If doing the "Tooth" both ways is too much, have a friend drop you off at Mount Evans, then pick you up at Guanella Pass after you descend Bierstadt's west flank. Another option is to climb Bierstadt via the Abyss Lake route (3.4.9), then return to Evans via the Sawtooth (3.4.5).

Summer after snow melt-off: Since climbing the Sawtooth to Mount Evans is described in route 3.4.5, this description will describe it as if climbed from Mount Evans.

Park at the summit of Mount Evans or climb Mount Evans from lower down. Hike down Evans' west ridge ¼ mile to 13,800'. Swing SW across a saddle to the start of the Sawtooth Ridge. Continue along the crest of the Sawtooth to an improbable drop. Take a ledge system down W, then follow ledges along the W side of the ridge. When the going gets improbable again, switch to the east side of the ridge and continue to a small saddle before several gendarmes. Turn the gendarmes on the east side to reach the Bierstadt/Sawtooth saddle (13,360'). Take Bierstadt's easy north ridge 700 vertical feet to the summit. Continue via any of the options mentioned above. If you choose to descend to Guanella Pass, the total route only involves 780 feet of gain.

Safety notes: While this route is short on miles and elevation gain, allow plenty of time for safe, methodical movement on The Sawtooth. For emergencies, carry a lightweight rope and light selection of rock hardware.

SECTION 3.5
Longs Peak (14,255')

When you visit Estes Park, the gateway town for Rocky Mountain National Park, you'll lock your eyeballs on the astounding monolith of Longs Peak rising to the southwest. The east face of Longs Peak, known as The Diamond, has long been a focal point for big wall climbing in Colorado. Contrary to its appearance, Longs Peak also has a fine "walk-up" route via The Keyhole (3.5.4), and several outstanding mountaineering routes that involve easy roped climbing. Many fine technical routes take the peak via The Diamond. Those routes are beyond the scope of this book.

While popular in the summer, the Keyhole Route holds little interest for snow climbers or skiers. Wind is Longs Peak's trademark, and most snow gets blown off the peak. Yet occasional spring seasons with heavy snow and less wind lard the Keyhole Route with enough snow for an enjoyable snow climb, and the North Face may have enough snow accumulation for a true summit ski descent. A complete ski descent from summit to parking lot has only been done several times and is a notable achievement. Skiing from Chasm View, however, is highly recommended. Most likely, you'll find the best skiing and snow climbing in the Trough Couloir and below (3.5.1). Pioneer mountaineer Enos Mills did a great deal of skiing on Longs Peak in the first decade of the 1900s, but it's doubtful that he skied from the summit due to the technical nature of the descent. For mixed snow (or ice) and rock, try Kieners Route.

Longs Peak is located in Rocky Mountain National Park, and climbers must conform to the Park's rules. At present, no registration is required for one-day adventures, but all camping and bivouacing in the Park requires registration. If you plan an overnight, it's best to call the Park well in advance and make reservations (see directory). During the peak tourist season (July and August), Estes Park and Rocky Mountain National Park are crowded. If your goal is a peaceful alpine holiday, visiting this area during tourist season may yield the opposite experience.

ROADS AND TRAILHEADS:

USGS Maps: Longs Peak, McHenrys Peak, Isolation Peak, Allens Park
USFS Forest Visitors Map: Roosevelt NF

Longs Peak Ranger Station Trailhead

Drive U.S. Highway 34 or 36 to the town of Estes Park. From the town's main street, drive S on Colorado Highway 7 for 8½ miles to the well-signed Longs Peak Campground Road. Follow the signs for one mile up the Campground Road to the Longs Peak Ranger Station and parking lot (9,410'). Parking is no problem. If you start early put a note on your vehicle explaining your purpose—parking at 2:00 AM could make the Rangers think you're camping with no permit.

Glacier Gorge Trailhead

Drive U.S. highway 34 or 36 to the town of Estes Park. Drive through Estes Park to the Beaver Meadows entrance to Rocky Mountain National Park. Once through the entrance, drive a few hundred yards and turn left on to the Bear Lake/Glacier Gorge Road (good signs). At 8.5 miles from the turnoff, park in an obvious parking area (9,300') enclosed by a hairpin turn. The trailhead is well signed but parking may be scarce, especially on weekends. If the Park is crowded, park at one of the shuttle bus stations lower on the road and take the bus to the trailhead.

3.5.1	**Longs Peak—Kieners Route**	
Ratings:	Summer Climb—Advanced	Snow Climb—Advanced
	Technical Rock Climb—5.2	
Season:	Summer or Spring Snow	
RT Data:	14 hours, 12½ miles, 4,845' ↑	
Start:	Summer: Longs Peak Ranger Station 9,410'	
1 Day from Rd:	Yes	
Map:	Longs Peak, pg. 185	
Photo:	pg. 187	

You want a more technical route for Longs Peak, but one that the "average" rock climber can handle? Consider Kieners Route.

Summer, or spring snow season: Park at the Longs Peak Ranger Station. Hike the beaten Longs Peak Trail 4½ miles to a low-angled area below Chasm Lake, then hike steep terrain W up a less established but obvious trail to Chasm Lake.

From Chasm Lake, your first goal is the Lambs Slide Couloir (known in short as Lambs Slide), a hidden snowfilled slot dropping from Long's southeast ridge into the basin above Chasm Lake. Glance at your map for clarification. To reach Lambs Slide hike around the north side of Chasm Lake, then climb 400 vertical feet SW to Mills Glacier, the permanent snowfield in the basin above the lake. As you climb trend to the left (S) and spot Lambs Slide Couloir, which becomes obvious once you near the upper reaches of the basin.

Climb Lambs Slide to its intersection with the Broadway Ledges at 13,000'. Exit right from the Lambs Slide Couloir onto the Broadway Ledges. Continue climbing a short distance to the higher ledges, then traverse right along the ledges (they quickly narrow) for a short distance to the Notch Couloir. One dicy move around a boulder is the crux of the traverse.

Cross the Notch Couloir with a climbing traverse, then leave the couloir and climb several easy 5th class rock pitches to easier ground. Climb west for several hundred feet to a headwall. Don't climb the headwall. Instead take an easy, but obscure, traverse right to an airy perch with a view of the famous Diamond Face. Flirt with the face, and after your heart descends to its proper location, climb easy ground to the summit. Descend the Keyhole Route or Cable Route (the latter can be rappelled in several short pitches with a doubled 150' rope).

Skilled mountain skiers enjoy the Lambs Slide Couloir and Chasm Lake Basin. The couloir already has a name, so don't slide like Lamb!

Safety notes: Be prepared for steep snow or ice climbing, as well as technical rock climbing. Lambs Slide can be quite a nice ice climb, altough the crux changes with season and conditions. It's wise for climbers attempting this route to know the descent routes—preferably by having climbed them. Many parts of this route are relatively easy, but a stumble could send you to your death. Use your rope.

3.5.2	**Longs Peak—Notch Couloir**	
	Ratings:	All Seasons—Advanced (Possible Technical Ice and Rock Climb)
		Technical Rock and Ice Climb—5.6
	Season:	Summer, or Spring Snow
	RT Data:	13 hours, 12 miles, 4,845' ↑
	Start:	Longs Peak Ranger Station 9,410'
	1 Day from Rd:	Yes
	Map:	Longs Peak, pg. 185
	Photo:	pg. 187

Spring or summer snow season, or fall ice season: Long famed as a terrific snow or ice climb, in recent history this lovely couloir had the kiss of skis. But it ends at a cliff below the Broadway Ledges—enough said. During some early summer seasons, after heavy winters, climbers on this route can plant their crampon points into real alpine ice—good practice for other parts of the world.

In a sense, this is a variation of the Kieners Route, but snow and ice climbers might say that the Notch Couloir is the route and Kieners the variation. Go figure, but go climb!

The route is simple. Follow Kieners Route (3.5.1) up Lambs Slide and along the Broadway Ledges to the Notch Couloir. Climb the Notch Couloir (snow or ice) to its terminus

Winter conditions, Longs Peak North Face.

at the notch. Climb a 5.6 pitch towards the summit out of the notch, then follow the ridge to the summit. For experienced climbers in good weather, this short section of ridge is easy ground. With snow or inexperience, however, it becomes a complex wander up the ridge through steep sections mixed with easy ground. Persevere and you'll get there. Descend the Keyhole Route (3.5.4) or Cable Route (3.5.3) (the latter can be rappelled with a doubled 150' rope).

   Safety notes: You must be familiar with mixed snow, ice, and rock climbing for this route. It's best to climb the Notch Couloir when it is completely filled with compacted snow or ice. To determine the couloir's condition, check with other climbers or the Rocky Mountain National Park rangers. Use standard sunrise to time your sunhit estimate, but remember that true sunrise will occur earlier than standard because of the lower horizon on the eastern plains.

3.5.3	Longs Peak—North Face Cable Route		
Ratings:	Summer Climb—Advanced		Ski Descent—Extreme
		Snow Climb—Advanced	
Season:	Summer, or Spring Snow		
RT Data:	12 hours, 12½ miles, 4,845' ↑		
Start:	Longs Peak Ranger Station 9,410'		
1 Day from Rd:	Yes		
Map:	Longs Peak, pg. 185		
Photos:	pgs. 187, 188, 190		

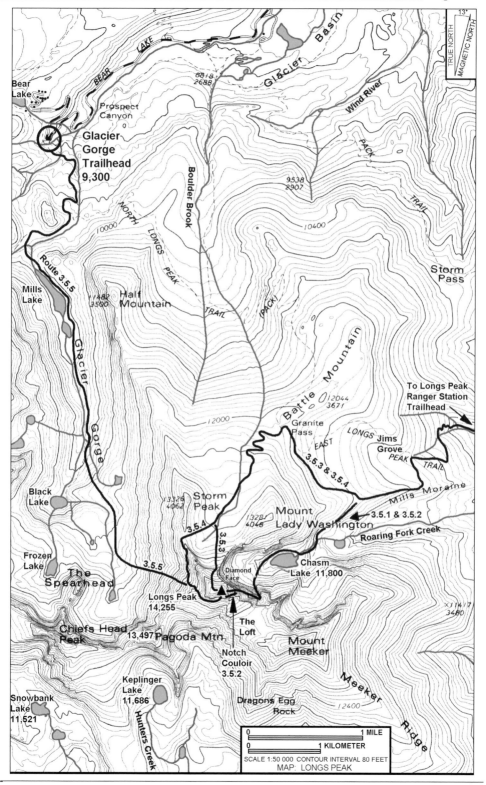

SCALE 1:50 000 CONTOUR INTERVAL 80 FEET
MAP: LONGS PEAK

The North Face of Longs Peak is a short wall of relatively solid granite that yields enjoyable and safe rock climbing. The face has an average angle of approximately 45 degrees, so on years when the snow sticks it serves as a summit ski route. Back in the 1920s, steel cable hand lines were set on the route, and hoards of people used the cables for a "tourist route" to the top. You can imagine what would have happened if lightning had struck during a crowded climb. The steel was later removed, and since then the standard route up the North Face has been called the "Cable Route." You can use the cable anchors as rappel anchors (but back them up—no rappel should ever rely on one anchor).

Summer after snow melt-off: The Cable Route is simple. Park at the Longs Peak Ranger Station (section introduction) and slog up the well beaten Longs Peak Trail to The Boulder Field; the vast rocky bowl at the 12,600' level below Longs Peak's north face.

Climb up to the flats at the head of The Boulder Field (below Long's broad north face). Head left (E), and avoid the steeper, wall-like portion of the face by hiking to the prominent notch in the ridge leading to the left (E) side of the face (13,490'). This is known as Chasm View, as it's your first good look down into the Chasm Lake amphitheater.

From Chasm View, climb the rock slabs above to the west. Several eyebolts from the old cables make good belay anchors. Back these up with a few nuts or slings. About 300 feet of roped climbing brings you to lower-angled slabs. Several obvious "paths of least resistance" take you to the summit. Though this route has no difficult rock climbing (it's rated at about 5.6), falls over the huge East Face are possible, so it's smart to use a rope on the steeper sections. For your descent, use the Keyhole Route (3.5.4) or do several short rappels on the cable anchors.

Spring snow season: Use the route above. Keep your map handy and begin careful navigation below timberline. It's easy to lose the snowcovered trail in the dark timber. The section from timberline up to the Boulder Field is straightforward but can be confusing in the dark. For a ski descent, start in one of several couloirs that drop from the ridge a few hundred feet N of the true summit. These are reasonable, but a fall will send you over the Diamond Face to certain death. This warning also holds for the lower-angled slabs. The skiing steepens as you get lower, with a final crux involving one rappel or several hops off small ledges. On good snow years the whole route can be one continuous snow pitch, but this is rare.

Winter climbing: This route above Chasm View is so steep and windscoured that slide danger is often minimal or totally absent. But roped climbing in arctic conditions requires a great deal of skill. You'll need astute avalanche hazard evaluation and avoidance on the slopes leading to Chasm View.

Safety notes: Other than the inherent dangers in roped climbing, be aware that rockfall is possible here. Consider a weekday for your outing, as fewer people will be climbing above you. Helmets are de rigueur. Remember the time that even a few rope pitches can add to a climb and factor such delays into your start time. During the winter or spring snow seasons, take care on the cornice at Chasm View. This is really a northeast face and gets sun from the

3.5.4	**Longs Peak—Keyhole Route**		
Ratings:	Summer Climb—Intermediate Snow Climb—Advanced		
Season:	Summer	Spring	Winter
RT Data:	10 hours, 16 miles, 4,845' ↑	13 hours, 16 miles, 4,845' ↑	overnight, 4,845' ↑
Start:	Longs Peak Ranger Station 9,410'		
1 Day from Rd:	Summer Yes	Spring Yes	Winter No
Map:	Longs Peak, pg. 185		
Photo:	pg. 190		

LONGS PEAK 14,255 FT

BOULDER FIELD

MOUNT LADY WASHINGTON

NORTH FACE 3.5.3

THE DIAMOND FACE

THE NOTCH

3.5.1

MILLS GLACIER

NOTCH COULOIR 3.5.2

LAMBS SLIDE

CHASM LAKE 11,800

ROUTES 3.5.1 & 3.5.2

TO LONGS PEAK RANGER STATION

THE LOFT

PEACOCK POOL

MOUNT MEEKER

N

Longs Peak from the east, summer.

eastern plains before standard sunrise.

This is the most popular line up Longs and could be called a hiking route without snow cover, although a stumble in several places could send you over cliffs. But be warned: With a coating of snow, the Keyhole route requires crampons, ice axe, and knowledge of snow craft. As a snow route it is stimulating and enjoyable for those seeking out the better snow climbs on the fourteeners. One couloir on the route, called the Trough (route 3.5.5), is skied quite often. But the Keyhole route has never been used as a summit ski descent, as the rock ledges and traverses eliminate any continuous line.

Summer after snow melt-off: Park at the Longs Peak Ranger Station (section introduction) and hike a hard 3,190 vertical feet up the Longs Peak Trail to The Boulder Field; the vast bowl at the 12,600' below the north face. When dry, this trail is a veritable interstate highway.

Climb N then W up through the Boulder Field to the Keyhole, an obvious keyhole-shaped notch at 13,160' on Longs' northwest ridge. Once through the Keyhole follow a climbing traverse S to the Trough Couloir. Climb the Trough to its top, then traverse E on the Narrow Ledges to the upper part of wide shallow couloir on the S side of the summit. This area is known as "The Homestretch". Climb the Homestretch to the summit.

Spring snow season: Use the summer route. Navigation can be tricky in the vast terrain around Jims Grove. Keep your map handy and begin careful navigation below timberline.

Winter: Whatever your route, you can be proud if you make Longs Peak in the winter. The peak is known for high winds and cold temperatures, and it certainly is far enough from the trailheads. Countless parties even fail to breach timberline due to severe winter conditions. In short, prepare for extreme arctic conditions.

All but the strongest climbers should consider a night out for a winter ascent of the Keyhole Route. If you set a high winter camp, prepare for wind with snowblock walls or dig a snow cave. Remember that snow for such projects may be scarce above timberline. Take care with avalanche danger in the Trough Couloir, and lower down on the steeper slopes above

Longs Peak from the Boulder Field, early summer.

Jims Grove. Use standard sunrise time for sunhit.

Safety notes: It is possible to take a nasty fall in the Trough Couloir. Also, since much of this route passes above cliffs, be careful on patches of snow that could break free and carry you down. Perhaps more often than any mountain in Colorado, Longs Peak picks up a coating of ice (verglas) during storms. This can change easy routes like the Narrows Ledges into treacherous passages. Avoid verglas as you do other summer storm hazards: get your climb done early. While snow or ice climbing on this route, beware of patches that could break away with your weight and launch you over cliff bands. If in doubt, get out your rope.

3.5.5	**Longs Peak—Trough Couloir**	
Ratings:	Ski Descent—Advanced	Snow Climb—Advanced
Season:	Spring or Summer Snow	
RT Data:	12 hours, 10½ miles, 4,955' ↑	
Start:	Glacier Gorge Trailhead 9,300'	
1 Day from Rd:	Yes, with broken trail or consolidated spring snow	
Map:	Longs Peak, pg. 185	
Photo:	pg. 190	

To the dismay of many climbers, when winter ends Longs Peak's eastern routes are mobbed. To avoid crowds snow climbers and skiers should consider the Trough Couloir route. This classic cut drops from just below the Longs Peak summit into a pristine alpine bowl. The route is possible as a day trip—albeit with 5,000 vertical feet of climbing. The keys during spring season are to use skis for approach and descent, and to catch a solid spring snow pack. Once the lower trail is melted out, it's probably best to camp at snow line.

Spring of summer snow season: Drive to the Glacier Gorge Trailhead (section introduction). If the trail is melted off, stick with it to snow line, then follow the right (E) side of Glacier Creek to timberline at the east edge of Black Lake. Swing left (E) here to avoid the headwall above Black Lake. At 11,000' turn right (S) and climb the Green Lake drain ½ mile to 11,400'. (Skier's who don't plan on skiing the couloir should leave their boards here). Take time here to examine the west face of Longs Peak. The Trough Couloir is the most conspicuous gully; it leads up then leans right to 13,600' on Long's southwest ridge. Put on your crampons, grab your ice axe, and climb the Trough. From the head of the trough (if you brought them, leave your skis here) traverse rock slabs on the Keyhole Route about ⅛ mile E across the south face of the Longs Peak summit cap, then climb left (N) to the summit. This latter section is often windscoured and dry, but may require crampon work.

Note: If you're on snow as soon as you leave the trailhead, use the "Skier's Short Cut" for a more direct start to the Glacier Gorge trail. To do so, head up the main trail several hundred yards. Just past the second bridge, turn right off the trail and ski directly up the drainage. Intersect the main trail in timber at 9,800'.

Safety notes: Because of rockfall from people on the popular Keyhole Route above the couloir, it's best to climb the Trough Couloir on a weekday. This entire route is exposed to many avalanche paths. Though an early spring might give you stable snow at low elevations, you could still encounter winter avalanche conditions above timberline. You may need to do hand-and-foot climbing on the rock slabs above the couloir, with dangerous fall potential. It's prudent to carry a rope and perhaps set a few belays. This route faces northwest and west, and thus gets a late sunhit several hours after sunrise.

You get a good view of Longs Peak from Highway 34, summer.

4

ELK
MOUNTAINS

Early spring snow on Capitol Peak's Knife Ridge.

USFS Forest Visitors Map: White River National Forest

Marked by sinuous aretes, towering monoliths, and steep technical north faces, Elk Mountains' fourteeners stand as classic peaks. Combine this with the Elks' good access, and you have a popular mountain playground.

If you're used to climbing on the solid granite of ranges such as Wyoming's Wind Rivers or California's Sierras, the loose rock of the perilous "slag heap" Elks will surprise you—even scare you. If you're uncomfortable with loose rock, stick to the trade routes that have had much rubble knocked away over the years. Better still, climb the Elk Range peaks during the spring snow season, when the slag is covered by a blanket of white. During spring you can explore the hundreds of steep snow-climbs, ski routes, and mixed snow and rock climbs that attract climbers to the Elks year after year.

The easiest access for the Elk Range fourteeners is from the north (Aspen & Glenwood Springs) side. If you're willing to make longer trips, you can use several backpack and 4-wheel-drive approaches from the south and west. While all the trailhead roads are open to varying degrees during the snow season, several are closed with gates until the powers-that-be proclaim them open. For gated roads a bicycle or small motorcycle can be useful after most of the snow has melted. Quite often winter climbers use snowmobiles for the Maroon Creek Road since it's packed and groomed by a rental operation. Purists stick with ski and foot travel, but often spend a night out because of the extra hours. Check with the Forest Service (see directory) about the status of your access road and consider doing a reconnaissance drive a few days before your trip.

SECTION 4.1
Capitol Peak (14,130'), Snowmass Mountain (14,092')

Though Snowmass Mountain and Capitol Peak stud the same massif, these are quite different mountains. Capitol is a monolith more attractive for snow and rock climbing than for skiing, while Snowmass presides over the huge snowbowl that gives it its name and provides one of the most sought after ski descents in the Elks. Snowmass Peak is the Elks' easiest summer fourteener climb—Capitol Peak is technically the hardest. But with its relatively solid rock, Capitol's technical problems seem tame in comparison to the tottering boulders of the Elks' other fourteeners.

Capitol Peak gives alpinists many choices. A good technical route, rated 5.9, takes the peak's northwest buttress via a crack system leading to a steep arete. The peak's north face directisima is seldom climbed—it's too loose. A less direct and more popular route, known as the Y Couloir, takes the right side of the north face via an icy couloir and several rock pitches. Many a local alpinist has tasted his first mixed climbing on this classic, which was first climbed in 1937 by Carl Blaurock. One caveat: though routes on Capitol might be termed "solid" relative to other Elk Range peaks, they still have much rockfall danger. Wear a helmet, take rest breaks under protective outcrops, and be aware of climbers above and below you.

While winter climbing on Capitol will never be as popular as it is on more accessible fourteeners, the peak has had many winter ascents. Fritz Stamberger and Gordon Whitmer made what is perhaps the boldest of Capitol's arctic climbs. In 1972 they climbed the direct North Face route in the middle of winter, bivouaced on the summit, and descended the next day. While others have challenged the wintry "nordwand," most use the the Knife Ridge for a winter route. After a dry spell in March, it's possible to safely ski up the Moon Lake drainage, crampon firm snow across the Knife, then enjoy a ski run from "K2" to your car. One undone "first" on Capitol is a one-day winter ascent.

ROADS AND TRAILHEADS

USGS Maps: Snowmass Mountain, Capitol Peak, Highland Peak (Marble for winter approach from west.)
USFS Forest Visitors Map: White River National Forest

Snowmass Creek Trailhead

To reach the Snowmass Creek trailhead, drive 15 miles down the valley from Aspen on Colorado Highway 82, or 27 miles up valley from Glenwood Springs, to a gas station and residential area officially called Snowmass. Locals call this "Old" Snowmass because the ski resort of Snowmass Village stole the town's name.

Following the cairns on the South Ridge of South Maroon Peak at about 13,800'. Snowmass Mountain in background.

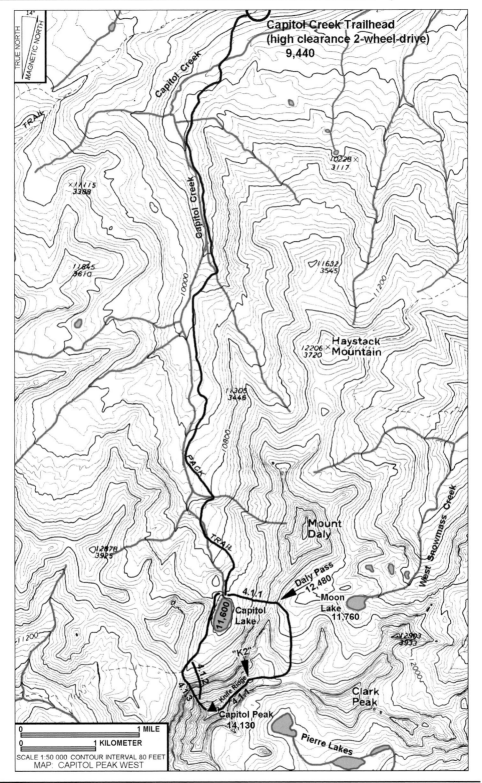

Capitol Creek Trailhead
(high clearance 2-wheel-drive)
9,440

At Old Snowmass, turn S off Highway 82 onto the Snowmass Creek Road. Drive the Snowmass Creek Road 1.6 miles to a "T" intersection. Take a left (still the Snowmass Creek Road) and drive 8.7 miles to another "T" intersection. Turn right and continue .8 mile to a closure gate and parking at the Snowmass Falls Ranch property (8,390'). Walk through a pedestrian gate, then follow a dirt road ¾ mile to the obvious trail, which climbs left from the road just before the road swings right and crosses the creek. Snow season closure will be lower, but varies. The lowest the plow will turn is at a bridge over Snowmass Creek (8,310'), 10 miles from Old Snowmass.

Capitol Creek Trailhead

At the Capitol Creek Trailhead, looking south at Capitol Peak.

Even if you don't need this trailhead for a route, it's worth visiting for the view of Capitol Peak's magnificent north face. Use the directions above for Old Snowmass, and drive the Snowmass Creek Road 1.6 miles to the aforementioned "T" intersection. Turn right on the Capitol Creek Road. At 6.2 miles from Highway 82 the road becomes dirt, but despite warning signs, when the road is dry you can drive a passenger car to parking on the right at 7.6 miles. Start hiking here, or with high clearance 2-wheel-drive you continue 1.8 miles to the trailhead in a beautiful meadow at 9,440'. The trailhead has good signs and you'll find plenty of parking. If the road is muddy, you'll need 4-wheel-drive past the warning signs. In winter the road is closed near mile 6.2, and most of the closed road is packed by ranchers' snowmobiles.

Lead King Basin Trailhead

Drive Colorado State Highway 82 W from Aspen or E from Glenwood Springs to the Carbondale stoplight near the Days Inn Motel. Turn S here onto Colorado State Highway 133, the road to Carbondale, Redstone, and McClure Pass. Drive 20.5 miles on Highway 133 and take the well-signed left turnoff to the town of Marble. Drive 6 miles to Marble, then follow signs through Marble for the Crystal & Schofield Pass Road. Continue 5.6 miles to Crystal, a small group of old buildings and summer residences (narrow road, 4-wheel-drive or high clearance 2-wheel-drive). Park 2-wheel-drive in an aspen tree grove just past Crystal (9,000')'. On foot or 4-wheel-drive, continue up the Schofield Pass Road .5 miles to an obvious intersection. Take the left (N) fork (the Lead King Basin Road) and follow it 1.5 miles to the trailhead on the west side of Lead King Basin at 9,700'. This section of road is awfully rough and better walked by all but expert 4-wheel-drive enthusiasts. Winter closure is at Marble. The road opens to Crystal sometime in late May or early June, while the road into Lead King Basin melts out sometime in June.

CAPITOL PEAK   14,130 FT.

UPPER
SPIRE

ROTTEN
SPIRE

UNICORN
SPIRE

NORTHWEST BUTTRESS
ROUTE 4.1.3

SLINGSHOT COULOIR
ROUTE 4.1.2

N

KNIFE RIDGE 4.1.1

K2

CAPITOL
LAKE
11,600 FT.

TO DALY PASS
AND MOON LAKE

Capitol Peak, North Face from Capitol Creek Trailhead, summer.

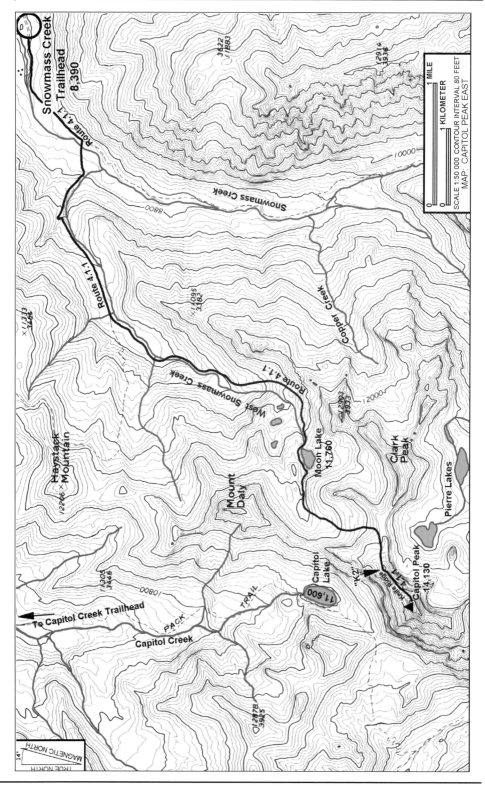

Snowmass Creek Trailhead
8,390

Route 4.1.1

Snowmass Creek

8800

×1,1333
3464

Route 4.1.1

×1,1095
3382

Copper Creek

West Snowmass Creek

Route 4.1.1

12000

×2,1202
3933

Moon Lake
×1,1760

Haystack Mountain
12206×
3714

Clark Peak

Pierre Lakes

Mount Daly

×1,1205
3446

Capitol Lake

10800

"K2"

Capitol Peak
14,130

Knife Ridge

Route 4.1.1

To Capitol Creek Trailhead

PACK

TRAIL

11,600

Capitol Creek

×12878
3925

3622
×1183

×2914
×1936

10000

SCALE 1:50 000   CONTOUR INTERVAL 80 FEET
MAP: CAPITOL PEAK EAST

1 MILE

1 KILOMETER

MAGNETIC NORTH
TRUE NORTH
14°

4.1.1 Capitol Peak—Knife Ridge

Ratings:	Summer Climb—Advanced		Snow Climb—Intermediate	
Season:	Late Spring / Summer		Winter / Early Spring	
RT Data:	14 hours, 14 miles, 5,740' ↑		overnight, 14½ miles, 5,920' ↑	
Start:	Snowmass Creek Trailhead, 8,390'		Snowmass Creek (winter), 8,310'	
1 Day from Rd:	Late Spring	Summer	Winter	Early Spring
	No	Yes; very long	No	No
Maps:	Capitol Peak East, pg. 196; Capitol Peak West, pg. 193			
Photo:	pg. 195			

In any season, with a standard route that's somewhat harder than the usual fourteener, Capitol Peak is an enjoyable challenge for rock or snow climbers. For skiers, the peak has too many cliff bands to be of interest to anyone but the "new-wave" extremist who's willing to link turns on 50 degree slopes above the cliffs. Nevertheless, a summit ski descent is possible. Intermediate level skiers enjoy the fabulous cruise from "K2" down into Moon Lake Basin.

The standard route for all seasons is the famous Knife Ridge. This thin arete makes an excellent snow climb in the early spring, and summer scramblers enjoy it as well. It's a cruise for expert climbers, but most novices should be protected by a rope while they dance on the edge. This route is feasible in winter, but many groups fail due to slow rope work and inclement weather. Thus, a winter ascent of Capitol is something you can be proud of. In winter and spring, most parties work from a high camp in the Moon Lake area, though it is possible to do the whole trip in one push, albeit with a "sub-alpine" start. The first such snow season one-day ascent was probably done by Michael Kennedy in March of 1991. He missed winter by a few days, so the peak still awaits the first winter one-day ascent. Have at it! Summer climbers can do the route in one day—but they should be fit and start early.

It's more expedient and less crowded to climb this route from the Snowmass Creek Trailhead. Nonetheless, many people do it from the Capitol Creek Trailhead by camping at Capitol Lake, then joining the route above Moon Lake by hiking over Daly Pass (12,480), the low-point between Mount Daly and Capitol Peak. (See route 4.1.2 for the Capitol Creek to Capitol Lake approach).

Summer after snow melt-off: The route to Moon Lake area follows a trail through dense timber and patchy meadows. You take a well-defined cut for 3 miles to 9,800', then leave the main trail for a less obvious path up to Moon Lake (11,760').

In detail, park at the Snowmass Creek Trailhead (section introduction). Hike up the Snowmass Creek valley, pass the famous beaver ponds, and cross Snowmass Creek somewhere within ¼ mile of the Snowmass Creek—West Snowmass Creek confluence. During spring spate this crossing can be hairy.

After you cross the creek, walk up through the aspen forest on the right (N) side of West Snowmass Creek. Take care to find the trailcut through the aspen forest as it switchbacks up several steep hillsides, then crosses a ravine at 9,160'. Be sure you're on the trail; any other route across the ravine involves unpleasant bushwhacking.

After crossing the ravine, the route follows the NW side of the valley to 9,800'.

At approximately 9,800' you'll reach a large meadow. From here you leave the main pack trail, which heads up the mountainside west to Haystack Mountain, and forge a route on an "un-improved" trail. Stay to the west of the creek for about ½ mile, then cross to the east side of the creek as the valley narrows and steepens. Loop away from the creek as you climb up the valley, then traverse back into the drainage on a shelf at timberline (11,150'). Follow the drainage from timberline to Moon Lake (11,760'). You'll find good camping at the lower lakes; reach these by continuing W from the 11,150' shelf just below timberline.

From Moon Lake or the upper of the smaller lakes, continue up the drainage, traverse the south side of an obvious depression, then climb the spectacular north facing basin to point 13,664' on Capitol's north ridge. This bump, which is your last break before the hand-and-foot climbing, is known as "K2."

Drop down K2 for a short distance, then shimmy or balance walk the knife ridge for 150 feet. After the knife ridge, continue up obvious scramble climbing to the summit. In general, work the east side (climber's left) of the summit ridge. Descend your ascent route.

Spring snow season: Use the summer route above with the following variations. To avoid the stream crossing, if you can obtain permission, cross Snowmass Creek using the bridge at the ranch (calibrate your altimeter here to 8,380'); ski up valley through the log corrals, then follow the south (creek) side of a fence that parallels the creek for about a quarter mile and leads to open meadows. Cross the meadows and intersect the summer route up through the aspen forest.

After crossing the ravine at 9,160', follow the northwest side of the valley, using the trail-cut, to 9,800'. The important thing to remember about the trail to this point is you'll find more open, easily traveled timber on the northwest side of the valley, while the timber in mid-valley and on the southeast side of the creek is extremely tight. So, if you're in doubt about the trail, or encounter difficult bushwhacking, work to the northwest and things will get easier.

At about 9,800' you'll ski into a large meadow. From here you forge your own trail the rest of the way to Moon Lake and beyond. Cross to the upper NW corner of the meadow. Enter the forest here, and ski though light timber directly up the valley until you encounter the creek bed. Cross to the left (E) side of the creek. From here on, if you are traveling during very low avalanche hazard and compacted snow, following the creek bed (if it is full of snow) makes a good route up and back from just below Moon Lake. Even with less snow, stick with the creek if possible.

If avalanche danger requires hazard avoidance, leave the creek bed to avoid exposure to steep banks on the north side of the ravine. These hazards are obvious. At 10,120' you'll enter a large cleared area resulting from avalanches off the east face of Mount Daly. Again, with safe conditions, continue up the creek bed; if slide hazard warrants, leave the creek bed and work left through heavy timber, then do a climbing traverse to intersect the drainage gut at 11,150'. By staying high on the east side of the valley, and utilizing dense timber, you avoid an avalanche-prone headwall. From 11,150', follow the main drain to 11,600' just below Moon Lake. Here, instead of following the actual creek, take a more direct line up to the lake.

Continue to K2 per the summer route. Leave your skis or snowshoes at K2—unless you intend a summit ski descent. Take the summer route to the summit. With avalanche danger, you can stick to the ridge and climb a 5.2 technical rock pitch up the last section to the summit. For a ski descent pick a day in early spring after a heavy snow year. Ski before late morning to avoid thawing snow on this eastern aspect. Drop S of the summit for 20 or 30 feet, then traverse to the east face. Ski a 50 degree gully for 150 or 200 feet, then begin a traverse to the knife ridge. With heavy cornicing the ridge is skiable all the way into the K2 notch. Snow conditions vary greatly from year to year, so plan your descent route during your ascent. Consider belaying while climbing and skiing, since most of the route passes above cliffs.

Winter: This is a challenging, but feasible route. Use the spring route described above. Plan on a high camp and be willing to turn back if avalanche conditions dictate.

Safety notes: Only experienced fourteener climbers, or those with a guide, should attempt Capitol Peak. Carry a rope and know how to use it. Snow seasons: The route to Moon Lake does not pass over any avalanche starting zones, but it does pass through runouts. Travel during times of lesser hazard, and remember the one-at-a-time rule. The basin below K2 has several lower-angled starting zones that slide on occasion but are usually windpacked or scoured. Use caution here. From K2 to the summit the snow is usually very windscoured, but belay if you're in doubt. During spring snow season, remember that the route past K2 faces east, with the poor snow conditions characteristic of that aspect. Be there early, and use standard sunrise for sunhit.

4.1.2 Capitol Peak—North Face via Slingshot Couloir

Ratings:	Summer Climb—Advanced Snow Climb—Advanced
	Technical Rock Climb—5.5
Season:	Spring Snow or Summer
RT Data:	overnight, 16 miles, 5,930' ↑
Start:	Capitol Creek Trailhead, 9,440'
1 Day from Rd:	No
Map:	Capitol Peak West, pg. 193
Photo:	pg. 195

This technical rock and snow route can be considered a classic because of its longevity. Indeed, it was first climbed in 1937 by a group that included the indomitable Carl Blaurock. What tends to diminish the route's classic standing is its abundant rockfall, both from natural causes and climbers above. For this reason, perhaps a better "classic" is the Northwest Buttress route (4.1.3). At any rate, many climbers have tasted their first alpine mixed climbing on the Slingshot Couloir, and doubtless many will continue to do so. Wear your helmet.

Summer or late spring: Drive to the Capitol Creek Trailhead (section introduction). While fit and experienced climbers have done this route in one push, most people camp near Capitol Lake. From the trailhead, take the Capitol Lake Trail as it drops south 420 vertical feet into the Capitol Creek drainage, then climbs a beaten path 5 miles to Capitol Lake (11,600').

While you pause at Capitol Lake, study Capitol's North Face. To the right of the face is the majestic Northwest Buttress, which drops to the pass at the head of the valley. The feature that defines your route is the slingshot-shaped couloir system on the Northwest Buttress, to the right of the huge North Face. That north face is going to catch your eye and whet your appetite. Just so you don't get deluded into thinking you'll bag a first ascent, the directisima on the NorthFace was first climbed in the winter of 1972 by Fritz Stamberger and Gordon Whitmer. Stamberger knew that the face had too much rubble for summer climbing, and his winter strategy gained him one of Colorado's plumb winter ascents. The first winter ascent of the Slingshot Couloir was done the next winter, via a direct variation up the left arm of the Slingshot, then up the North Face to a saddle just to the west of the Summit Cone.

For the standard route, hike around the west side of Capitol Lake (use the pack trail where appropriate) and continue up boulders and talus (or snow) to the bottom of the Slingshot. Climb the Slingshot via the right arm (crampons and axe), then trend up and left though a series of ledges interspersed with steeper hand-and-foot climbing up to 5.7 in difficulty. As you near the crest of the buttress, the climbing eases in difficulty but stays loose and dangerous. Stick with the Northwest Buttress to the summit, generally staying to the left of any obstacles. Use the Knife Ridge route for your descent, with a return over Daly Pass, the low point between Mount Daly and Capitol. Remember, you'll have about 400 vertical feet of work back up to Daly Pass.

Safety notes: As with many of the fourteener face routes, it's best that at least one party member has previously climbed the descent route, in this case the Knife Ridge. You'll need a rope, rock hardware, crampons and ice axe . Your leader should be comfortable with 5.7 rock climbing, and all party members should be capable of deft movement over extremely loose rock. The Slingshot Couloir gets little sun, but don't let yourself be deceived by this fact. You'll want to start early anyway, so you'll have plenty of time for the technical climbing. There is extreme rockfall danger in the couloir.

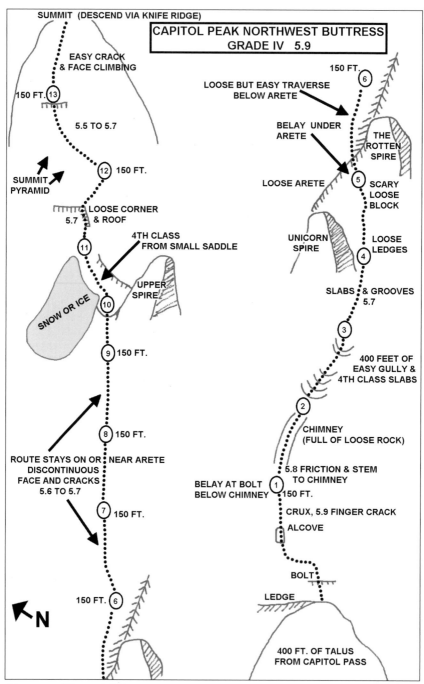

SUMMIT (DESCEND VIA KNIFE RIDGE)

**CAPITOL PEAK NORTHWEST BUTTRESS
GRADE IV 5.9**

EASY CRACK
& FACE CLIMBING

150 FT. (6)

LOOSE BUT EASY TRAVERSE
BELOW ARETE

150 FT. (13)

5.5 TO 5.7

BELAY UNDER
ARETE

THE
ROTTEN
SPIRE

(12) 150 FT.

LOOSE ARETE (5) SCARY
LOOSE
BLOCK

SUMMIT
PYRAMID

LOOSE CORNER
5.7 & ROOF

UNICORN
SPIRE

LOOSE
LEDGES

(11)

4TH CLASS
FROM SMALL SADDLE

(4)

UPPER
SPIRE

SLABS & GROOVES
5.7

(10)

SNOW OR ICE

(3)

(9) 150 FT.

400 FEET OF
EASY GULLY &
4TH CLASS SLABS

(2)

(8) 150 FT.

CHIMNEY
(FULL OF LOOSE ROCK)

ROUTE STAYS ON OR NEAR ARETE
DISCONTINUOUS
FACE AND CRACKS
5.6 TO 5.7

5.8 FRICTION & STEM
TO CHIMNEY

BELAY AT BOLT
BELOW CHIMNEY

(1) 150 FT.

(7) 150 FT.

CRUX, 5.9 FINGER CRACK

ALCOVE

BOLT

150 FT. (6)

LEDGE

N

400 FT. OF TALUS
FROM CAPITOL PASS

Diagram of Route 4.1.3.
Based on a topo by Glen Parker.

4.1.3 Capitol Peak—Northwest Buttress

Ratings:	Summer Climb—Advanced Technical Rock Climb—5.9
Season:	Spring Snow or Summer
RT Data:	overnight, 16 miles, 5,930' ↑
Start:	Capitol Creek Trailhead, 9,440'
1 Day from Rd:	No
Map:	Capitol Peak West, pg. 193
Photo:	pg. 195

This is one of the best technical routes on the Elk Range fourteeners. Nonetheless, it's a loose, dangerous route—only expert mountaineers should attempt it.

Summer or late spring: From the Capitol Creek Trailhead (section introduction), follow the directions in route 4.1.2 to Capitol Lake. Continue S on the pack trail around the west side of the lake, then follow the trail ½ mile up to Capitol Pass (12,080'). Leave the trail at the pass and make a short approach SE up the ridge to the base of the buttress. Traverse about 30 feet left on a ledge to the base of an obvious crack system leading to a chimney.

Climb the crack system (the crux of the route at 5.9) to the chimney. Do this as one pitch so your belayer is not exposed to rockfall by being stuck in the middle of the face below the chimney. Climb the chimney. After the chimney, the route follows an obscure but easy line 400 feet through a low-angled slab area. After the slabs, work to the right of Unicorn Spire, then climb to the right of a prominent arete that connects Unicorn Spire with another rotten spire. Cross to the left side of the rotten spire, then climb 3 pitches (150' each) to a small saddle on the ridge proper. From the saddle, take several 5.7 pitches to the summit. The upper part of this route follows the same line as the Slingshot Couloir (route 4.1.2). Descend the Knife Ridge (route 4.1.1).

Safety notes: Several people have been rescued off this route after being hosed by falling rock. For your descent, at least one party member should be familiar with the Knife Ridge (route 4.1.1).

4.1.4 Snowmass Mountain—The Big Bowl from Snowmass Lake

Ratings:	Summer Climb—Intermediate Ski Descent—Intermediate	
	Snow Climb—Intermediate	
Season:	Summer	Winter Spring
RT Data:	overnight, 23 miles, 5,702' ↑	overnight, 23½ miles, 5,782' ↑
Start:	Snowmass Creek Trailhead, 8,390'	Snowmass Creek (winter), 8,310'
1 Day from Rd:	No; use high camp at Snowmass Lake	
Map:	Snowmass North, pg. 202	
Photo:	pg. 203	

Snowmass Mountain is in the middle of the Maroon Bells Snowmass Wilderness. As such, access to the peak is up eight miles of wilderness trail to Snowmass Lake (10,980'). All but climbing "gods" will need a high camp at the lake. It's 2½ miles and 3,112 vertical feet from a lake camp to the summit. That should leave time for fishing! This is a good "first teener" for backpackers looking to expand their horizons.

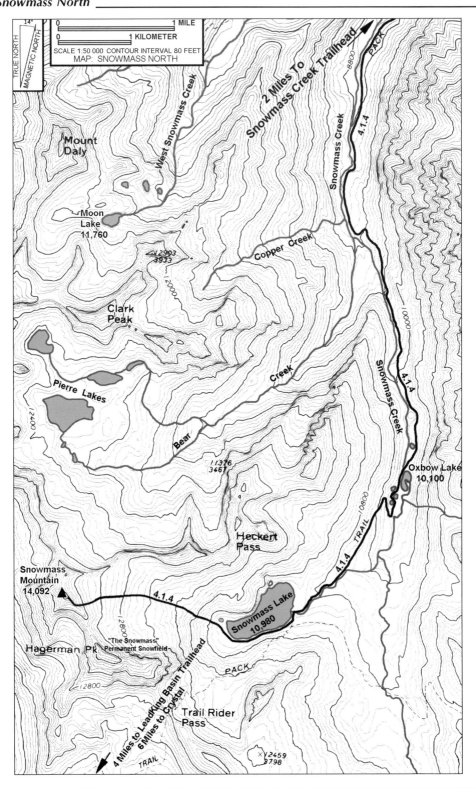

Snowmass Mountain from the east, winter.

Summer after snow melt-off: Park at the Snowmass Creek Trailhead (section introduction), and hike the long Snowmass Creek pack trail 8 miles to Snowmass Lake. At the lake, take time and identify the summit of Snowmass Mountain, which is the less majestic summit up at the head of the bowl containing the "snowmass" permanent snowfield. (At least one climber has mistaken other, more majestic peaks for the mundane summit at the head of the bowl). Hike a fisherman's trail around the south side of the lake, then climb the bowl's lower talus slopes via a stable area to the right (N). Once you're in the bowl proper (with summer snow, boulders and scree) head for a point on the ridge midway between the summit and the Snowmass/Hagerman Saddle. Take a short jaunt N along the ridge to the summit and descend your ascent route.

Spring snow season: For mellow terrain in a spectacular setting, this is one of the best fourteener ski descents. As a snow climb it is easy and safe enough to make a good "first teener." Yet the short, optional northeast face can add a thrill if you are so inclined. For good, safe snow work, you'll need need a high camp at Snowmass Lake or camp at about 10,000' elevation in the main Snowmass Creek valley.

To begin, park at the Snowmass Creek Trailhead (section introduction). Follow the route of the pack trail (an obvious cut) to the small oxbow lake (10,100') at six miles. If you deem it necessary because of slide danger, just before the oxbow lake, switch to the east side of the valley to avoid the runouts of several huge avalanche slopes coming down from the west. About ¼ mile past the oxbow lake, a dense spruce forest fills the valley. Skirt the trim line of this forest back to the west side of the valley. Here the summer trail switchbacks up the huge avalanche path that threatens the oxbow lake area. Again, with any avalanche danger, stick to the forest trim line. In the summer, stick to the trail. It is an obvious highway.

If you used the forest trim line to avoid the avalanche slope, you now have a critical juncture. At approximately 10,400', find the summer trail where it enters into the forest from the avalanche path. If you have trouble with this you must persevere; any other route involves impossible bushwhacking. Once you find it, stay on the summer trailcut the remainder of the way to Snowmass Lake.

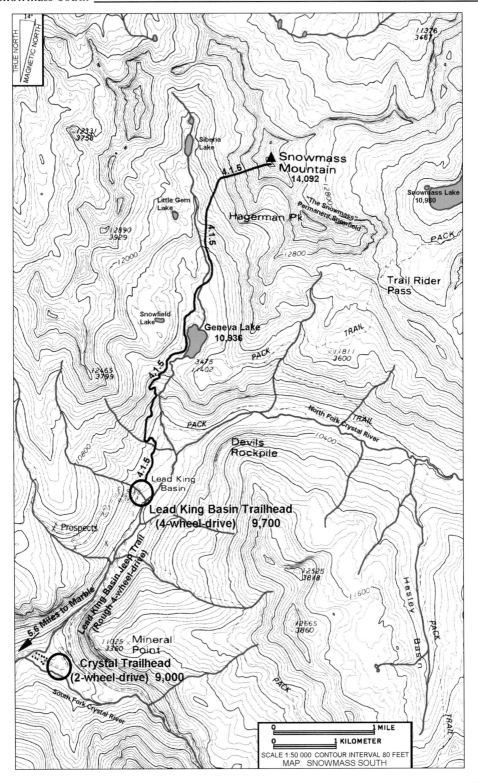

SNOWMASS MOUNTAIN 14,092 FT.

4.15

4.15

GENEVA
LAKE

TO LEAD KING BASIN
AND CRYSTAL TRAILHEADS

N

Snowmass Mountain from the south, summer.

From Snowmass Lake the route is fairly obvious. Travel to the west end of the lake, then climb up the snow bowl to the obvious shoulder to the south of the summit. Be very careful to identify the correct peak as the summit—it does not look high enough when you're in the bowl! From the shoulder follow a rocky ridge to the summit. Most parties ski the bowl from the shoulder. For a summit ski descent you can ski the short northeast face into the bowl, or ski a short way down the N ridge, then drop into the bowl. Both these summit routes have inconsistent snow cover, so if you want a summit descent be there in early spring.

Winter: Snowmass Mountain is a major expedition in the winter. Use the approach tips in the spring description above (calibrate your alitmeter at the ranch bridge to 8,380') . Take care with the avalanche prone headwall leading up from the west end of Snowmass Lake. An astute evaluation of snow stability is necessary to make a decision about your ascent, as the headwall has no safe lines. Because of this, and the expedition style of any attempt, Snowmass Mountain has been climbed few times in the winter.

Safety notes: Though Snowmass Mountain is considered an easy summer fourteener, summer hike/climbers should still have a reasonable level of skill in mountain-craft. You may encounter patches of steep icy snow at any time of the year, so you should carry, and know how to use, your ice axe. Those with ice axe and crampons might enjoy exploring the permanent snowfield at the base of Hagerman Peak. A deep bergschrund here is similar to crevasses in true glaciers. Spring snow climbers should note that this is another east facing route with its typical early sun-hit and poor snow conditions. Be there early and do not tarry. Use standard sunrise for sunhit (see Appendix 5).

4.1.5	**Snowmass Mountain from Geneva Lake**	
Ratings:	Summer Climb—Advanced	Snow Climb—Advanced
Season:	Summer or Spring Snow	Winter
RT Data:	12 hours, 12 miles, 5,092' ↑	multiday, 22 miles, 6,132' ↑
Start:	Lead King Basin Trailhead, 9,000'	Marble, 7,960'
1 Day from Rd:	Yes, for very fit, but overnight recommended	No, multi-day
Map:	Snowmass South, pg. 204	
Photo:	pg. 205	

Geneva Lake is a popular goal for backpackers, but above the lake, you'll see few souls on this side of Snowmass Mountain. The route is not a technical climb. You'll need patience and skill, however, to find a line that avoids dangerous steep rock that's too loose to be climbable.

Summer after melt-off, or spring snow: Follow the directions (see section introduction) for the Lead King Basin Trailhead. From the true trailhead in Lead King Basin (9,700'), climb a well-used pack trail 1¾ miles to Geneva Lake, then continue up the trail a short distance to 11,000', where the trail loops back to the southeast. Leave the trail at this point, and climb N up the drainage to 11,300'. Continue climbing and detour to the right to avoid a small gorge. Continue on a climbing traverse about ½ mile to the huge talus and cliff studded west face of Snowmass Mountain. Take care not to start up the face too soon; stay on your climbing traverse until you're at about 12,200' and directly below the summit. Start climbing towards the summit, then trend slightly to the right as you climb. If you're stymied by cliffs, traverse with care and look for a safe line. At least one climber on this face has been injured by falling rock. A steep section near the summit is the crux. The correct route takes you to a point on the south summit ridge just a few feet from the summit. Descend your ascent route.

Winter: While any winter climb of Snowmass Mountain is a major endeavor, this route might be slightly safer than doing the Big Bowl. Wind strips the snow on this side, and the approach is about the same. You'll need at least one night out, considering the long approach

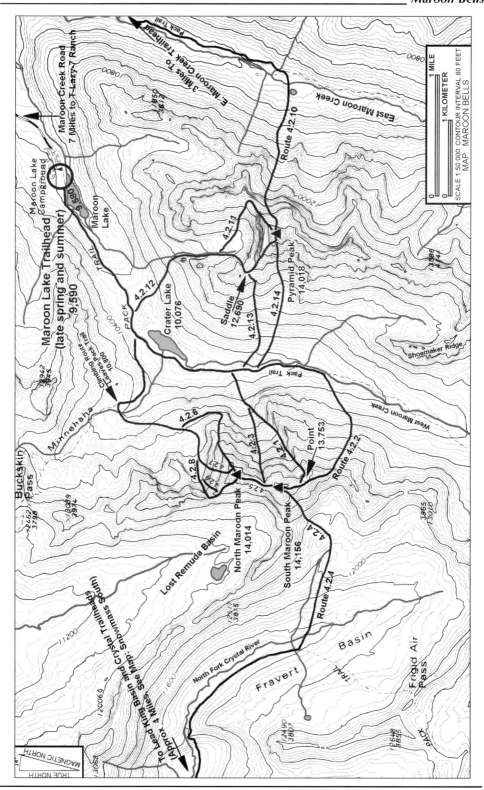

from road closure in Marble. The closed road is lightly used in winter, and not popular with snowmobilers because of rocky sections and side-hills.

SECTION 4.2
South Maroon Peak (14,156'), North Maroon Peak (14,014'), Pyramid Peak (14,018)

South and North Maroon Peaks, connected by a jagged ½ mile ridge, are known as the Maroon Bells. Pyramid Peak stands vigil over "The Bells" across a classic glacial valley. Hard and dangerous summer climbs, challenging snow ascents, and the most intricate skiing in Colorado; that sums up mountaineering on these peaks. All the routes place you above vertical cliffs—on the most perilous loose rock many mountaineers will ever encounter. Pyramid is covered with ribs and pillars that teeter like a stack of dinner plates balanced by a harried waiter. The Maroon Bells are slightly less convoluted, but every ledge is covered with piles of loose rocks. On both peaks gigantic "widow maker" boulders hang by Damocles' threads.

To make matters worse, cliff bands are common in this striated rock, but rope work on these cliffs is fraught with problems. Anchoring a belay is often impossible, and any use of a rope knocks rocks onto the climber below. The difficulty of rope work is the reason more technical routes have never been done on these peaks. For example, though the north face of Pyramid Peak has been climbed by several routes to the summit block, all the routes exit from here along a ledge to the west ridge—the north face of the summit block has never been climbed. Indeed, these are nasty mountains—but they have their own special beauty.

The sight of The Bells rising up from Maroon Lake, with their tilted bell-like shape and myriad gullies and ledges, makes tourists grab for their cameras—and mountaineers yearn. After melt-off, the summer routes up Pyramid and the Maroon Bells, in many climbers' opinion, are little more than dangerous scree hikes. But with a cover of hardened spring snow to eliminate loose rock, these routes are some of the best climbs in the state. Moreover, look no farther if you want extreme skiing. These peaks have some of the most exciting ski routes on the fourteeners. Less aggressive skiers can carry skis as high as they dare, snow climb to the summit, downclimb, then enjoy carving the bonus bowls. Neither of the Maroons has reasonable winter routes. The first winter ascent of North Maroon Peak was done by Peter Hofer and a group of friends in January of 1958 via the Northeast Ridge. The safest winter route for South Maroon Peak is the South Ridge—but that route is so long that winter ascents are rare.

The way most peak baggers "ring" both bells is to climb North Maroon Peak first, climb South Maroon via the connecting ridge (4.2.5), then return via the same route. It's not exaggerating to say this is one of the most dangerous climbs in Colorado and should only be attempted by experienced, well-equipped parties. You must understand the importance of an early start, and be willing to turn back. If in doubt, hire a guide (see directory).

Technically, the South Ridge (4.2.2) is the easiest route to the summit of South Maroon Peak. It's rough and long, however, and should only be attempted by strong groups. South Maroon's east facing couloirs are popular Extreme ski descents (4.2.1).

ROADS AND TRAILHEADS

USGS Maps: Maroon Bells, Highland Peak, Snowmass Mountain
USFS Forest Visitors Map: White River National Forest

Maroon Creek Road, East Maroon Creek Trailhead, Maroon Lake Trailhead

Drive W (downvalley) out of Aspen on Colorado State Highway 82. Less than a mile out of town you will come to a three way stoplight at the well-signed turnoff to the Castle Creek and Maroon Creek Roads. The Aspen Municipal Golf course will be on your right, and you'll see a church to the left. Take the left turnoff from Highway 82, then bear right up the well-signed Maroon Creek Road. Until mid-May the road is gated three miles up at the T-Lazy-

7 Guest Ranch. Later in the spring, and in the summer, the road is open the next 3½ miles to the East Maroon Creek Wilderness Portal and Trailhead, then on to the Maroon Lake Campground and Maroon Lake parking lot at 7 miles from T-Lazy-7 ranch. While parking varies according to which lots are open, you usually start your climb from just above Maroon Lake at 9,590'.

During summer season (usually starts in June), the Maroon Creek Road is only open to vehicles other than buses in early morning or late evening, and the bus runs too late in the morning for a safe starting time. Time your drive accordingly.

When the Maroon Creek road is closed, how do you make these peaks a reasonable one day tripwithout slogging up a snowcovered, or gated and dry, paved road? In the winter one solution is to use a snowmobile. After all, this is one of the most pounded snowmobile trails in the state. T Lazy 7 Ranch's snowmobile business (at the winter snowclosure) will ferry climbers to the end of the road. That option is pricey, so many climbers find a friend with a "sled." Cruising back down the packed snowmobile track on skis is a snap. The road dries early in the spring, but stays gated—a frustrating situation. Mountaineers have been known to use bicycles, motorcycles, or just spend an extra couple of hours walking (and waking even earlier). For information on road closure and conditions call the Forest Service Aspen office (see Appendix 3.4).

4.2.1	South Maroon Peak—East Face Couloirs		
Ratings:	Summer Climb—Advanced		Ski Descent—Extreme
	Snow Climb—Advanced		
Season:	Spring or Summer Snow		
RT Data:	8 hours, 6 miles, 4,566' ↑		
Start:	Maroon Lake Trailhead, 9,590'		
1 Day from Rd:	Yes, with road open or mechanical transport		
Map:	Maroon Bells, pg. 207		
Photo:	pg. 210		

These snow gullies are excellent climbs, and you can reach them with minimal effort after the Maroon Creek Road opens in late May (see section introduction). Ice axe, rope and crampons (and knowledge of their use) are mandatory for this ascent.

Spring or summer snow season: From the Maroon Lake parking area, hike or ski (depending on snow cover) 1¼ miles to Crater Lake (9,580' elevation). Follow the route of the West Maroon Creek Pack Trail for another ¼ mile south from the lake to the point where the trail crosses an intermittent stream (10,280'). Leave the trail and climb an apron E towards an obvious huge slot in the mountainside. This slot is known as the "Garbage Chute." You can climb through the Garbage Chute, or on a good snow year you can climb around it to the right. Later in the spring, the snow in the Garbage Chute can be dangerously undermined by the stream. You can identify this situation by the sound of water flowing under the snow. To be safe, climb near the sides of the slot.

Above the Garbage Chute you'll climb into a small basin (12,000' elevation). From here you can climb either the right or left gully. The right gully is steeper and more technical, and sometimes has discontinuous snow. The left gully has a more consistent pitch and usually has better snow; it is the more popular of the two. Follow either gully to the south ridge of South Maroon Peak, then traverse the east side of point 13,753' to a comfortable saddle. Follow a climbing traverse up the west face to the summit.

For your descent, downclimb the route, or downclimb the South Ridge (route 4.2.2).

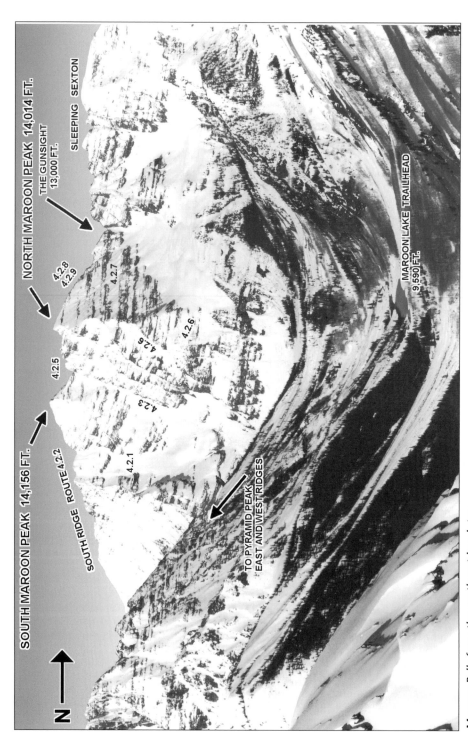

SOUTH MAROON PEAK 14,156 FT.

SOUTH RIDGE ROUTE 4.2.2

NORTH MAROON PEAK 14,014 FT.

THE GUNSIGHT 13,000 FT.

SLEEPING SEXTON

MAROON LAKE TRAILHEAD 9,590 FT.

TO PYRAMID PEAK EAST AND WEST RIDGES

4.2.1

4.2.3

4.2.5

4.2.6

4.2.7

4.2.8

4.2.9

N

Maroon Bells from the northeast in winter

The south ridge is an endless trek over tottering boulders and miserable scree, so downclimb the couloir if you can do it safely. Use crampons and ice axe, and gingerly test your footing when you start down—many people have been surprised by ice hidden under a thin layer of slush. Still others have fallen because their crampons balled up. Many of these unfortunates are dead.

For a ski descent, the southern-most couloir is most popular, but the other couloir has been skied during heavy snow years. Early in the spring it is possible to make a run from the summit down to the saddle, then down the south gully to the valley floor. Unfortunately, the snow on the lower portion of the route melts quickly; consequently most parties do their skiing above the 11,000' level and finish by hiking down the lower portion of the route. Another factor to consider is that during late spring, deep melt channels form in the snow in the lower and middle portions of these gullies. These may be too deep and narrow to ski, yet too wide to jump across without making daredevil moves. A fall down these melt channels can be very dangerous because they make performing a self arrest nearly impossible.

Safety notes: These gullies should only be climbed on compacted spring snow early in the morning. Remember that an east face such as this gets early sun, and thus may become unstable just after sunrise. Several climbers were killed in a late morning avalanche here during June of 1992. They would still be alive if they'd been climbing tightly frozen spring snow.

You can climb or descend these gullies in fall or early summer, provided they still have snow in them. If you chose to descend after climbing a different route, you may encounter patches of ice hidden under a thin layer of snow. Do not glissade; always use crampons, and proceed with caution. Do not climb these gullies if they are dry; the rockfall is too dangerous. For sunhit use standard sunrise.

4.2.2	South Maroon Peak—South Ridge		
Ratings:	Summer Climb—Advanced	Snow Climb—Intermediate	
Season:	Summer / Spring	Winter	
RT Data:	12 hours, 12 miles, 4,566' ↑	multiday, 5,920' ↑	
Start:	Maroon Lake Trailhead, 9,590'	T Lazy 7 Guest Ranch, 8,236'	
1 Day from Rd:	Yes, with open road or snowmobile over closed road	No, multi-day	
Map:	Maroon Bells, pg. 207		
Photos:	pgs. 210, 212		

This is the safest non-snow route for South Maroon Peak. Even so, the last 1,000 vertical feet require a mile of traversing along a drop-off studded mountainside covered with dangerous loose rock. In addition, this is one of the most time consuming routes in this book, and the route finding for that last 1,000 vertical feet is tedious at best. A springtime snow ascent of this route is more enjoyable, and you'll find good skiing down from the first 13,300' bump. In terms of comparison, this ridge is longer than the connecting ridge between North and South Maroon Peaks, but less technical.

Summer after snow melt-off: Get an early "alpine" start from the Maroon Lake Trailhead (section introduction). Slower groups may need to start from a high camp in West Maroon Basin. Follow the West Maroon Creek Pack Trail (a highway) about 3½ miles to its first crossing of West Maroon Creek at 10,490' elevation. Leave the trail here and do a southerly climbing traverse up the west side of the valley. You'll encounter several scree and talus-filled ravines, but for the most part you'll be traversing patches of willows and grass. Traverse for about ¾ of a mile to the 11,400' level on grassy, rock-studded slopes at the base of the prominent southeast ridge dropping from South Maroon's south ridge.

First, ascend grassy slopes on the south side of this ridge; then at about the 12,100'

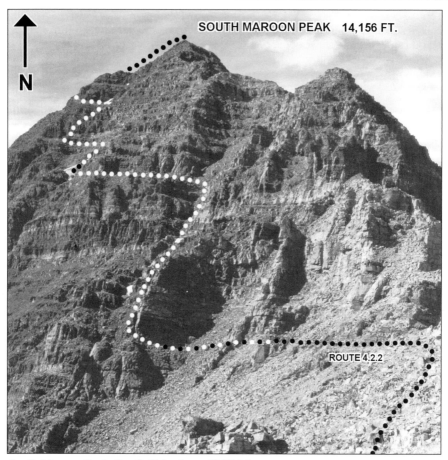

SOUTH MAROON PEAK   14,156 FT.

N

ROUTE 4.2.2

South Maroon Peak, South Ridge from 13,300 feet, summer

level, work your way back to the ridge crest (it becomes more and more rocky as you get higher), and follow the ridge crest to Point 13,300 on South Maroon's true south ridge. Now the fun begins.

The remainder of the route is loose, steep, and dangerous. It should only be attempted by very experienced or guided parties. Helmets are mandatory. First, follow the crest of the south ridge N for about 500 feet, then drop a short way down on the west side of the ridge. Next, follow a long, tedious traverse for about ¼ mile. This traverse hovers around the 13,300' level taking several frustrating downhill ledge systems and the occasional optimistic climb. As you traverse, use an intricate series of ledges, small gullies, and the occasional chimney to get to the more pronounced couloir that drops into Fravert Basin from the north saddle of point 13,753'. You enter this couloir at about the 13,400' level.

"Hike" loose talus and scree up the couloir. About 50 vertical feet below the saddle at the top of the couloir, traverse left (N) on a ledge system that takes you around to the true-southwest face of the peak. Follow more ledges and short vertical steps up to the crest of the south ridge about 400 feet before the summit. Walk the south ridge to the summit. Other than this short section, and the other just past Point 13,300, this route uses the south side of the south ridge. Because it is so intricate, it's almost always marked with cairns, so skilled route finding involves cairn spotting as much as terrain evaluation. Be forewarned that false trails are cairned by well meaning but misguided climbers. Also, a cairned route follows the crest of the south ridge but is not recommended.

Descend your ascent route. Follow existing cairns or ones you built on the way up. Many parties report that the route is easier to find while downclimbing. Be careful to exit the point 13,753 couloir at the correct level—too high or low will put you in steeper terrain.

Winter: This climb is rarely done in winter and is an admirable accomplishment. The problem is finding a route safe from avalanches but easy enough to climb on a short winter day without being held up by technical climbing problems. Your best bet is to establish a high camp in the West Maroon Valley above Crater Lake. From there use a route up various ribs to the crest of the south ridge, which you follow to the summit. In the 1970's Fritz Stamberger did a winter ascent of South Maroon's East Face via a line north of the gullies described in route (4.2.1) This route is steep enough not to have severe slide danger, but the approach involves a great deal of avalanche exposure.

Safety notes: The safe time to ascend this route is when the loose rock is hidden by a blanket of frozen spring snow. Even so, such a long route requires a very early start. Winter climbers should note that, because the best lines do not usually follow the ridge crests, it would be very difficult to do this route safely with unstable snow. Use standard sunrise for sun-hit.

4.2.3 South Maroon Peak—Bell Cord Couloir

Ratings:	Ski Descent—Extreme Snow Climb—Advanced
Season:	Spring or Summer Snow; possible mid-summer ice
RT Data:	7 hours, 6 miles, 4,566' ↑
Start:	Maroon Lake Trailhead, 9,590'
1 Day from Rd:	Yes, with road open or mechanical transport
Map:	Maroon Bells, pg. 207
Photo:	pg. 210

Spring or summer snow season: This snow route takes the classic couloir between the two Maroon Bells. During mid-summer and early fall it may come into condition as a technical ice climb.

From the Maroon Lake parking area, hike or ski (depending on snow cover) 1¼ miles to Crater Lake (10,076').Follow the route of the West Maroon Creek Pack Trail for another ½ mile S from the lake, to the point where the trail crosses an intermittent stream (10,280' elevation). Leave the trail here and follow the route of the intermittent stream up to an obvious huge slot that leads to the South Maroon Gullies (route 4.2.1). Do not climb through the slot; instead head to the right (N) and climb the obvious gully, the Bell Cord Couloir, that leads to a notch in the ridge just north of the South Maroon Peak summit. You need ice axe and crampons for this route, and rope work may be necessary.

For your descent downclimb your route or downclimb the South Ridge of South Maroon Peak (4.2.2) for a mile, then drop to West Maroon Creek. Downclimbing the south ridge involves tiptoeing around dicy tottering boulders and hiking miserable scree. So, if you have the skill to downclimb this couloir, that is your best option. Use crampons and ice axe , and gingerly test your footing when you start down—several people have been fatally surprised by ice patches disguised under several inches of benign looking snow. The Bell Cord Couloir is usually too narrow, rock studded, and melt channeled for skiing, yet it has been done. At least one aspiring extreme skier has fallen down the couloir, and landed hanging upside-down in the bergschrund. He survived—others have not.

Safety notes: This couloir must be filled with ice or snow to reduce rockfall. Even so, it's a shooting gallery. Use standard sunrise time for sunhit and remember that you must start early for snow climbing on this east face.

4.2.4 South Maroon Peak—Southwest Face Direct

Ratings:	Ski Descent—Extreme Snow Climb—Extreme
Season:	Spring or Summer Snow
RT Data:	multi-day, 15 miles, 4,456' ↑
Start:	Lead King Basin Trailhead, 9,700'
1 Day from Rd:	No
Map:	Maroon Bells, pg. 207
Photo:	pg. 214

As a snow climb or extreme ski, this is a wilderness classic. For the best skiing, you should do this route early in the season, perhaps in May. In this case, the road may be closed below Crystal. For all but the mountain gods, this is at least an overnight.

Spring or summer snow season: Walk, ski, bike, or drive to the Lead King Basin Trailhead (see section 1 introduction). Follow the pack trail for a long 6 miles to 11,200' in Fravert Basin, a stupendous amphitheater. This is a good area for your camp.

Leave the pack trail and climb for just over a mile towards South Maroon Peak. The obvious direct couloir begins at 12,600', and leads to the summit pyramid several hundred feet below the summit. You can also start the climb via a slanting couloir farther to the left (W). Sections of the climb have been measured at 70 degrees, so be prepared for steep snow or ice. Heavy snow build-up will even the contours and may reduce the maximum angle. Descend your ascent route, or follow the south ridge back towards Bellview and drop W down obvious scree or snow slopes into Fravert Basin. A complete ski descent of this couloir is a worthy goal

SOUTH MAROON PEAK 14,156 FT.

Peter Kelley Photo

N

4.2.2

4.2.4

FRAVERT BASIN 12,400 FT.

South Maroon Peak, Southwest Face, early spring.

but is seldom accomplished because of steep, inconsistent snow. One party reported that early June was too late in the season, and that skiable conditions would have been more likely in May. Climbing should be best from late April through June, depending on the winter's snowfall.

Safety notes: Beware of rockfall later in the spring. For sunhit add 2 hours to standard sunrise. This route is only safe as a snow climb and you may need a rope.

4.2.5	South Maroon Peak via North Maroon Peak	
Ratings:	Summer Climb—Advanced	Snow Climb—Advanced
Season:	Summer or Spring Snow	
RT Data:	12 hours, 9 miles, 5,066' ↑	
Start:	Maroon Lake Trailhead, 9,590'	
1 Day from Rd:	Yes, with open road	
Map:	Maroon Bells, pg. 207	
Photo:	pg. 210	

Bag North and South Maroon Peaks in the same day? This is your route. The connecting ridge is intricate and challenging and is a worthy goal whether you're going for all the four-teeners and need to check two off, or you're simply out for a fine mountaineering challenge. Climbers who know the route can make it without a rope, but most climbers end up tying in a few times. If in doubt hire a guide.

Summer, or spring snow season: Climb any of the routes in this chapter to the summit of North Maroon Peak. The Northeast Ridge (route 4.2.6) is the most popular. Now the real work begins! From the summit of North Maroon Peak, downclimb south to the ridge proper, then stick with the ridge crest, with a few variations to your right (W), to the lowest point on the ridge. Trend a bit left (E), then climb an obvious ridge line to the summit of South Maroon Peak.

For the safest descent reverse your route. You'll need a few minor variations on the ridge, but for the most part a reverse takes the same line. Parties also descend the South Ridge of South Maroon Peak (route 4.2.2), but this option is long on miles and requires intricate route finding. If someone in your party knows the route, then consider it. Otherwise stick with what you know. The same goes for downclimbing the East Face Couloirs from South Maroon Peak. These gullies are treacherous, and you should only descend them after you've climbed them. They are too steep and inconsistent for safe glissading—don't be tempted.

Safety notes: The ridge portion of this route is extremely dangerous. You'll be exposed to weather and steep dropoff. In places you swing below the crest of the ridge—with loose rock above you. Make a pre-dawn start and be willing to turn back if you're moving too slow. Use standard sunrise time for sunhit. If you are extremely careful with route finding, this route can be easy and relatively safe. But woe to the climber who moves without forethought, ignoring steep drop-offs and being led into cul-de-sacs with no easy egress. Carry a lightweight rope and a few pieces of rock hardware. If you find the perfect route you can leave your rope coiled—but it's an imperfect world.

4.2.6 North Maroon Peak—Northeast Ridge

Ratings:	Summer Climb—Advanced Snow Climb—Advanced
Season:	Summer, or Spring Snow
RT Data:	10 hours, 8½ miles, 4,424' ↑
Start:	Maroon Lake Trailhead, 9,590'
1 Day **from Rd:**	Yes, with open road or mechanized transport
Map:	Maroon Bells, pg. 207
Photo:	pg. 210

Summer after snow melt-off: Drive to the parking area at Maroon Lake at the end of the Maroon Creek Road (see section introduction). Follow the West Maroon Pass Trail from the Maroon Lake parking area (see section introduction) to its intersection with the Buckskin Pass Trail a short distance before Crater Lake. Climb the Buckskin Pass Trail to the 10,800'. Take a left off the trail, cross Minnehaha Creek, then take a climbing traverse up and left along several prominent shelves that lead to timberline just below the flank of the Northeast Ridge. Move to just above timberline and traverse S along a shelf at about the 11,500' level into the "Grassy Gully," a huge east facing chute studded with rocks and alpine flora. Climb the Grassy Gully to steep rock, then traverse left into another large gully that will lead you to the crest of the Northeast Ridge several hundred feet below the summit (you'll be at about 13,300'). Continue along the ridge, then just below the summit, traverse a few feet towards the north face, then climb one of several short chimneys to the summit.

The route is usually cairned and may be marked by ugly blobs of paint. The latter practice is discouraged since this peak is located in legal wilderness, and cairns do the job without defacing the rock. Indeed, painting rocks in wilderness is, at the least, uncouth!

Spring snow season: Use the summer route above. Start early, and enjoy cramponing firm snow in the Grassy Gully (which won't have much grass). Because this easterly route gets early sun, consider descending the Gunsight Ridge (route 4.2.8). Bring a lightweight rope in case you need a rappel into the Gunsight Notch. In early spring, skis make for an efficient approach.

Winter: Winter climbers use the summer route, with minor variations to avoid wading through waist deep snow. While this route has seen many winter climbs, the approach is exposed to dozens of avalanche paths. Moreover, the Grassy Gully on the route proper is a major slide path. Thus, the crux of a winter ascent is avoiding avalanche hazard. To do so, climb during a stable period in late winter. Anyone who makes this climb in winter should be proud.

Safety notes: This route is the least technical and most popular for summer climbs of North Maroon. Route finding is hard, and a mistake can lead you onto loose steep rock where technical climbing is impossible because of the lack of solid anchors. If you stray from the route, backtrack immediately to safer ground. Many people have been hurt or killed trying to force a route. Intermediate and novice climbers should climb with a guide or experienced friend. Use standard sunrise for sunhit.

4.2.7	**North Maroon Peak—North Face Direct**	
Ratings:	Ski Descent—Extreme	Snow Climb—Advanced+
Season:	Spring or Summer Snow	
RT Data:	10 hours, 8¼ miles, 4,424' ↑	
Start:	Maroon Lake Trailhead, 9,590'	
1 Day from Rd:	Yes, with open road or mechanized transport	
Map:	Maroon Bells, pg. 207	
Photo:	pg. 210	

The direct North Face of North Maroon Peak provides one of the classic extreme ski descents in the Elks; it is also one of the best advanced snow climbs. What distinguishes this route from the average is that the face is more complex than the usual escalation up a clean snowfilled couloir. It involves finding your way past several rock steps, and most of the route exposes you to possible falls over cliffs.

The first ski descent of the North Face was done by Fitz Stamberger in the spring of 1971. In those days few people had even considered extreme skiing in Colorado, or even knew what the sport was. Stamberger's feat amazed people all over Colorado and spurred a spate of ski descents. After Stamberger's, the most radical descent of the face was Ted Miners, decent. He slipped while negotiating the tricky traverse onto the lower snow field and was launched into the air over the lower headwall for a ride that included several hundred feet of flight. He survived because of a gradual runout on the steep snow at the base of the cliff. The lower headwall has been dubbed "Miners Ski Jump" to honor his feat.

Spring or summer snow season: To climb or ski the North Face of North Maroon Peak, follow the West Maroon Pack Trail from the Maroon Lake parking area (see section introduction) to its intersection with the Buckskin Pass Trail a short distance before Crater Lake. Follow the Buckskin Pass Trail to 10,800'. Leave the trail here and cross Minnehaha Creek; then take a climbing traverse up and left along several prominent shelves that lead to the snow bowl below the north face.

Observed from the snow bowl, the face has three obvious features. They are the first cliff band (A.K.A. Miners Ski Jump), the long snowfield that stretches from left to right above Miners Ski Jump, and a narrow gully that rises from the right end of the snowfield. This gully forms part of route (4.2.8). The features in the middle of the face, above the long snowfield, form a steep gully system broken by several rock bands. This is the central gully and provides a ski and climbing route.

Begin the climb by moving up the snow bowl to the right side of the face, then up onto the right end of the long snowfield (there may be a bergschrund to cross). Traverse the snowfield to the left until you are below the central gully. The route then heads up the gully and becomes slightly devious. If you run into problems here remember, due to the horizontal stratification of the rock, a short traverse will lead around most obstacles.

At the top of the Central Gully the angle eases up and the route becomes less technical. You will encounter a second large snowfield topped by another broken rock band. There are several ways through this band, usually a bit to the right. Above this rock band you will come to a third snowfield capped by a more forbidding, less broken rock band, called the Punk Rock Band. This is only 30 to 60 feet high, but it has stymied many parties. Avoid it by traversing to the left and climbing the last portion of the easier Northeast Ridge route (4.2.6) to the summit

If you're not skiing, descend one of the summer routes in this section. The Northeast Ridge (route 4.2.6) is less technical, but the route finding is tricky. The Gunsight Ridge (route 4.2.8) is more straightforward, but may involve a rappel into the Gunsight Notch and downclimbing steep snow in the Gunsight Gully.

Fritz Stamberger is the only person to have skied directly off the summit to the face. Legend holds that to accomplish this he jumped over the Punk Rock Band. All subsequent descents have been made by climbing (or skiing) down the northeast ridge to the point where it is possible to ski out onto the snowfield under the Punk Rock Band. From here you ski the climbing route, the crux being snow steeper than 48 degrees in the central gully. Because of the cliff bands, this route is dangerous to ski; consider belaying the crux sections, and only attempt the ski descent if you are an *experienced* extreme skier.

Safety notes: With snow cover to cement the rubble, the North Face of North Maroon is a good spring, early summer, or late fall climb. Without snow the rockfall potential is too extreme for safe climbing. During spring or early summer, attempt this route only early in the morning on frozen snow. Though this is a "north face" in climbing terms, it is east facing enough for an early sunhit. Thus, you must time your ascent as if it were an east face, with a sunrise sunhit. Skiers must hit this face after the spring consolidation but while the snowcover is still thick; otherwise they risk portions of the route being unskiable. Most ski descents are made during May or early June, depending on the snowfall and temperatures.

4.2.8	North Maroon Peak—Gunsight Ridge	
Ratings:	Summer Climb—Advanced	Ski Descent—Extreme
	Snow Climb—Advanced	
Season:	Summer, or Spring Snow	
RT Data:	10½ hours, 9 miles, 4,424' ↑	
Start:	Maroon Lake Trailhead, 9,590'	
1 Day	Yes,	
from Rd:	with open road or mechanized transport	
Map:	Maroon Bells, pg. 207	
Photo:	pg. 210	

Also known as the "Dike Route." the Gunsight Ridge more or less follows North Maroon's northwest ridge from the slot (the Gunsight) at the head of the north face snow bowl. This route is more technical than the Northest Ridge, but the route is slightly easier.

Summer after snow melt-off: To begin, drive the Maroon Creek Road to the Maroon Lake parking area. Follow the directions in route 4.2.7 to reach the talus and boulder-filled bowl below the North Maroon's north face. At the upper west end of the bowl, climb an obvious gully into the prominent Gunsight Notch. You can encounter ice in this gully during any season, so bring crampons. To get out of the notch, do a direct technical pitch (4th class) to your left up the ridge, or an easier, (but still technical) traverse on the west side of the ridge.

Once out of the notch, follow a winding route up the ridge to the summit. You rarely follow the ridge crest. Instead, make a series of climbing traverses on the west side of the ridge and return nearer the ridge crest when it is logical to do so. The rock is very loose in this whole area, so do not attempt any technical climbing other than getting in and out of the notch. Descent is via the same route.

Spring snow season: Use the summer route described above. You can ski the Gunsight Couloir, but be prepared for difficult, or impossible, skiing later in the spring. The upper part of the route has been skied, and connects to a couloir on the north face which can be climbed and skied as a variation (see the North Face & West Face Combo, route 4.2.9).

Safety notes: Take the usual precautions for loose rock. Bring, and know how to use, your crampons and ice axe. Use standard sunrise for sunhit.

4.2.9	**North Maroon Peak—North Face & West Face Combo**	
Ratings:	Ski Descent—Extreme	Snow Climb—Advanced
Season:	Spring or Summer Snow	
RT Data:	10 hours, 8½ miles, 4,424' ↑	
Start:	Maroon Lake Trailhead, 9,590'	
1 Day from Rd:	Yes, with open road or mechanized transport	
Map:	Maroon Bells, pg. 207	
Photo:	pg. 210	

Spring snow season: Snow climbers might prefer this gem instead of the Gunsight Route (4.2.8). It uses a similar but longer gully to reach a point higher on the same ridge. The gully is an exciting ski route. It's "easy" as extreme routes go and makes good preparation for more radical descents. With good snow cover, it's possible to make a complete summit ski descent via this route.

Summer or spring snow season: To climb or ski this route, follow the West Maroon pack trail from the Maroon Lake parking area (see section introduction) to its intersection with the Buckskin Pass Trail a short distance before Crater Lake. Follow the Buckskin Pass Trail to 11,800'. Leave the trail here, cross Minnehaha Creek, then traverse up and left along prominent shelves that lead to the snow bowl below the North Face of North Maroon Peak (4.2.7).

Observed from the snow bowl, the north face has three obvious features. These are the first cliff band (A.K.A. Miners Ski Jump), the long snowfield that stretches from left to right above the Miners Ski Jump, and a narrow gully that rises from the right end of the snowfield. This gully is hidden from view at certain angles but becomes obvious as you get closer to the face.

Climb the gully to the crest of the northwest ridge. It has a maximum angle of about 48 degrees and narrows significantly at one point.

When you exit the gully onto the ridge, you'll be on the standard Gunsight Ridge route (4.2.8), which you then follow to the summit. This route follows a winding line mostly on the western flank of the peak, making a series of climbing traverses. Return nearer to the crest of the northwest ridge when it is logical to do so, but remember that the best route never follows the crest. Eventually, the correct route intersects the southwest corner of the summit pyramid a short distance below the summit. The rock is very loose on this route—do not attempt any technical climbing.

Descend the same route. You can ski from the summit with enough snow. None of the skiing is steeper than 50 degrees, but exposure to many cliffs makes skiing this route a serious endeavor that only the most expert should undertake. Many people ski the lower portion of the gully.

Safety Notes: Rockfall is always a concern, and the snow in the couloir is only avalanche-safe after the spring consolidation. Climb or ski before mid-day thawing commences. Though the west facing parts of the route receive a late sunhit, the couloir on the north face (which has an eastern aspect) gets early morning sun. Use standard sunrise time, but in order to hit the couloir early enough, you'll have to be on the western aspects before they get sun.

4.2.10	**Pyramid Peak—East Face**	
Ratings:	Ski Descent—Extreme	Snow Climb—Advanced
Season:	Spring Snow	
RT Data:	13 hours, 12 miles, 5,318' ↑	
Start:	East Maroon Creek Trailhead, 8,700'	
1 Day from Rd:	Possible; but high camp recommended	
Map:	Maroon Bells, pg. 207	
Photo:	pg. 220	

As a snow climb, the East Face of Pyramid Peak is rarely in condition. Nonetheless, those who accomplish this climb report it to be rewarding. For the skier, this is one of the most dangerous, intricate descents yet done in Colorado. As such, and considering the unpredictable nature of east facing snow, it should only be attempted by the elite extreme skier.

Spring snow season: Follow the Maroon Creek Road (section introduction) three miles up from the T Lazy 7 Ranch to the East Maroon Creek Trailhead. Cross the creek over a foot bridge and follow the pack trail up the valley to a small pond (9,640'). This is a good area for a high camp (do not camp in the avalanche runout).

PYRAMID PEAK 14,018 FT.

NORTHEAST RIDGE ROUTE 4.2.11

N →

Peter Kelley photo

EAST FACE ROUTE 4.2.10

APPROX. 11,000 FEET

EAST MAROON CREEK

Pyramid Peak east face, winter.

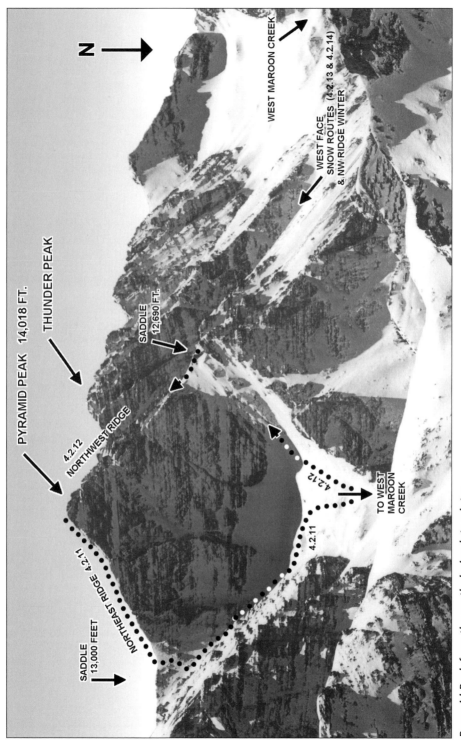

N

WEST MAROON CREEK

WEST FACE
SNOW ROUTES (4.2.13 & 4.2.14)
& NW RIDGE WINTER

PYRAMID PEAK 14,018 FT.

THUNDER PEAK

SADDLE
12,690 FT.

4.2.12
NORTHWEST RIDGE

4.2.12

TO WEST
MAROON
CREEK

4.2.11

NORTHEAST RIDGE 4.2.11

SADDLE
13,000 FEET

Pyramid Peak from the north during late winter.

If Maroon Creek Road is open and you're driving (or you're using a bicycle, motorcycle, or snowmobile), you can eliminate a few miles of travel by heading farther up the Maroon Creek Road past the East Maroon Creek Trailhead. Walk a short distance through meadows to the confluence of Maroon Creek and Castle Creek, then intersect the East Maroon pack trail. Sadly, this variation requires wading across Maroon Creek. Is it worth it? Only you can judge.

At any rate, from the pond at 9,640', climb directly W up the huge amphitheater couloir dropping from the summit of Pyramid. Take care to identify the proper amphitheater; it's easy to mistakenly go for the larger amphitheater upvalley from the correct one. The climbing is easy up to the 11,800' level. After that the amphitheater narrows and steepens, and you're faced with two choices: either continue up the main couloir, which takes you to the 13,880' saddle just south of the summit; or head up patchy snow and rock to the right, then up a steep, fairly wide couloir that leads to the 13,000' level on the Northeast Ridge (4.2.11). Both routes stay on their respective ridges to the summit, with small traverses and the occasional "hands for balance" move over a rock step. The former route (to the left) is a more classic line.

Descent is problematic. The only way to ski from the true summit is to ski near or on the Northeast Ridge (4.2.11) to the aforementioned 13,000' level, then work your way down the couloir to the amphitheater. The descent has only been done once and required a section of downclimbing. A ski descent of the gigantic east facing snow chute dropping from the south side of the summit would be the classic line. Thus far, this has never been attempted.

Climbers face two interrelated problems with this route: an early sunhit and snow steep enough to require a belay for all but the most experienced climbers. You must be off this route before the sun heats the snow. Because of the time problem, it is best to descend the peak via the Northwest Ridge (4.2.12) into West Maroon Creek. To do so, you reverse the northwest ridge down to the saddle at 13,000'. Leave the ridge at the saddle and drop W down scree or snow gullies into the bowl at the base of the Pyramid's great North Face. Descend the bowl drainage to timberline, then use a series of descending SW (upvalley) traverses to drop into the West Maroon Creek Valley. Follow the West Maroon Creek Pack Trail down to the Maroon Lake parking lot (section introduction). The problem with this scenario is getting back to your high camp. A solution would be to carry light weight bivouac gear—or make a super early start and do the whole traverse in one push.

Safety notes: This east facing mountain side, with a preponderance of dark rock and cliffs, begins to thaw just minutes after sunhit. Consequently, time your climb to be off the face at sunhit. Also, the snow on this face stabilizes earlier in the spring than many other east faces. Because of loose rock, this route is not safe after snow melt-off. Use standard sunrise for sunhit. Carry a rope and climbing hardware.

4.2.11	**Pyramid Peak—Northeast Ridge**	
Ratings:	Ski Descent—Extreme	Snow Climb—Advanced
Season:	Summer or Spring Snow	
RT Data:	8 hours, 6½ miles, 4,428' ↑	
Start:	Maroon Lake Trailhead, 9,590'	
1 Day from Rd:	Yes, with open road or mechanical transport	
Map:	Maroon Bells, pg. 207	
Photo:	pg. 221	

After snow melt-off, this is certainly the less complex of Pyramid's two ridge routes (the other being the Northwest Ridge Keyhole Route (4.2.12) described above). Nonetheless, it still takes you above scary cliffs on dangerous loose rock. With a tight spring snow cover it is much safer, but still exposes you to plenty of fall potential. This route has been used for a complete ski descent of Pyramid, but it is not recommended for skiing in its entirety. The lower couloir and cirque, however, yield excellent skiing.

Summer after snow melt-off: Drive to the Maroon Lake Campground parking area (see section intro). Hike upvalley on the well beaten Crater Lake Trail 1 mile to 10,120'. As you hike look up and left to identify Pyramid's incredible North Face and the steep drainage leading up through a deep notch to the cirque below the face. This notch is your first goal.

Turn left off the trail at 10,200', and hike S across glacial moraine ¼ mile towards the imposing north flanks of Pyramid Peak. A few faint trails exist here, but don't waste time trying to find them. Swing southeast and climb steep dirt, scree, and grass towards the aforementioned notch. Again, you'll find various sections of trail, but they all fizzle out, so just take the most logical route—usually straight up and slightly to the left. Once through the notch the angle eases into the spectacular North Face Cirque. Stay right and hike up an obvious ravine through the cirque. In the upper part of the cirque, at about 12,100', swing left (E) and cross to the east side of the bowl. Climb E up a system of scree filled couloirs to a notch on Pyramid's northeast ridge (13,000').

Now the real climbing begins. In general, stick to the ridge S then SW to the summit—with variations to the left. In detail: follow the ridge about ¼ mile to a steep-sided intimidating notch. The pitch just past this is the crux and involves a bit of hand-and-foot work on a wall of pale-colored rock. Most parties forgo a rope here, but it could come in handy. After the crux, to reach the summit (after the crux) stick to the ridge as the angle eases off and veer left each time you get stymied by a steep section. Enjoy the occasional glimpse of the North Face. This face has been climbed via several routes on the right side but has never had a "directisima"—because of the rotten rock such a climb might be impossible.

Move slowly and carefully. You can't help but notice that the right (W) side of the ridge exposes you to thousand foot falls, while going too far to the left brings you uncomfortably close to other nasty drops. Descend the same route, or use the Keyhole Route if you are familiar with it.

Spring snow season: Use the summer route above. This can be a good snow climb. Yet much of it faces east, with related early sunhit and rotten snow. Bring a rope, rock anchor devices in the small to medium size range, and a snow anchor such as a fluke or snow-stake.

Safety notes: With coatings of slippery snow or verglas, this route can be deadly because the rock strata create sloping ledges that will eject you over cliffs. In general, the route finding is easier than the Keyhole Route, but you'll encounter more places where a trip could send you flying to oblivion. Take precautions for rockfall in the gullies leading from the bowl to the ridge. Use standard sunrise time for sunhit.

4.2.12	**Pyramid Peak—Keyhole Route (Northwest Ridge)**	
Ratings:	Summer Climb—Advanced	Snow Climb—Advanced
Season:	Summer, or Spring Snow	
RT Data:	9 hours, 7 miles, 4,428' ↑	
Start:	Maroon Lake Trailhead, 9,590'	
1 Day from Rd:	Yes, with road open or mechanical transport	
Map:	Maroon Bells, pg. 207	
Photos:	pgs. 221, 224	

For a summer or spring climb of Pyramid Peak, this is the most popular route. In the opinion of many climbers, however, the Northeast Ridge (4.2.11) is a better choice. The problem with the Keyhole Route is the intricate series of gullies you must follow on the upper portion of the route. It's easy to get lost in this maze. Ask most climbers, and you'll find that their first Pyramid climb was done with someone who knew the route. Unless you are highly

Upper west face of Pyramid Peak, early winter. Where route appears to descend, in photo, it actually traverses.

competent, you should do the same, or hire a guide.

Summer, or spring snow season: Drive to the the Maroon Lake parking lot at the Maroon Lake Campground (see section intro). Hike upvalley on the well beaten Crater Lake Trail 1 mile to 10,120'. As you hike look up and left to identify Pyramid's incredible North Face and the steep drainage leading up through a deep notch to the cirque below the face. This notch is your first destination.

Turn left off the main trail at 10,200', and hike S across glacial moraine ¼ mile towards the imposing north flanks of Pyramid Peak. A few faint trails exist here; don't waste time trying to find them, but use them if you do. Swing southeast and climb steep dirt, scree, and grass towards the aforementioned notch. Again, you'll find various sections of trail, but they all fizzle out, so just take the most logical route: usually straight up and slightly to the left. Once through the notch the angle eases into the spectacular North Face Cirque. Stay right, and hike up an obvious ravine through the cirque. Near the upper end of the cirque, at at about 11,900', swing right (W) and climb a wide couloir up to a major saddle (12,690') on the crest of the Northwest Ridge.

From here to the summit, your route follows a tricky series of rubble-filled (or snow filled) couloirs linked with traverses, usually to the right (S). Only short portions of the route actually follow the ridge crest. Indeed, this could be the hardest route to find of any of the fourteeners. Parts of the route are marked with cairns, but these disappear. Worse yet, cairns get set in the wrong places.

In more detail: from the first saddle on the ridge, follow the ridge crest southeast for a few hundred feet, then trend to the right of the ridge to the base of a rubble-filled couloir. Climb this couloir (rockfall danger, stay to the sides) to its head at the base of a short vertical pitch to the right. At the left head of the couloir is the "Keyhole," which looks out on the infamous North Face and cirque below. Be careful here if you explore, as the terrain is deceptively steep and loose. The Keyhole is the last time you are near the actual crest of the Northwest Ridge.

Climb the vertical pitch at the right head of the couloir, then take a series of southern traverses, interspersed with short climbs, to a small amphitheater on the west side of the summit block. At this point you are only a few hundred vertical feet below the summit. Traverse SE through the amphitheater to an obvious notch that breaks the South Ridge. Gain the South Ridge via this notch, then climb the South Ridge several hundred feet to the summit. If you are new to the mountain, descend your ascent route.

Spring: Use the summer route above. With snow cover, this route can be much safer and more enjoyable. But you must carry and know how to use crampons and ice axe . Timing is crucial, since unstable thawing snow could avalanche you over any of hundreds of cliffs.

Safety notes: The hazards of this route can not be overemphasized. Because many parts of the route pass above vertical cliffs, many climbers have died from simple slips or from rock giving way. Still others have died from sliding falls on snow that took them over cliffs. The key to safe climbing on Pyramid Peak is to keep a keen awareness about how exposed you are. With any fall potential, move slowly and test each hand and foothold. Don't climb while others are climbing above you, and give your party plenty of time by starting early. A rope can be handy on the vertical pitch at the head of the Keyhole Couloir. Indeed, all parties should carry a rope on these peaks. But, as with most other climbs on Pyramid Peak and the Maroon Bells, using a rope may cause more problems than it solves. For approximate sunhit, add three hours to standard sunrise.

4.2.13	Pyramid Peak—West Face Snow & Ski Route	
Ratings:	Ski Descent—Extreme	Snow Climb—Advanced
Season:	Spring or Summer Snow	
RT Data:	10 hours, 8 miles, 4,428' ↑	
Start:	Maroon Lake Trailhead, 9,590'	
1 Day from Rd:	Yes, with road open or mechanical transport	
Map:	Maroon Bells, pg. 207	
Photo:	pg. 221	

Though it's a fine snow climb with several sections of good skiing, this route is poor after snow melt-off because of endless scree slopes. Instead, use the Keyhole Route (4.2.12) or the Northeast Ridge (route 4.2.11).

Spring snow season: With good snow cover this route is challenging, intricate, and rewarding. You'll find the best conditions sometime in May—earlier, you'll be post holing a winter snowpack; later the snow will be patchy. You can ski from about 100 vertical feet below the summit, with another small unskiable section in a gully too narrow for turns. Thus, taking skis high on this route is probably not worth the trouble. Nonetheless, the first long gully described below makes a spectacular ski, so take your skis at least part way up—and enjoy the snow climbing.

From Maroon Lake (see section introduction) follow the route of the pack trail 2 miles to 10,240', ½ mile past Crater Lake. Cross to the east side of the valley through a spruce forest, then climb an obvious, deeply cleft couloir to 12,200' where it widens and splits. Stay to the right and climb to 12,880'. Here traverse right above a steep bowl to a beautiful hidden couloir; climb the couloir. At a split stay right, climb to its top where it widens considerably, then traverse right again into another narrower and steeper couloir.

Climb this couloir to a small snow bowl just below the crest of Pyramid's west ridge. Again, traverse right through the small snow bowl, then across a shoulder and into the larger steep snow bowl below the rocky summit crest. Climb directly up this snow bowl to the base of the summit cliffs, then traverse right and gain the south ridge through a steep-sided notch.

Follow the rocky and exposed south ridge several hundred feet to the summit. Descend your ascent route.

Winter: For a winter route you can climb windblown ribs to the north of the first couloir. Take these all the way to the crest of the west ridge, then follow the Keyhole Route (4.2.12) to the summit snow bowl mentioned above. The Keyhole Route is inconsistent: at times easy; at times too loose and steep to be safe. The route follows another series of ledges and small couloirs on the right (S) side of the ridge. Connecting these can be trying, but persevere and look for the occasional cairn built by helpful climbers. A traverse right (S) will usually lead you out of a dead end. Remember that rope work is next to impossible, so think before you climb.

Safety notes: Without snow these couloirs are rock filled shooting galleries—and you are the target. Also, all the upper couloirs are above cliff bands, so being carried down by an avalanche, however small, will yield a dire outcome. The same goes for falls while climbing. Remember, you can't place good protection in the rock on the sides of these couloirs, so anyone climbing here should be comfortable with unprotected steep snow climbing—both up and down. Maximum angle on this route is 55 degrees. For sunhit, add 3 hours to standard sunrise (see Appendix 5).

4.2.14	Pyramid Peak—West Face Direct Snow Route
Ratings:	Snow Climb—Extreme
Season:	Spring Snow
RT Data:	10 hours, 9½ miles, 4,428' ↑
Start:	Maroon Lake Trailhead, 9,590'
1 Day from Rd:	Yes
Map:	Maroon Bells, pg. 207
Photo:	pg. 221

While only safe during the spring snow season, for the true alpinist this is a fourteener plumb. Many a climber has gazed down this couloir while downclimbing the standard Keyhole (West Ridge) route. If you're in that category, and have the skill, pick a spring day and satisfy your curiosity. The route is rated extreme because of steep snow (over 55 degrees), and the possibility of combined technical rock climbing and snow climbing. Bring a rope and a small amount of rock hardware.

Spring snow season: Follow the approach directions for the West Face Snow Climb & Ski route (4.2.13). Instead of taking this route, continue up the valley another ⅛ mile to 10,280'. Leave the valley at this point and climb directly up Pyramid's west flanks to a large shelf at 11,600'. Pause here to evaluate snow conditions and your timing. Are you late? If so, turn back.

While several couloirs lead up directly from the upper end of the shelf, the one you want is slightly to the left (N) and leads to the small snow bowl several hundred feet below the summit. Climb the couloir to the snow bowl. Traverse up and right through the snow bowl to a notch in the south summit ridge, then scramble the south ridge several hundred feet north to the summit ; this finish is the same as that for the Keyhole Route (4.2.12). Descend the Keyhole route to the 12,690' saddle, then drop west down Pyramid's flank to the valley where you began.

Safety notes: The snow and rock on this route are steep enough to warrant rope work for all but elite climbers. Problem is, more than occasional use of a rope will slow you down, thus exposing you to rockfall. Be extra cautious and time your ascent so you reach the summit 2 hours after standard sunrise. With this being a west facing route, that will allow you a slight margin for error. Remember that such timing will mean climbing in the dark, so it might be best to approach the route the evening before, identify it, and fix it in your memory. A headlamp only throws light so far! Wear a helmet. One other caveat: at least one person in your party *must* have previously climbed one or preferably both ridge routes on the mountain, so you can safely find the descent. Pyramid Peak is a confusing, dangerous mountain.

SECTION 4.3
Castle Peak (14,265'), Conundrum Peak (14,022')

Castle Peak and its subpeak Conundrum Peak are located between the towns of Crested Butte and Aspen at the head of the Castle Creek, Brush Creek, and Conundrum Creek valleys. With names like Precarious, Cathedral, and Electric, the peaks and basins of this area in the Elks form one of the most rugged mountain areas in Colorado. The region was trampled in the mining days, and has the prolific road access you come to expect from mining areas in the Rockies. In the summer, you can drive the Montezuma Mine 4-wheel-drive Road to 12,500' at the base of Castle Peak. The road ends just below the Montezuma Glacier, a huge permanent snow field that yields good snow climbing and skiing most of the summer.

In terms of access, the Montezuma Road makes Castle Peak almost in league with Pikes Peak and Mount Evans (with their roads to the summit). Indeed, the Montezuma Road probes the lands of the Maroon Bells Snowmass Wilderness area and makes for unique access to alpine wilderness. As with the other peaks' high roads, this one allows you to tailor the climb to your physical ability. Start at timberline for the classic "3,000 vertical" or drive to the road's end for ultimate access.

With such good summer access, the options for high altitude hiking in the Montezuma area are terrific. You can enjoy the high ridges or do the pass between Conundrum Peak and Castle Peak that drops you down to famed Conundrum Hot Springs (4.3.5). Both peaks have good summit hike routes and are excellent "first teeners." Practice your ice axe technique on Montezuma Glacier.

Technical climbers will find very little of interest on these peaks, though early season ascents of the south and north faces of Castle Peak can yield good snow routes—given an average winter and a strong spring melt-freeze cycle to mature the snow. In the summer, Castle and Conundrum are easy hikes (see summer routes). But as with any fourteener, proper equipment and knowledge are musts for safe alpine hiking.

Castle and Conundrum give skiers plenty of options. In particular, spring and summer skiing have been popular for decades on Montezuma Glacier. Most people ski the lower portion of Montezuma. But the upper part of this basin snowfield is worth exploring. With good conditions it is possible to ski off the summit of Castle, down a beautiful couloir (route 4.3.3), then down the basin and the lower snowfield—a classic ski descent.

Another amenity of note are the Alfred Braun Huts located on the Pearl Pass Road just past its junction with the Montezuma Road. These huts are open in winter and early spring and make a good base for the climbs described below. The Braun huts are closed later in the spring and in the summer. For information call the 10th Mountain Hut Association (see Appendix 3.9).

ROADS AND TRAILHEADS

USGS Maps: Hayden Peak, Maroon Bells, Pearl Pass, Gothic
USFS Forest Visitors Map: White River National Forest

Castle Creek Road

Drive W out of Aspen on Highway 82. Less than a mile out of town you'll come to a stop light and good signs at the turnoff for Castle Creek and Maroon Creek (both to the left). The Aspen Municipal Golf Course will be on your right and you'll see a church to your left. Take a

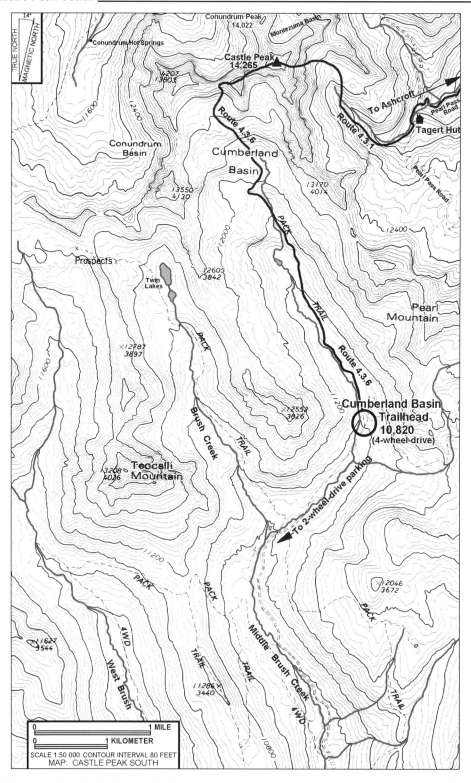

CASTLE PEAK 14,265 FT.

NORTHEAST RIDGE
ROUTE 4:3:2

EAST FACE
4:3.1

RIDGE OF
GENDARMES

TO TAGERT HUT
& PEARL PASS ROAD

N

Castle Peak east face, winter.

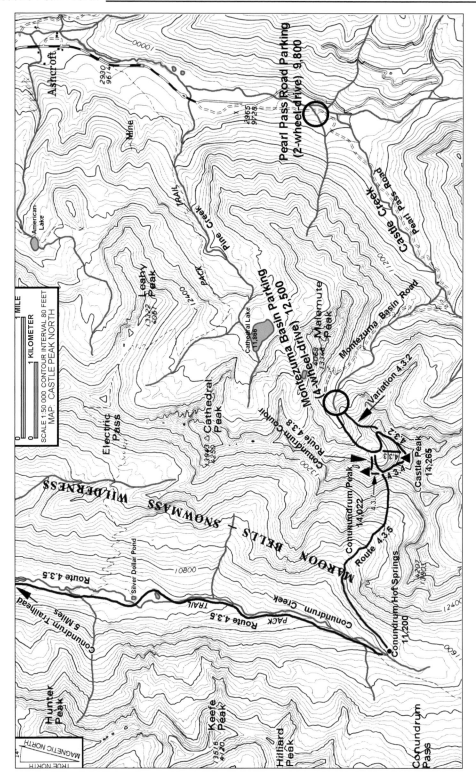

hard left onto the Castle Creek Road (the left of the two forks, the right is the Maroon Creek Road). Drive 11 miles to the ghost town of Ashcroft. Park here during snow closure.

In the summer, continue driving up the valley 1.9 miles to a Y intersection. The left fork of the Y takes you to the fenced mining operation of the Ashcroft Transfer Station; the right fork is the Pearl Pass Road. From the Highway 82 turnoff to the Y is approximately 12.9 miles.

Pearl Pass Road

Take the right fork of the Y and drive the Pearl Pass Road .7 mile to 2-wheel-drive parking (9,800') at the base of a steep hill that's obvious 4-wheel-drive terrain. With 4-wheel-drive, continue 3.2 miles up the famed Pearl Pass Jeep Trail to another fork (usually signed) where the Pearl Pass Road heads up to the left, and the Montezuma Road continues straight ahead. For the East Face route on Castle (4.3.1) take a left on the Pearl Pass Road; to get to Montezuma Basin continue straight ahead.

Montezuma Road

The Montezuma Road gets rougher the higher you go, and terminates at a large turnaround (12,500') below the Montezuma Glacier permanent snowfield. If you're concerned about abusing your 4x4, park just past where the road splits into the Pearl Pass and Montezuma Roads. Now and then, the Montezuma Road is graded and it's a reasonable 4-wheel-drive route. When the road is in poor condition, however, only expert four-wheelers should plan on driving all the way.

Snow closure is at Ashcroft. In the spring and early winter the road may be open to another snow closure 1 mile farther up the road at the Pine Creek Cookhouse, a restaurant that is part of the ski touring operation. Full melt-out varies every year because of avalanche debris. Usually, you can drive up to the Pearl Pass/Montezuma intersection by late May, with the Montezuma Road open sometime in June. In early winter (depending on snowfall), climbers and skiers use their chained 4-wheel-drive vehicles to drive as high as 10,900' on the Pearl Pass Road, just before the road crosses Castle Creek. It's best to be conservative here, since a dangerous ice flow forms over the road.

Conundrum Creek Road

Follow the directions above for the Castle Creek Road, and drive the Castle Creek Road 5 miles from the stoplight. At this point turn right (W) on the poorly signed Conundrum Creek Road (the only sign says, RESTRICTED BRIDGE), head down and to the right, cross Castle Creek, then head up the Conundrum Valley. The summer Forest Service closure gate is about 1½ miles from the Castle Creek Road. Parking is abundant. Winter snow closure is about a mile from the Castle Creek Road. Parking is sparse in winter, so park up on the Castle Creek Road and walk to the snow closure.

Brush Creek Road, Cumberland Basin Trailhead

Climbers probably reach this trailhead with bicycles as often as they do with cars. From the town of Crested Butte, drive 2 miles SE on Highway 135. Take a left off the highway on the well signed Brush Creek Road (signs for Skyland Ranch and Airport). Drive the Brush Creek Road 7½ miles (high clearance 2-wheel-drive) to 2-wheel-drive parking (9,400') before crossing Middle Brush Creek. Continue by foot or 4-wheel-drive ¼ mile to a well-signed intersection. Here the Pearl Pass jeep trail continues up Middle Brush Creek, and the Block & Tackle Jeep Trail turns off to the right. Continue on the Pearl Pass jeep trail (reasonable 4-wheel-drive) 3½ miles to the Cumberland Basin Trailhead (10,820'). This trailhead has no signs, so use your altimeter, map, and perhaps your vehicle odometer for positive identification.

Winter snow closure is usually at the Cold Spring Ranch (8,960') three miles from the highway, and far from the summit of Castle Peak. Snowmobiles pack the road up several miles, but after that it's a ski route due to sidehills and switchbacks that snowmobiles can't handle.

4.3.1	**Castle Peak—East Face**	
Ratings:	Ski Descent—Extreme	Snow Climb—Advanced
Season:	Spring Snow	
RT Data:	7 hours, 6 miles, 3,665' ↑	
Start:	Pearl Pass Road snow closure ≈10,600'	
1 Day from Rd:	Yes, or stay at the Braun Huts	
Maps:	Castle Peak South, pg. 228; Castle Peak North, pg. 230	
Photo:	pg. 229	

Spring snow season: Viewed from Pearl Basin, with a coating of spring snow, the East Face of Castle Peak inspires lust in the hearts of snow climbers and extreme skiers. It's a plumb—sought by many but plucked by few. Problem is, the route faces east and is rarely in condition.

Snow climbers should start early after a cold clear night and time their ascent to be off the route by sunrise. Skiers must be even more fanatical with their timing— late enough in the season to be safe from avalanches (late April or early May) ice runnels form soon after every snow storm. Later on, deep melt-channels form and the route becomes unskiable. The trick is to wait for a warm late April or early May storm followed by cold weather; then get on the route about 48 hours after the last snowfall. If you time it right, the recent storm will have smoothed out the snow. The key is being flexible with your timing. Be willing to come back another day if it looks bad.

The route is simple. Park at snow closure on the Pearl Pass Road (section introduction). Follow the Pearl Pass Road to its last intersection with Castle Creek at 11,280' (at a foot bridge near the Tagert Hut). Leave the road here just before crossing the foot bridge and follow the Castle Creek drainage up W then NW to the base of the east face of Castle Peak. Stay a bit right (N) as you climb to here. While ascending the drainage, be sure to pick the exact snow you will climb on the face, as the couloir branches higher up. Around 13,000' work left onto an obvious snow slope that leads to the more narrow couloirs (maximum angle 48 degrees) about midway up the face. This lower portion of the climb is hidden from view until you are beside it. It faces a bit more to the north than the east face above. When the couloirs fade, work left and continue directly toward the summit, eventually following the last several hundred feet of the Northeast Ridge (route 4.3.2).

Snow climbers should descend the Northeast or Northwest Ridge routes (4.3.2 & 4.3.4). The ski descent follows the ascent route, with minor variations in and out of the upper gullies.

Safety notes: This route should be climbed or skied on stable spring snow. Plan to be off the face by sunrise. Remember the problematic nature of east facing spring snow. This route is not safe for summer climbing because of rockfall, nor in winter because of avalanche danger.

Michael Kennedy Photo

Descending the northeast ridge of North Maroon Peak after a winter ascent.

4.3.2	**Castle Peak—Northeast Ridge**		
Ratings:	Summer Climb—Intermediate		Ski Descent—Intermediate
		Snow Climb—Intermediate	
Season:	Summer	Spring	Winter
RT Data:	4 hours, 2 miles, 1,765'↑	7 hours, 6 miles, 3665'↑	overnight, 13 miles, 4,767'↑
Start:	Montezuma Basin, 12,500'	Pearl Pass Road, snow closure ≈10,600'	Ashcroft, 9,498'
1 Day from Rd:	Yes	Yes	No
Map:	Castle Peak North, pg. 230		
Photos:	pgs. 229, 236		

Most climbers going for a "Grand Slam" use this route on Castle Peak. It's well-worn, and you'll often meet other climbers.

Summer after snow melt-off: Drive to the Montezuma Basin parking area, or park lower down depending on your vehicle and how hard you want the climb to be. If you park lower down, simply hike the jeep trail to the parking area.

From the Montezuma Basin parking area (12,500'), climb E then SE up the swooping snow slopes of the Montezuma Basin permanent snowfield to a rocky moraine (13,400') that separates lower Montezuma Basin from the upper basin tucked beneath Castle Peak's north face. Swing left (S) here, and ascend a well-worn trail up the scree covered flank of Castle Peak's northeast ridge. Once you gain the ridge crest, stick with it to the summit, with a few obvious variations to avoid rocky clefts in the ridge. Descend via the same route, and enjoy a glissade down the snowfield.

You can do a variation by climbing the Northeast Ridge direct form the parking lot. This avoids all the snow climbing.

Spring snow season: Use the route above, with variations for snow cover and your mode of travel. Skiers should stash their boards when they reach the ridge.

Winter: Fortunately, the flank of Castle's northeast ridge is often blown clear of snow. Not so fortunately, climbing up through Castle Creek and Montezuma Basin in winter has been called "the journey through the valley of death." Only attempt this route during the most stable times. Consider using one of several Alfred Braun huts in this area; see the *Colorado High Routes* guidebook for details.

Safety notes: You don't need technical climbing skills for this route. You should have an ice axe and know how to use it. Crampons may be useful for early morning starts or for ice patches in fall and early winter. Use standard sunrise for sunhit, since the lower slopes in Montezuma Basin face east.

4.3.3	**Castle Peak—North Face Couloir**	
Ratings:	Ski Descent—Advanced	Snow Climb—Intermediate
Season:	Spring or Summer Snow	
RT Data:	5½ hours, 6 miles, 3,665' ↑	
Start:	Pearl Pass Road snow closure ≈10,600'	
1 Day from Rd:	Yes	
Map:	Castle Peak North, pg. 230	

Spring or summer snow season: This is an excellent entry-level snow climb and a fine ski descent. Maximum angle is 40 degrees. Follow the directions in route 4.3.2 to the basin at the base of Castle Peak's north face. The couloir is easily spotted to the left of the summit, on the northwest face of the peak's northeast ridge. It leads to a notch below and to the northeast of the summit. From the notch follow the ridge to the summit. The couloir and upper route are obvious. With good snow cover, it's possible to ski from the summit to the couloir entrance—a grand summit ski descent!

Winter: The summer routes above are both good winter routes, provided avalanche danger is at a minimum. The route up the scree to the northeast ridge is commonly windscoured. The Conundrum Creek route (4.3.5) is also used in the winter.

Safety notes: This route should be climbed or skied on stable spring snow. You can time your ascent for a late sunhit in the couloir, but starting a little earlier is best because the snow on the summit ridge gets sun at sunrise.

N

TO CASTLE PEAK
ROUTE 4.3.5

Conundrum Hot Springs.

4.3.4	**Castle Peak—Northwest Ridge**	
Ratings:	Summer Climb—Intermediate Ski Descent—Intermediate	
	Snow Climb—Intermediate	
Season:	Summer/Spring	Spring Snow
RT Data:	4½ hours, 2¼ miles, 1,765' ↑	7½ hours, 6¼ miles, 3,665' ↑
Start:	Montezuma Basin 12,500'	Pearl Pass Road snow closure ≈10,600'
1 Day from Rd:	Yes	
Map:	Castle Peak North, pg. 230	
Photo:	pg. 236	

While similar to Castle's Northeast Ridge route (4.3.2), in the spring the Northwest Ridge allows you to stay on snow to the ridge crest. Thus, you avoid painful scree slogging and cause less erosion. In summer after melt-off, either route involves scree, with the Northeast Ridge route being slightly more worn and perhaps easier. A fun option is to climb one route and descend the other.

Summer season, or spring snow season: Follow route 4.3.2 up the Montezuma Glacier into upper Montezuma Basin below Castle Peak's north face. Swing right (W) and climb 400 vertical feet up snow or scree to the obvious saddle (13,800') separating Castle Peak from Conundrum Peak. From the saddle walk a well-defined rocky trail ¼ mile along Castle's Northwest Ridge to the summit. Skiers should leave their boards at the saddle. Consider doing a big loop by descending from the saddle to Conundrum Hot Springs (route 4.3.5).

Safety notes: If the pitch up to the saddle is dry, it has extremely steep scree that can produce rockfall and be hard for inexperienced climbers to ascend. Use standard sunrise time for sunhit and see route 4.3.2 for more notes.

4.3.5	**Castle Peak from Conundrum Hot Springs**
Ratings:	Summer Climb—Intermediate Ski Descent—Intermediate
	Snow Climb—Intermediate
Season:	All
RT Data:	overnight, 20 miles, 5,545' ↑
Start:	Conundrum Creek Trailhead 8,720'
1 Day from Rd:	No; (possible for the very fit)
Map:	Castle Peak North, pg. 230
Photo:	pg. 234

Unique in Colorado fourteener climbing, this route includes a wilderness camp with a hot bath! Highly recommended—winter, spring or summer. Bear in mind that the hot springs are crowded on summer weekends and holidays. Winter brings solitude.

Summer after snow melt-off: From parking at the Conundrum Creek Wilderness gate and trailhead (8,720') (section introduction), follow the Conundrum Creek Valley to Conundrum Hot Springs (11,200'). The trail is well traveled and obvious.

From the hot springs, take a slightly climbing traverse NE ½ mile along the east side of the valley. This will place you at the entrance to a giant amphitheater that drops west from the

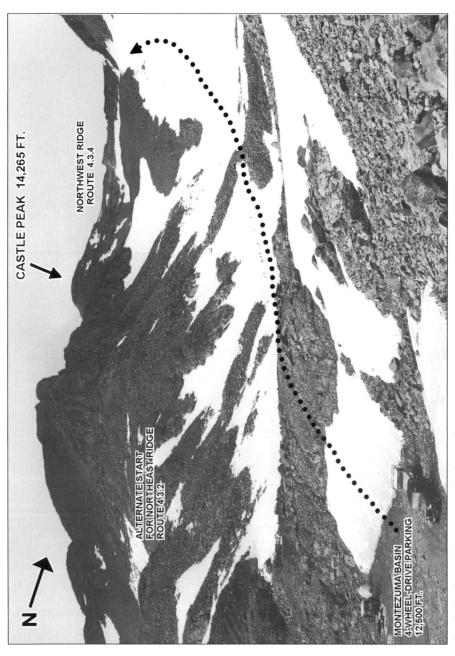

CASTLE PEAK 14,265 FT.

NORTHWEST RIDGE
ROUTE 4.3.4

ALTERNATE START
FOR NORTHEAST RIDGE
ROUTE 4.3.2

MONTEZUMA BASIN
4-WHEEL-DRIVE PARKING
12,500 FT.

N

Castle Peak and Montezuma Basin, early summer.

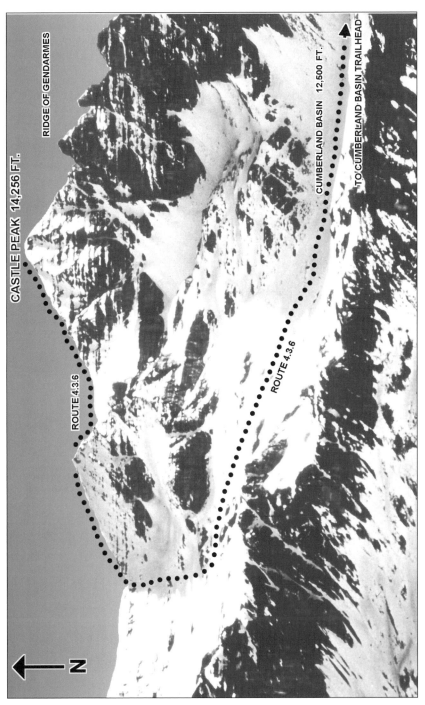

RIDGE OF GENDARMES

CASTLE PEAK 14,256 FT.

CUMBERLAND BASIN 12,500 FT.

TO CUMBERLAND BASIN TRAILHEAD

ROUTE 4.3.6

ROUTE 4.3.6

N

Castle Peak and Cumberland Basin from the south, spring.

summit of Castle. Follow the amphitheater to the Castle/Conundrum saddle (13,800'), then climb the obvious ridge to the summit. You can also climb to the summit of Conundrum Peak from this saddle (route 4.3.7). Neither route has technical climbing.

Spring snow season: Use the summer route above. The best strategy for enjoying this route is to set a high camp near Conundrum Hot Springs. While the lower portion of the trail up Conundrum Creek will be melted out, the upper portions of the trail lead through dense snowfilled timber. When hidden by snow the trail is hard to follow, and a high camp gives you a whole day for route finding. Get an early start on your first day so you'll hit snowline in the morning while it's still hard.

Winter: A winter trip up the Conundrum Valley is a highly technical orienteering problem. A wrong turn will expose you to extreme avalanche danger. Losing the trailcut can place you in impassable dark forest. The *Colorado High Routes* guide book includes a detailed description of the winter route up the Conundrum Creek Valley (see bibliography, Appendix 4)

Safety notes: Summer climbers should beware of rockfall on the steep slopes in the amphitheater. During spring snow season, get an early start. It's possible to do a winter ascent of this route that is relatively safe from avalanches. To do so, choose a time when the snow on the route has been stripped and compacted by wind—a regular occurrence on this exposure. Figure a sunhit for a west face.

Climbing Castle Peak's northwest ridge, early summer.

4.3.6	Castle Peak from Cumberland Basin	
Ratings:	Summer Climb—Advanced Ski Descent—Intermediate Snow Climb—Advanced	
Season:	Summer	Spring Snow
RT Data:	9 hours, 8 miles, 3,445' ↑	12 hours, 10 miles, 4,865' ↑
Start:	Cumberland Basin Trailhead, 10,820'	Brush Creek Road spring closure 9,400'
1 Day from Rd:	Yes	
Map:	Castle Peak South, pg. 228	
Photo:	pg. 237	

If you'd like to climb an Elk Range fourteener from the south (town of Crested Butte), and you only have a day—and mortal legs—this is your route.

Summer after snow melt-off: Four-wheel-drive, bicycle, or walk to the Cumberland Basin Trailhead (section introduction). If you walk it adds 6 miles round trip and 1,400' gain to your climb. Follow the Cumberland Basin pack trail to 12,000' in Cumberland Basin. Identify the summit of Castle Peak to the north at the head of the basin. Next, spot the major buttress which juts south into the basin from a false summit on the west ridge of Castle Peak. This buttress splits the upper part of the basin. Climb the basin to the left (W) of this buttress, eventually gaining the west ridge of Castle Peak at 13,400'.

Stick with the ridge and, taking care with dangerous loose rock, tiptoe ⅛ mile to the false summit, then continue along the ridge to the summit of Castle Peak. Return via the same route.

Spring snow season: Use the summer route above. Leave your skis in upper Cumberland Basin.

Safety notes: Loose rock is the limiting factor on this route. The route may not be cairned; allow extra time for "micro" route finding around sections of dangerous loose rock. Figure for a south face sunhit.

4.3.7	Conundrum Peak—South Ridge	
Ratings:	Summer Climb—Intermediate Ski Descent—Intermediate Snow Climb—Intermediate	
Season:	Summer	Spring Snow
RT Data:	3½ hours, 2 miles, 1,522' ↑	6½ hours, 6 miles, 3,422' ↑
Start:	Montezuma Basin, 12,500'	Pearl Pass Road spring closure ≈10,600'
1 Day from Rd:	Yes	
Map:	Castle Peak North, pg. 230	
Photo:	pg. 238	

While not an "official" fourteener, Conundrum Peak is a fine summit that is often combined with a Castle Peak climb. It's also a good peak for those not quite up for the summit of Castle.

Summer after snow melt-off: Follow route 4.3.4 to the Castle/Conundrum saddle (13,800') between Castle Peak and Conundrum Peak. From the saddle, take the easy ridge ⅛ mile N to the summit of Conundrum Peak. Descend your ascent route.

Spring snow season: Use the summer route above. Leave your skis at the saddle. For a summit ski descent use the Conundrum Couloir (route 4.3.8).

Safety notes: Use standard sunrise for sunhit.

4.3.8	**Conundrum Peak—Conundrum Couloir**	
Ratings:	Ski Descent—Advanced	Snow Climb—Advanced
Season:	Summer	Spring Snow
RT Data:	4 hours, 2 miles, 1,522' ↑	6 hours, 5 miles, 3,422' ↑
Start:	Montezuma Basin, 12,500'	Pearl Pass Road spring closure ≈10,600'
1 Day from Rd:	Yes	
Map:	Castle Peak North, pg. 230	
Photo:	pg. 238	

Summer snow season or spring snow season: From the Montezuma Road (section introduction), continue up the Montezuma Glacier to 13,600' into the the bowl under the north face of Castle Peak. If you're looking up at Castle Peak, Conundrum Peak and the Conundrum Couloir will be behind you. The deep cleft of the couloir makes it easy to spot. Climb the couloir (maximum angle 47 degrees). The crux is working around the cornice at the top.

For your descent ski the couloi or descend the South Ridge of Conundrum Peak (route 4.3.7) down to the 13,800' saddle. From the saddle drop E down scree and snow into the bowl where you began.

Safety notes: This route should only be climbed and skied on stable spring snow. If you choose to climb after the lower portion of the route melts out and exposes a rock field (which it does early in the spring), remember that a fall into rocks—rather than down a snow runout—can be a fatal mistake. Only climb this couloir when scree in the upper couloir is covered by snow. Use standard sunrise time for sunhit.

Appendix 1
ROUTE NUMBERS AND NAMES LISTED BY DIFFICULTY

Asterisks indicate recommended routes.
If you want the best of the fourteeners, and aren't so concerned with the number of peaks you climb, the asterisks indicate suggestions for enjoyable hikes, climbs and ski routes.

1.1   Summer Climbs—Novice
* 1.2.3   Mount Massive via the Mount Massive Trail
  1.2.6   Mount Elbert—Northeast Ridge
* 1.2.7   Mount Elbert Trail
* 1.4.1   Mount Belford from Elkhead Basin via Elkhead Pass
  1.6.4   Mount Harvard from Missouri Basin
  2.3.2   Mount Antero via Baldwin Creek
* 3.1.1   Mount Sherman—South Ridge from Iowa Gulch
  3.1.2   Mount Sherman from Fourmile Creek (Leavick)
* 3.1.4   Mount Lincoln—East Ridge
  3.1.6   Mount Bross from Kite Lake
  3.1.7   Mount Bross—East Flank
  3.1.9   Mount Bross via Quartzville Creek
  3.1.10 Mounts Lincoln and Bross via Quartzville Creek
* 3.2.3   Quandary Peak—East Ridge
* 3.4.1   Mount Evans—Northeast Ridge
* 3.4.6   Mount Bierstadt West Flank from Guanella Pass

1.2   Summer Climbs—Intermediate
  1.1.1   Mount of the Holy Cross—North Ridge
  1.2.2   Mount Massive from North Halfmoon Lakes
  1.2.4   North Mount Massive from the Fryingpan Drainage
  1.2.5   Mount Elbert—South Halfmoon Creek
  1.2.9   Mount Elbert from Echo Canyon
  1.3.1   La Plata Peak—Northwest Ridge
* 1.3.4   La Plata Peak—South Face from Vicksburg
  1.4.2   Mount Belford—Northwest Flank
  1.4.5   Mount Oxford via Mount Belford
* 1.4.6   Mount Oxford—East Ridge from Pine Creek
  1.4.8   Missouri Mountain—South Ridge from Missouri Basin
  1.4.10 Missouri Mountain—Northwest Ridge from Elkhead Basin
  1.4.11 Missouri Mountain—West Ridge from Lake Fork Creek
  1.5.1   Huron Peak—Southwest Face from South Fork of Clear Creek
  1.5.2   Huron Peak—Direct West Face from South Fork of Clear Creek
  1.5.3   Huron Peak —East Face from Lake Fork Creek
* 1.6.1   Mount Harvard—South Ridge
  1.6.5   Mount Columbia from Three Elk Creek
  1.6.6   Mount Columbia—West Flank to South Ridge
* 1.6.7   Mount Columbia—Southeast Ridge
  2.1.1   Mount Yale from Kroenke Lake
* 2.1.2   Mount Yale—East Ridge
  2.1.3   Mount Yale via Denny Creek & Delaney Gulch
  2.2.1   Mount Princeton from Merriam Creek
* 2.3.4   Mount Shavano—The Angel Snowfield
  3.1.11 Mount Lincoln and Mount Bross from Kite Lake
* 3.1.12 Mount Democrat from Kite Lake
  3.1.13 Mount Democrat—North Flank
  3.3.1   Grays and Torreys Peaks via Trail from Stevens Gulch
  3.3.2   Grays and Torreys Peaks via Chihuahua Gulch
* 3.3.3   Grays Peak from Horseshoe Basin
* 3.4.3   Mount Evans—Northwest Ridge from Summit Lake
  3.4.4   Mount Evans West Ridge from Guanella Pass
  3.4.9   Mount Bierstadt from Mount Evans via Abyss Lake
* 3.5.4. Longs Peak—Keyhole Route
* 4.1.4   Snowmass Mountain—The Big Bowl from Snowmass Lake
* 4.3.2   Castle Peak—Northeast Ridge
  4.3.4   Castle Peak—Northwest Ridge
* 4.3.5   Castle Peak from Conundrum Hot Springs
  4.3.7   Conundrum Peak —South Ridge

1.3   Summer Climbs—Advanced
  1.1.4   Mount of the Holy Cross—Halo Route
  1.2.1   Mount Massive Direct from North Halfmoon Creek
  1.2.8   Mount Elbert via Black Cloud Gulch
* 1.3.3   La Plata Peak—Ellingwood Ridge
  1.4.7   Mount Oxford—South Flank from Pine Creek
  1.6.3   Mount Harvard—Mount Harvard Trail
* 2.2.2   Mount Princeton from Grouse Canyon
  2.3.5   Mount Shavano via Tabeguache Peak
  2.3.6   Tabeguache Peak—Southwest/West Ridge from Jennings Creek
  2.3.8   Tabeguache Peak via Mount Shavano
  3.1.5   Mount Lincoln—Lincoln Amphitheater
  3.2.1   Quandary Peak—West Ridge
* 3.3.5   Torreys Peak Northeast (Kelso) Ridge from Stevens Gulch
* 3.3.7   Torreys Peak from Loveland Pass
  3.4.5   Mount Evans from Mount Bierstadt via Sawtooth Ridge
  3.4.8   Mount Bierstadt from the Abyss Lake Trail
  3.4.10 Mount Bierstadt from Mount Evans via Sawtooth Ridge
* 3.5.1   Longs Peak—Kieners Route (Technical Rock—5.2)
  3.5.2   Longs Peak—Notch Couloir (Technical Rock—5.5)
  3.5.3   Longs Peak—North Face Cable Route
* 4.1.1   Capitol Peak—Knife Ridge
  4.1.2   Capitol Peak—North Face via Slingshot Couloir (Technical Rock—5.5)
* 4.1.3   Capitol Peak—Northwest Buttress (Technical Rock—5.9)
  4.1.5   Snowmass Mountain from Geneva Lake
  4.2.1   South Maroon Peak—East Face Couloirs
* 4.2.2   South Maroon Peak—South Ridge
  4.2.5   South Maroon Peak via North Maroon Peak
  4.2.6   North Maroon Peak —Northeast Ridge

4.2.8   North Maroon Peak—Gunsight Ridge
4.2.12   Pyramid Peak—Keyhole Route (Northwest Ridge)
* 4.3.6   Castle Peak from Cumberland Basin

RECOMMENDED SKI ROUTES
(may not be skiable from summit)

1.4   Ski Descents—Novice

3.1.1   Mount Sherman—South Ridge from Iowa Gulch
3.1.4   Mount Lincoln—East Ridge
3.1.7   Mount Bross—East Flank
* 3.2.3   Quandary Peak—East Ridge
3.3.2   Grays and Torreys Peaks from Chihuahua Gulch
* 3.4.1   Mount Evans—Northeast Ridge

1.5   Ski Descents—Intermediate

1.1.1   Mount of the Holy Cross—North Ridge
1.2.7   Mount Elbert—Mount Elbert Trail
1.4.1   Mount Belford from Elkhead Basin via Elkhead Pass
1.4.6   Mount Oxford—East Ridge from Pine Creek
1.4.8   Missouri Mountain—South Ridge from Missouri Basin
1.5.1   Huron Peak—Southwest Face from South Fork of Clear Creek
1.5.2   Huron Peak—Direct West Face from South Fork of Clear Creek
* 1.6.2   Mount Harvard—South Face Snow Route
* 1.6.5   Mount Columbia from Three Elk Creek
2.1.1   Mount Yale from Kroenke Lake
2.1.2   Mount Yale—East Ridge
2.1.3   Mount Yale via Denny Creek & Delaney Gulch
2.2.1   Mount Princeton from Merriam Creek
* 2.3.4   Mount Shavano—The Angel Snowfield
2.3.5   Mount Shavano via Tabeguache Peak
2.3.8   Tabeguache Peak via Mount Shavano
3.1.2   Mount Sherman from Fourmile Creek (Leavick)
3.1.6   Mount Bross from Kite Lake
3.1.9   Mount Bross via Quartzville Creek
3.1.10   Mount Lincoln and Mount Bross via Quartzville Creek
3.1.12   Mount Democrat from Kite Lake
* 3.3.1   Grays and Torreys Peaks via Trail from Stevens Gulch
3.3.5   Torreys Peak—Northeast (Kelso) Ridge from Stevens Gulch
3.4.4   Mount Evans West Ridge from Guanella Pass
* 3.4.6   Mount Bierstadt West Flank from Guanella Pass
* 4.1.4   Snowmass Mountain—The Big Bowl from Snowmass Lake
4.3.2   Castle Peak—Northeast Ridge
4.3.4   Castle Peak—Northwest Ridge
* 4.3.5   Castle Peak from Conundrum Hot Springs
4.3.7   Conundrum Peak—South Ridge

1.6   Ski Descents—Advanced

1.1.3   Mount of the Holy Cross—Holy Cross Ridge
1.2.1   Mount Massive Direct from North Halfmoom Creek
1.2.2   Mount Massive from North Halfmoon Lakes
* 1.2.3   Mount Massive via the Mount Massive Trail

* 1.2.4   North Mount Massive from the Fryingpan Drainage
* 1.2.5   Mount Elbert—South Halfmoon Creek
1.2.6   Mount Elbert—Northeast Ridge
1.2.8   Mount Elbert via Black Cloud Gulch
1.3.1   La Plata Peak—Northwest Ridge
1.3.4   La Plata Peak—South Face from Vicksburg
* 1.4.3   Mount Belford—West Face Central Couloir
1.4.4   Mount Belford—Northwest Gulch
1.4.5   Mount Oxford via Mount Belford
1.4.7   Mount Oxford—South Flank from Pine Creek
1.4.10   Missouri Mountain—Northwest Ridge from Elkhead Basin
1.4.11   Missouri Mountain—West Ridge from Lake Fork Creek
* 1.5.3   Huron Peak—East Face from Lake Fork Creek
1.6.8   Mount Columbia—West Face Snow Route
2.3.2   Mount Antero via Baldwin Creek
2.3.3   Mount Shavano—Southeast Couloir
2.3.6   Tabeguache Peak—Southwest/West Ridge from Jennings Creek
* 3.1.3   Mount Lincoln—Russian Couloir
3.1.5   Mount Lincoln—Lincoln Amphitheater
* 3.1.8   Mount Bross—Moose Creek Gulch
3.1.11   Mount Lincoln and Mount Bross from Kite Lake
3.1.13   Mount Democrat—North Flank
* 3.2.2   Quandary Peak—South Gully (Cristo Couloir)
* 3.3.6   Torreys Peak Northwest Face from Grizzly Gulch
3.3.7   Torreys Peak from Loveland Pass
* 3.4.2   Mount Evans—Summit Lake Bowl
3.4.7   Mount Bierstadt Snow Route from Frozen Lake
3.4.9   Mount Bierstadt from Mount Evans via Abyss Lake
3.5.2   Longs Peak—Notch Couloir
* 3.5.5   Longs Peak—Trough Couloir
* 4.3.3   Castle Peak—North Face Couloir
4.3.8   Conundrum Peak—Conundrum Couloir

1.7   Ski Descents—Extreme

1.1.2   Mount of the Holy Cross Cross Couloir
* 1.3.2   La Plata Peak—North Face
1.4.9   Missouri Mountain—North Face from Elkhead Basin
2.3.1   Mount Antero—Direct North Face from Chalk Creek
2.3.7   Tabeguache Peak—North Face
3.1.14   Mount Democrat—North Face Snow Route
3.1.15   Mount Democrat—West Face Snow & Ski Route
* 3.3.4   Torreys Peak—Dead Dog Couloir from Stevens Gulch
3.5.3   Longs Peak—North Face Cable Route
4.2.3   South Maroon Peak—Bell Cord Couloir
4.2.4   South Maroon Peak—Southwest Face Direct
* 4.2.7   North Maroon Peak—North Face Direct
4.2.8   North Maroon Peak—Gunsight Ridge
* 4.2.9   North Maroon Peak—North Face & West Face Combo

	Couloir
4.1.5	Snowmass Mountain from Geneva Lake
* 4.2.1	South Maroon Peak—East Face Couloirs
4.2.3	South Maroon Peak—Bell Cord Couloir
4.2.5	South Maroon Peak via North Maroon Peak
4.2.6	North Maroon Peak—Northeast Ridge
4.2.7	North Maroon Peak—North Face Direct (this borders on an Extreme snow climb)
* 4.2.8	North Maroon Peak—Gunsight Ridge
4.2.9	North Maroon Peak—North Face & West Face Combo
4.2.10	Pyramid Peak—East Face
4.2.11	Pyramid Peak—Northeast Ridge
4.2.12	Pyramid Peak—Keyhole Route (Northwest Ridge)
* 4.2.13	Pyramid Peak—West Face Snow & Ski Route
4.3.1	Castle Peak—East Face
4.3.6	Castle Peak from Cumberland Basin
4.3.8	Conundrum Peak—Conundrum Couloir

1.11   Snow Climbs —Extreme

* 2.3.1	Mount Antero—Direct North Face from Chalk Creek
4.2.4	South Maroon Peak—Southwest Face Direct
* 4.2.14	Pyramid Peak—West Face Direct Snow Route

Appendix 2
2.1. SUMMER CLIMBER'S GRAND SLAM ROUTES

If your goal is simply to have climbed all the 54 official fourteeners, use this list of the most efficient summer routes in this volume.

4.1.1	Capitol Peak—Knife Ridge
4.3.4	Castle Peak—Northwest Ridge,
3.3.1	Grays and Torreys Peak via Trail from Stevens Gulch
1.5.1	Huron Peak—Southwest Face
1.3.1	La Plata Peak—Northwest Ridge
3.5.4	Longs Peak—Keyhole Route
1.4.10	Missouri Mountain—Northwest Ridge from Elkhead Basin
2.3.2	Mount Antero via Baldwin Creek
1.4.2	Mount Belford—Northwest Flank
3.4.6	Mount Bierstadt West Flank from Guanella Pass
3.1.10	Mount Lincoln and Mount Bross via Quartzville Creek
1.6.6	Mount Columbia—West Flank to South Ridge
3.1.12	Mount Democrat from Kite Lake
1.2.7	Mount Elbert—Mount Elbert Trail
3.4.1	Mount Evans—Northeast Ridge
1.6.1	Mount Harvard—South Ridge
3.1.10	Mount Lincoln and Mount Bross via Quartzville Creek
1.2.3	Mount Massive via the Mount Massive Trail
1.4.5	Mount Oxford via Mount Belford
2.2.1	Mount Princeton from Merriam Creek
2.3.4	Mount Shavano—The Angel Snowfield
3.1.1	Mount Sherman—South Ridge from Iowa Gulch
2.1.3	Mount Yale via Denny Creek & Delaney Gulch

1.1.1	Mount of the Holy Cross—North Ridge
4.2.6	North Maroon Peak—Northeast Ridge
4.2.11	Pyramid Peak—Northeast Ridge
3.2.3	Quandary Peak—East Ridge
4.1.4	Snowmass Mountain—The Big Bowl from Snowmass Lake
4.2.2	South Maroon Peak—South Ridge
2.3.8	Tabeguache Peak via Mount Shavano
3.3.1	Grays and Torreys Peaks via Trail from Stevens Gulch

2.2. SKIER'S GRAND SLAM ROUTES

If your goal is to ski all 54 fourteeners, here are the routes you need for the 30 official fourteeners (plus North Maroon Peak, since most people count it as official) covered in this volume. These recommended routes aren't always the most aesthetic, but they're the ones that leave from the summit and have the best access.

4.1.1	Capitol Peak—Knife Ridge
4.3.3	Castle Peak—North Face Couloir
3.3.1	Grays and Torreys Peaks via Trail from Stevens Gulch
1.5.1	Huron Peak—Southwest
1.5.2	Huron Peak—Direct West Face
1.3.2	La Plata Peak—North Face
3.5.3	Longs Peak—North Face Cable Route
1.4.9	Missouri Mountain—North Face from Elkhead Basin
2.3.2	Mount Antero via Baldwin Cree,
1.4.3	Mount Belford—West Face Central Couloir
3.4.6	Mount Bierstadt West Flank from Guanella Pass
3.1.8	Mount Bross—Moose Creek Gulch
1.6.5	Mount Columbia from Three Elk Creek,
1.6.8	Mount Columbia—West Face Snow Route
3.1.12, 3.1.15	Mount Democrat From Kite Lake or West Face
1.2.7	Mount Elbert—Mount Elbert Trail
3.4.2	Mount Evans—Summit Lake Bowl
1.6.2	Mount Harvard—South Face Snow Route
3.1.4	Mount Lincoln—East Ridge
1.2.3	Mount Massive via the Mount Massive Trail
1.4.5	Mount Oxford via Mount Belford
2.2.1	Mount Princeton from Merriam Creek (descend east face bowl)
2.3.4	Mount Shavano—The Angel Snowfield
3.1.1	Mount Sherman—Iowa Gulch
2.1.2	Mount Yale—East Ridge (descend Avalanche Gulch Bowl)
1.1.1	Mount of the Holy Cross—North Ridge
4.2.7	North Maroon Peak—North Face Direct
4.2.10, 4.2.11	Pyramid Peak—East Face Pyramid Peak—Northeast Ridge combination,
3.2.2, 3.2.3	Quandary Peak—Cristo Couloir, or East Ridge
4.1.4	Snowmass Mountain—The Big Bowl
4.2.1	South Maroon Peak—East Face Couloirs
2.3.7, 2.3.6	Tabeguache Peak—North Face, or Jennings Creek

3.3.1	Grays and Torreys Peaks via Trail from Stevens Gulch

2.3. WINTER GRAND SLAM ROUTES

To date only one man, Tom Mereness of Boulder Colorado, has climbed all 54 official fourteeners in winter. If you want to be the next, here are the best winter routes for the 30 official fourteeners covered in this volume. Remember, "winter" means any day during "official" winter between the winter solstice and the vernal equinox.

4.1.1	Capitol Peak—Knife Ridge
4.3.2	Castle Peak—Northeast Ridge
3.3.2	Grays and Torreys Peaks from Chihuahua Gulch
1.5.1	Huron Peak—Southwest Face from South Fork of Clear Creek
1.3.1	La Plata Peak—Northwest Ridge
3.5.4	Longs Peak—Keyhole Route
1.4.11	Missouri Mountain—West Ridge from Lake Fork Creek
2.3.2	Mount Antero via Baldwin Creek
1.4.2	Mount Belford—Northwest flank
3.4.6	Mount Bierstadt West Flank from Guanella Pass
3.1.4	Mount Bross—East Ridge, then ridge to Bross
1.6.5,	Mount Columbia from Three Elk Creek,
1.6.7	Mount Columbia—Southeast Ridge
3.1.4	Mount Lincoln—East Ridge
1.2.6,	Mount Elbert—Northeast Ridge,
1.2.7	Mount Elbert—Mount Elbert Trail
3.4.4	Mount Evans West Ridge from Guanella Pass
1.6.1	Mount Harvard—South Ridge
3.1.4	Mount Lincoln—East Ridge
1.2.3	Mount Massive via the Mount Massive Trail
1.4.5	Mount Oxford via Mount Belford
2.2.1	Mount Princeton from Merriam Creek
2.3.4	Mount Shavano—The Angel Snowfield
3.1.1	Mount Sherman—South Ridge from Iowa Gulch
2.1.3	Mount Yale via Denny Creek & Delaney Gulch
1.1.1	Mount of the Holy Cross—North Ridge
4.2.6	North Maroon Peak—Northeast Ridge
4.2.12	Pyramid Peak—Keyhole Route (Northwest Ridge)
3.2.3	Quandary Peak—East Ridge
4.1.4	Snowmass Mountain—The Big Bowl from Snowmass Lake,
4.1.5	or from Geneva Lake
4.2.2	South Maroon Peak—South Ridge,
4.2.5	or from North Maroon
2.3.6	Tabeguache Peak—Southwest/West Ridge from Jennings Creek
3.3.2	Grays and Torreys Peaks from Chihuahua Gulch

2.4 RECOMMENDED WINTER CLIMBS

HARD
3.2.3	Quandary Peak—East Ridge
3.4.6	Mount Bierstadt West Flank from Guanella Pass
3.1.1	Mount Sherman—South Ridge from Iowa Gulch
3.1.7	Mount Bross—East Flank

HARDER
1.2.6	Mount Elbert—Northeast Ridge,
1.4.11	Missouri Mountain—West Ridge from Lake Fork Creek
2.1.3	Mount Yale via Denny Creek & Delaney Gulch
2.3.2	Mount Antero via Baldwin Creek
2.3.4	Mount Shavano—The Angel Snowfield
3.1.4	Mount Lincoln—East Ridge
3.3.2	Grays and Torreys Peaks from Chihuahua Gulch
3.4.4	Mount Evans West Ridge from Guanella Pass
4.2.13	Pyramid Peak—West Face Snow & Ski route (no skiing in winter)
4.3.2	Castle Peak—Northeast Ridge

DESPERATE
1.1.4	Mount of the Holy Cross—Halo Route
4.2.6	North Maroon Peaks—Northeast Ridge
4.2.5	South Maroon Peaks via North Maroon Peak
1.3.3	La Plata Peak—Ellingwood Ridge
3.5.3	Longs Peak—North Face Cable Route
4.1.1	Capitol Peak—Knife Ridge

Appendix 3
RESOURCE DIRECTORY

3.1. COUNTY PHONE NUMBERS FOR ROAD INFORMATION AND EMERGENCIES

In Colorado the County Sheriff handles emergency calls; try 911 first—if there is no response call the sheriff directly.

Boulder County   (county seat: Boulder)
County office	(303)441-3131
Sheriff	(303)441-4609

Chaffee County   (county seat: Salida)
County office	(719)539-4004
Sheriff	(719)539-2814

Clear Creek County   (county seat: Georgetown)
County office	(303)534-5777
Sheriff	same

Costilla County (county seat: San Luis)
County office	(719)672-3962
Sheriff	(719)672-3302

Custer County   (county seat: Westcliffe)
County office	(719)783-2441
Sheriff	(719)783-2270

Dolores   (county seat: Dove Creek)
County office	(719)677-2383
Sheriff	(719)677-2257

Eagle County   (county seat: Eagle)
County office	(303)328-7311
Sheriff	(303)328-6611

El Paso County (county seat: Colorado Springs)
County office	(719)630-2800
Sheriff	(719)520-7100

Fremont County (county seat: Canon City)
    County office   (719)275-7521
    Sheriff   (719)275-2000
Gunnison County (county seat: Gunnison)
    County office   (303)641-0248
    Sheriff   (303)641-1113
Hinsdale County (county seat: Lake City)
    County office   (303)944-2225
    Sheriff   (303)944-2291
Huerfano County (county seat: Walsenberg)
    County office   (719)738-2370
    Sheriff   (719)738-1600
Lake County (county seat: Leadville)
    County office   (719)486-1410
    Sheriff   (719)486-1249
La Plata County (county seat: Durango)
    County office   (303)259-4000
    Sheriff   (303)247-1157
Larimer County (county seat: Fort Collins)
    County office   (303)221-7000
    Sheriff   (303)498-5101
Las Animas County (county seat: Trinidad)
    County office   (719)846-3481
    Sheriff   (719)846-2211
Mineral County (county seat: Creede)
    County office   (719)658-2440
    Sheriff   (719)658-2600
Montezuma County (county seat: Cortez)
    County office   (303)565-8317
    Sheriff   (303)565-8441
Park County (county seat: Fairplay)
    County office   (719838-7509
    Sheriff   (719)836-2494
Pitkin County (county seat: Aspen)
    County office   (303)920-5180
    Sheriff   (303)920-5300
Saguache County (county seat: Saguache)
    County office   (719)655-2231
    Sheriff   (719)655-2544
San Juan County (county seat: Silverton)
    County office   (303)387-5671
    Sheriff   (303)387-5531
San Miguel County (county seat: Telluride)
    County office   (303)728-3954
    Sheriff   (303)728-4442
Summit County (county seat: Breckenridge)
    County office   (303)453-2561
    Sheriff   (303)453-2232

3.2 MECHANIZED ACCESS
Aspen
    T Lazy Seven Ranch, Snowmobile Rentals
    303-925-7254
Buena Vista
    Buena Vista Snowdrifters (snowmobile club)
    Bx. 3133, Buena Vista, CO, 81211
Lake City
    Continental Divide Snowmobile Club
    Bx. 797, Lake City CO, 81235
    Lake City Nordic Association 944-2625
Leadville
    High Riders Snowmobile Club
    400 E. 6th St., Leadville, CO 80461

Westcliff
    Sangre Snow Runners
    Bx 145, Silvercliff, CO 81249
Minturn
    Nova Guides (303)949-4232
Durango -Silverton Railroad
    Animas River Railway 303-247-9349

3.3. CHAMBERS OF COMMERCE PHONE NUMBERS
Lake City   (303)944-2527
Aspen   1-800-26-ASPEN
Durango   1-800-525-8855
Leadville   1-800-933-3901
Estes Park   1-800-44-ESTES

3.4. FOREST SERVICE and PARK SERVICE
The supervisor's office can give you the numbers of appropriate district offices for your trip.
Arapaho/Roosevelt National Forests
    (303)498-1100 Ft. Collins
Pike/San Isabel National Forests
    (719)545-8737 Pueblo
White River National Forest
    (303)945-2521 Glenwood Springs
Rocky Mountain National Park
    (303)586-2371 Estes Park

3.5. COLORADO STATE PATROL
Road conditions   (303)639-1234

3.6. GUIDE SERVICES
Adventures to the Edge
Bx 1965
Crested Butte, CO (303)349-6351

Antoine Savelli Guides
Bx 2411
Telluride, CO 81435 (303)728-3705

Aspen Alpine Guides
Bx 7937
Aspen, Co 81611 (303)625-6618

Elk Mountain Guides
Bx 10327
Aspen, CO 81612 (303)923-6131

Fantasy Ridge
Bx 1679
Telluride, CO (303)728-3546

Kent Mountain Adventure Center
Bx 835
Estes Park, CO (303)586-5990

Paragon Guides
Bx 130
Vail, CO 81658 (303)949-4272

3.7. FOREST SERVICE REGIONAL AVALANCHE INFORMATION FOR COLORADO

Front Range	(303)236-9435
Northern (Longs Peak)	(303)482-0457
Southern (Pikes Peak)	(719)520-0020
Vail Area	(303)827-5687
Dillon Area	(303)468-5434
Aspen Area	(303)920-1664

3.8. WEATHER

The avalanche information numbers provide good weather information.

Denver area weather	(303)398-3964
Weather radio VHF band	162.55 MHZ

(this is the best source of current information)

3.9 LODGING

HUTS

Fred Braun Huts and Friends Hut
c/o Tenth Mountain Trail Association
(hut reservations)
1280 Ute Avenue
Aspen, CO 81612 (303)925-5775

Colorado Mountain Club
3375 W. 31st Ave.
Denver CO 80211 (303)477-6343

Appendix 4
BIBLIOGRAPHY

Barnett, Steve. _Cross Country Downhill, 3rd ed._ Seattle: Pacific Search Press, 1983.

Bein, Vic. _Mountain Skiing._ Seattle: The Mountaineers, 1982.

Borneman and Lampert. _A Climbing Guide to Colorado's Fourteeners, 3rd. ed._ Boulder: Pruett Publishing, 1988.

Bueler, William. _Roof of the Rockies._ Boulder, Colorado: Pruett, 1974.

Dawson, Louis. _Colorado 10th Mountain Trails._ Aspen: WHO Press, 1991.

Dawson, Louis. _Colorado High Routes._ Seattle: The Mountaineers, 1987.

Kelner, Alexis and Hanscom, David. _Wasatch Tours._ Salt Lake City: Wasatch Publishers, Inc., 1976.

LaChapelle, Edward R. _The ABC of Avalanche Safety, 2nd ed._ Seattle: The Mountaineers, 1985.

Litz, Brian and Lankford, Kurt. _Skiiing Colorado's Backcountry._ Golden: Fulcrum, 1989

Peters, Ed, ed. _Mountaineering: The Freedom of the Hills._ Seattle: The Mountaineers, 1991

Perla, Ronald and Martinelli, M. _Avalanche Handbook._ Washington, D.C.: U.S. Department of Agriculture #489, 1976.

Roach, Gerry. _Colorado's Fourteeners._ Golden: Fulcrum Press, 1992.

Tejada-Flores, Lito. _Backcountry Skiing._ San Francisco: Sierra Club Books, 1981.

Watters, Ron. _Ski Camping._ San Francisco: Solstice Press/Chronicle Books, 1979.

Williams, Knox and Armstrong, Betsy. _The Snowy Torrents - Avalanche Accidents in the United States 1972-1979._ Jackson, Wyoming: Teton Bookshop Publishing Company.

Williams, Knox and Armstrong, Betsy. _The Avalanche Book._ Golden, Colorado: Fulcrum, 1986.

Appendix 5
TIMING YOUR ASCENT

The following suggestions, combined with the sun chart, will help you time your route for the most enjoyment and safety.

During the spring compacted snow season, when the snowpack is undergoing the a daily melt-freeze cycle, use the following rules of thumb:
- be off E by 9:00 MST
- be off S by 11:00 MST
- be off W by 12:30 MST
- be off N by 2:00 MST

You must be certain that north facing snow is in the spring melt-freeze. Otherwise, you're dealing with a winter snowpack, and possible soft slab avalanches. If the north facing snow is in the spring cycle, your safety depends on the air temperature during the day and how well it froze the night before. That's because, even in the spring, north facing snow doesn't get much sun. Beware, however, of how much sun the east and west sides of a north facing gully are getting. If the temperature at timberline, before sunrise, is warmer than 32 degrees F, abort your trip with no question. During years with a deep snowpack, the snow may mature to a point where it can be skied safely without being frozen. Such snow is very dense, and rare before June.

Roughly speaking, the sun will hit the east side of a fourteener at sunrise time. An intervening peak that is high and close will delay east sunhit. But few east facing routes are blocked significantly in this fashion. Of more concern is that a peak facing out over the eastern plains will have an earlier sunhit – sometimes 45 minutes earlier than standard sunrise.

South facing mountain sides will receive sunhit several hours after sunrise time. The exact delay depends on the date. During the shortest winter days the delay is shorter; towards the longer days of spring, the delay increases. Intervening mountains are not a factor, since by the time the sun moves around to the south it is high enough in the sky to be above any mountains.

In the winter, most north faces get little or no sun. In the spring, north faces get hit early in the morning or in the late afternoon, depending on exact aspect and horizon angle, how deeply the face is cupped, and how deep the gullies are. A deep gully on any face will receive a later sunhit than an equivalent smooth slope. But remember that couloirs usually open out onto less riven areas near the summit, and the snow here will still receive sun, even while the more deeply cleft portions of the gully are shaded. For example, the North Face of North Maroon Peak gets its spring sun-hit at sunrise.

SUNRISE AND SUNSET TIMES

These times these are figured for an average latitude and longitude of Colorado's fourteeners. The differences possible because of variation from this average amount only to minutes. Of more concern are variations due to your horizon. In other words, the horizon when you're in a valley is the ridge above you, and the sun will hit the vally later than standard sunrise.

Conversely, if you're on the side of a mountain above the horizon, the sun will hit earlier.

SUNRISE TIMES FOR CENTRAL COLORADO TIMES: MOUNTAIN STANDARD AND MOUNTAIN DAYLIGHT AS NOTED

TIMES BELOW:
MOUNTAIN STANDARD

DATE	SUNRISE	SUNSET
1 JAN	7:27	16:54
5 JAN	7:27	16:57
10 JAN	7:27	17:02
15 JAN	7:25	17:07
20 JAN	7:23	17:13
25 JAN	7:20	17:19
30 JAN	7:16	17:25
5 FEB	7:10	17:32
10 FEB	7:04	17:38
15 FEB	6:58	17:43
20 FEB	6:52	17:49
25 FEB	6:45	17:55
1 MAR	6:39	17:59
5 MAR	6:33	18:03
10 MAR	6:25	18:09
15 MAR	6:18	18:14
20 MAR	6:10	18:19
25 MAR	6:02	18:24
30 MAR	5:54	18:29
5 APR	5:44	18:35

TIMES BELOW:
DAYLIGHT SAVINGS

10 APR	6:36	19:40
15 APR	6:29	19:45
20 APR	6:22	19:50
25 APR	6:15	19:55
30 APR	6:08	19:59
5 MAY	6:03	20:04
10 MAY	5:57	20:09
15 MAY	5:52	20:14
20 MAY	5:48	20:18
25 MAY	5:45	20:23
1 JUN	5:41	20:28
5 JUN	5:40	20:30
10 JUN	5:39	20:33
15 JUN	5:39	20:35
20 JUN	5:39	20:37
25 JUN	5:41	20:38
1 JUL	5:43	20:38
5 JUL	5:45	20:37
10 JUL	5:48	20:35
15 JUL	5:52	20:33
20 JUL	5:56	20:29
25 JUL	6:00	20:25
1 AUG	6:06	20:19
5 AUG	6:10	20:14
10 AUG	6:14	20:08
15 AUG	6:19	20:02
20 AUG	6:24	19:55
25 AUG	6:28	19:48
5 SEP	6:39	19:31
10 SEP	6:43	19:23
15 SEP	6:48	19:15
20 SEP	6:52	19:07
25 SEP	6:57	18:58
1 OCT	7:03	18:49
2 OCT	7:04	18:47
3 OCT	7:05	18:46
4 OCT	7:06	18:44
5 OCT	7:07	18:42
6 OCT	7:08	18:41
7 OCT	7:09	18:39
8 OCT	7:10	18:38
9 OCT	7:11	18:36
10 OCT	7:12	18:35
11 OCT	7:13	18:33
12 OCT	7:14	18:32
13 OCT	7:15	18:30
14 OCT	7:16	18:29
15 OCT	7:17	18:27
16 OCT	7:18	18:26
17 OCT	7:19	18:24
18 OCT	7:20	18:23
19 OCT	7:21	18:21
20 OCT	7:22	18:20
21 OCT	7:23	18:19
22 OCT	7:24	18:17
23 OCT	7:25	18:16
24 OCT	7:26	18:15
25 OCT	7:27	18:13

TIMES BELOW:
MOUNTAIN STANDARD

26 OCT	6:28	17:12
27 OCT	6:29	17:11
28 OCT	6:31	17:09
29 OCT	6:32	17:08
30 OCT	6:33	17:07
31 OCT	6:34	17:06
1 NOV	6:35	17:05
2 NOV	6:36	17:04
3 NOV	6:37	17:02
4 NOV	6:38	17:01
5 NOV	6:39	17:00
6 NOV	6:41	16:59
7 NOV	6:42	16:58
8 NOV	6:43	16:57
9 NOV	6:44	16:56
10 NOV	6:45	16:55
11 NOV	6:46	16:54
12 NOV	6:47	16:54
13 NOV	6:49	16:53
14 NOV	6:50	16:52
15 NOV	6:51	16:51
16 NOV	6:52	16:50
17 NOV	6:53	16:50
18 NOV	6:54	16:49
19 NOV	6:55	16:48
20 NOV	6:56	16:48
21 NOV	6:58	16:47
22 NOV	6:59	16:47
23 NOV	7:00	16:46
24 NOV	7:01	16:46
25 NOV	7:02	16:45
26 NOV	7:03	16:45
27 NOV	7:04	16:44
28 NOV	7:05	16:44
29 NOV	7:06	16:44
30 NOV	7:07	16:43
1 DEC	7:08	16:43
2 DEC	7:09	16:43
3 DEC	7:10	16:43
4 DEC	7:11	16:43
5 DEC	7:12	16:43
6 DEC	7:13	16:42
7 DEC	7:14	16:42
8 DEC	7:15	16:42
9 DEC	7:15	16:43
10 DEC	7:16	16:43
11 DEC	7:17	16:43
12 DEC	7:18	16:43
13 DEC	7:19	16:43
14 DEC	7:19	16:43
15 DEC	7:20	16:44
16 DEC	7:21	16:44
17 DEC	7:21	16:44
18 DEC	7:22	16:45
19 DEC	7:22	16:45
20 DEC	7:23	16:46
21 DEC	7:24	16:46
22 DEC	7:24	16:47
23 DEC	7:24	16:47
24 DEC	7:25	16:48
25 DEC	7:25	16:48
26 DEC	7:26	16:49
27 DEC	7:26	16:50
28 DEC	7:26	16:50
29 DEC	7:26	16:51
30 DEC	7:27	16:52
31 DEC	7:27	16:53

Appendix 6
FOURTEENER LISTS IN ALPHABETICAL ORDER & ELEVATION ORDER

6.1 ALL COLORADO'S 54 OFFICIAL FOURTEENERS, ALPHABETIC.

Blanca Peak, 14,345
Capitol Peak, 14,130
Castle Peak, 14,265
Crestone Needle, 14,197
Crestone Peak, 14,294
Culebra Peak, 14,047
El Diente Peak, 14,159
Ellingwood Peak, 14,042
Grays Peak, 14,270
Handies Peak, 14,048
Humboldt Peak, 14,064
Huron Peak, 14,003
Kit Carson Mountain, 14,165
La Plata Peak, 14,336
Little Bear Peak, 14,037
Longs Peak, 14,255
Missouri Mountain, 14,067
Mount Antero, 14,269
Mount Belford, 14,197
Mount Bierstadt, 14,060
Mount Bross, 14,172
Mount Columbia, 14,073
Mount Democrat, 14,148
Mount Elbert, 14,433
Mount Evans, 14,264
Mount Harvard, 14,420
Mount Lincoln, 14,286
Mount Lindsey, 14,042
Mount Massive, 14,421
Mount Oxford, 14,153
Mount Princeton, 14,197
Mount Shavano, 14,229
Mount Sherman, 14,036
Mount Sneffels, 14,150
Mount Wilson (S.), 14,246
Mount Yale, 14,196
Mount of the Holy Cross, 14,005
North Maroon Peak, 14,014
Pikes Peak, 14,109
Pyramid Peak, 14,018
Quandary Peak, 14,265
Redcloud Peak, 14,034
San Luis Peak, 14,014,
Snowmass Mountain, 14,092
South Maroon Peak, 14,156
South Mount Eolus, 14,083
Sunlight Peak, 14,059
Sunshine Peak, 14,001
Tabeguache Peak, 14,155
Torreys Peak, 14,267
Uncompahgre Peak, 14,309
Wetterhorn Peak, 14,015
Wilson Peak (N.), 14,017
Windom Peak, 14,082

6.2 ALL COLORADO'S 54 OFFICIAL FOURTEENERS, BY ELEVATION.

Mount Elbert, 14,433
Mount Massive, 14,421
Mount Harvard, 14,420
Blanca Peak, 14,345
La Plata Peak, 14,336
Uncompahgre Peak, 14,309
Crestone Peak, 14,294
Mount Lincoln, 14,286
Grays Peak, 14,270
Mount Antero, 14,269
Torreys Peak, 14,267
Castle Peak, 14,265
Quandary Peak, 14,265
Mount Evans, 14,264
Longs Peak, 14,255
Mount Wilson (S.), 14,246
Mount Shavano, 14,229
Crestone Needle, 14,197
Mount Belford, 14,197
Mount Princeton, 14,197
Mount Yale, 14,196
Mount Bross, 14,172
Kit Carson Mountain, 14,165
El Diente Peak, 14,159
South Maroon Peak, 14,156
Tabeguache Peak, 14,155
Mount Oxford, 14,153
Mount Sneffels, 14,150
Mount Democrat, 14,148
Capitol Peak, 14,130
Pikes Peak, 14,109
Snowmass Mountain, 14,092
South Mount Eolus, 14,083
Windom Peak, 14,082
Mount Columbia, 14,073
Missouri Mountain, 14,067
Humboldt Peak, 14,064
Mount Bierstadt, 14,060
Sunlight Peak, 14,059
Handies Peak, 14,048
Culebra Peak, 14,047
Ellingwood Peak, 14,042
Mount Lindsey, 14,042
Little Bear Peak, 14,037
Mount Sherman, 14,036
Redcloud Peak, 14,034
Pyramid Peak, 14,018
Wilson Peak (N.), 14,017
Wetterhorn Peak, 14,015
North Maroon Peak, 14,014
San Luis Peak, 14,014
Mount of the Holy Cross, 14,005
Huron Peak, 14,003
Sunshine Peak, 14,001

Appendix 7
USGS 7.5-MINUTE MAPS COVERING ROUTES AND ROUTE ACCESS IN THIS GUIDE

including sequence number useful for ordering from USGS (the sequence number is simply where the map is in the alphabetic sequence of all Colorado maps; it is also called the file number).

Allens Park, 22
Alma, 24
Breckenridge, 281
Buena Vista West, 2104
Capitol Peak, 286
Climax, 377
Copper Mountain, 414
Garfield, 2105
Georgetown, 733
Gothic, 759
Granite, 784
Grays Peak, 790
Harris Park, 846
Harvard Lakes, 2111
Hayden Peak, 862
Highland Peak, 882
Idaho Springs, 953
Independence Pass, 960
Isolation Peak, 973
Leadville South, 1138
Longs Peak, 1184
Marble, 1212
Maroon Bells, 1218
Maysville, 2147
McHenrys Peak, 1236
Minturn, 1289
Montezuma, 1305
Mount Antero, 2148
Mount Elbert, 1337
Mount Evans, 1366
Mount Harvard, 2106
Mount Massive, 1345
Mount Sherman, 1351
Mount Yale, 2109
Mount of the Holy Cross, 1346
Pearl Pass, 1481
Snowmass Mountain, 1770
South Peak, 1780
St. Elmo, 2112
Winfield, 2113

To mail order maps, write for a Colorado catalog from the U.S. Department of the Interior, Geological Survey, Reston Virginia, 22092. This catalog provides excellent order forms and lists of all the maps available for Colorado.

PRESERVE OUR FOURTEENERS!

Colorado's fourteeners are priceless resources that give us immeasurable benefit. The increased popularity of climbing these peaks, however, is taking its toll: the fragile alpine environment is being damaged by erosion and crowding. As climbers, we must reduce the impact of our visits—we must climb with care and sensitivity. The following recommendations will help you reduce your impact.

1. Before your trip, learn about problems for the area you'll be in. Is there undue trail erosion? A riparian area that's being damaged? Wildlife you should avoid? Crowding? Parking problems? Private land?

2. Keep your group under 6 people.

3. If you camp, plan your itinerary to avoid over-used sites, and avoid camps during times of high use.

4. Don't use campfires in the backcountry; pack a stove.

5. Avoid traveling through undisturbed areas. Instead, use designated trails and established paths (unless you travel over snow).

6. When climbing or camping, do not build structures such as wind breaks, large cairns, rock walls, and fire rings.

7. Deposit human feces in holes 6 to 8 inches deep a minimum of 75 paces from water or camp. Burn or pack out your toilet paper.

8. Pack out what you pack in—litter and orange peels!

9. Don't feed wildlife.

10. Leave your pets at home—just the smell of a dog disturbs wildlife.

11. If possible, climb during snow seasons so that snow cover minimizes all your impacts.

12. Be courteous: wait for climbers below you to move out of rockfall areas. Don't ski above other climbers. Keep noise to a minimum (except for summit yodels). Be friendly and share information about routes that prevent erosion and rockfall. Share new routes, since they spread use. Remember—we're all in this together.

13. Support—or join—organizations that help preserve our fourteeners.